Jan. 1981.

FISHING FLIES
AND
FLY TYING

*American Insects, Including Nymphs
and Crustaceans*

BY WILLIAM F. BLADES

Illustrations By The Author

STACKPOLE BOOKS

FISHING FLIES AND FLY-TYING

Copyright © 1951 by Stackpole and Heck Inc.
Copyright © 1962, 1979 by The Stackpole Company

Limited facsimile edition, March 1979 $20.00

Published by
STACKPOLE BOOKS
Cameron and Kelker Streets
P.O. Box 1831
Harrisburg, Pa. 17105

Published simultaneously in Don Mills, Ontario, Canada by Thomas Nelson & Sons, Ltd.

Library of Congress Catalog Card No. 61-17665

ISBN 0-8117-0613-3

Printed in the U.S.A.

To my wife,
DOROTHY BLADES

To the memory of
my grandfather,
STEPHEN HARTLEY STONES,
Artist and fisherman

And to my sister,
JESSIE ROBINSON

FOREWORD

It was my second trip in two weeks to Diamond Lake, although I must confess that I didn't return because I had been particularly lucky the first time but merely, I am sure, because of the beauty and relaxed atmosphere. The lake region just north of Chicago seemed totally unaffected by the buzzing sounds and hectic life of the big city, and I needed the peace that a fishing trip alone brings.

Diamond Lake is one of the smallest in the area and somewhat isolated from the rest, but it was full of bluegills and largemouth bass. The shallow, soft-bottomed shoreline with overhanging tree branches and large heavy patches of lilypads made ideal breeding grounds and the result was a good population of fish. I was still new to the country, having been stationed in South America for several years, and I was thinking of the large river valleys of the Andes as I drove through the countryside. The Illinois landscape was so different from the subtropical environment I was used to, with the majestic mountains and dirt roads.

I snapped out of my dream when I reached the lake. Turning sharply into a small parking lot off the winding blacktop road, I was surprised to see only one other car on the lot, and equally surprised that the small boathouse and restaurant at the shore looked almost deserted. I got out of the car and stood for a moment to drink in the silence and solitude. I began to wonder if all the fishermen I had met here the last time knew something I didn't.

A slam of the boathouse door ripped me out of my reverie of having the whole lake for myself. I turned and saw a woman standing on the small veranda facing the shore. She swung the bell in her hand and called in the direction of a fisherman in a boat not far from shore, "Bill, your lunch is ready!"

The sound echoed across the small lake. The fisherman started to move the boat with long solid strokes and nearly rowed it up on the shore.

I watched as the boat came to rest and an elderly man stepped ashore and walked in the direction of the boathouse. The wide-brimmed Stetson shaded his sharply featured face; only part of his white hair was visible under the rim. His gold-rimmed glasses glittered in the shade as he removed the jacket and wiped some perspiration off his neck.

I finished assembling my rod and gathered up the rest of my gear before walking down to the boathouse myself. When I entered the small room, the inviting smell of fried bacon and fresh coffee greeted me. Sitting at a corner table, the summoned fisherman was already halfway through his lunch. I got some coffee and walked over to his table.

"Do you mind?" I asked politely.

"No, not at all," the fisherman replied gesturing at a chair in front of him. "Sit down. My name is Bill—Bill Blades."

I introduced myself and sat down.

We talked pleasantly about the weather and the fishing, but neither of us mentioned anything about flies. Bill had told me that he wasn't going to fish in the afternoon. He'd had enough, he said; besides it was too hot. I offered to help him carry his gear from the boat to his car. The trunk of his Cadillac was empty except for a spare tire and a tray with insects carefully positioned on top of a bundle of blankets in the corner.

"Oh, I see you are collecting insects."

"These are not real insects," Bill explained and picked up the tray. "They are artificials. See the hook there?"

"They are unbelievable," I gasped, scarcely trusting my eyes. "They look so real. Where did you get them?"

"I tied them myself," he said, somewhat surprised that I didn't know. "I wrote a book about it."

"My goodness Mr. Blades, why didn't you tell me during lunch."

"I didn't think of it—but you can still call me Bill," he replied with a grin.

I wanted to buy his book right then and there, but unfortunately he didn't have any with him, so I gave Bill a check and he promised to send me one.

I was on the road for the following two weeks and couldn't fish, but I didn't forget the beautiful flies Bill had shown me, so different from the ones I was used to buying in the store. When I returned home the book had been delivered—by a small, white-haired gentleman with an English accent, I was told. It was carefully autographed on the front flyleaf above a hand drawing of one of his incredibly realistic mayfly imitations. I read it from cover to cover that night and studied every fly on each page. I was hooked! I bought a vise and some beginning fly tying materials the same week.

A few months later I somehow managed to get up enough courage to telephone Bill and ask him a couple of questions about patterns in his book. Much to my surprise he invited me to come over to his house in Wilmette, not too far from Glenview where I lived. I spent an unforgettable evening with Bill and his wife, Dorothy, in his tying room upstairs. There were flies all over, neatly arranged in large, homemade, plexiglass trays. A number of bridge tables set end to end were filled with bottles of natural insects and boxes of hooks, silk, and God knows what else. Some fine paintings and drawings of mayflies were set on top of a dresser in front of a row of books that were mostly about flies and fishing. His bed and closets were lined with boxes of all descriptions and sizes, filled with feathers and fur from every bird and animal in existence. It was way past midnight before I left. But I had seen it all, or so I thought.

The seven years that followed hold some of my most cherished personal memories, as I got to know Bill Blades as one of the finest fly tyers in the world, and as a man and good friend. Bill was born in Sheffield, England, and immigrated to the United States shortly after the turn of the century. He was a young mason then, but his skill and drive soon enabled him to emerge as an independent contractor, building some of the many fine residential homes that still exist on Chicago's northern lake shore. The depression in the twenties curtailed his building efforts, but unlike others, his success had left him comfortably situated. So Bill retired to pursue his love for fly tying, and he fished for months at a time both in Canada and Florida.

During World War II he was active in organizing and teaching fly tying in various hospitals as a therapy for the patients, a gesture that was greatly appreciated by the many who were fortunate enough to participate despite their wounds.

Bill was a good teacher, but he was tough, and he was a perfectionist. I clearly remember the first two things he gave me: a brown rooster neck and a razor blade. "In case you are wondering what the razor blade is for, I'll tell you," he said while looking for something on his small tying table standing next to the bridge tables. He held up a hook and continued, "This hook here goes with it, and every time the stuff you tie on it is not to my liking, the razor blade goes into action." He was not kidding. Nor was he kidding about the penny he asked for the hook, which was a superstition of his. Like all artists, he was also a great individualist.

Even today, as I look through the pages of his book, it becomes very clear again that Bill Blades was indeed a master. His mayfly imitations are masterpieces, and his stoneflies have never been equalled. But his energy and talent were evident in everything he did—from his vise to the canvas and paintbrush, and from his fly rod to tournament bait casting (not to forget his cellar and his wine making). Once I saw him spin Duco cement on the hook with thread, pouring it on top of the hook shank and winding the silk from a spool on the floor before a drop could fall. And I saw him do a belly dance in the entrance hall of his home on Greenwood Avenue, laughing and saying to his wife, ''Not bad for an old man, eh?''

I lost a great friend—the fishing world lost a great friend—when Bill died rather suddenly in 1962 of a heart attack, not long after the publication of the second and revised edition of his book. His talents as a fly tyer and an artist earned him a place in the fishing hall of fame, and are very much in evidence on the pages that follows.

To this day I can still hear him say, ''Poul, if you ever write a book, dedicate it to me, will you.'' I know he was joking when he said it, but somehow I had an inner feeling that I might someday do just that. In 1973 it became reality when I dedicated my first book, *Dressing Flies for Fresh and Salt Water* (Freshet Press, New York), to my tutor and good friend, William F. Blades.

His book *Fishing Flies and Fly Tying* has long been a collector's item, and autographed copies are rare and costly. They will still be rare and costly even now that it has been reissued. The purpose of this reprint is to put the work of Bill Blades within reach of the many fly tyers that have emerged since the original went out of print. In that way, everyone has a chance to learn from an old master who surely was ahead of his time.

POUL JORGENSEN

ACKNOWLEDGMENTS

I would like to take this opportunity to thank the many leading fly tyers who have given me the privilege of making flies originated by them and mentioning their names.

I would like to acknowledge the assistance given me by several people in preparation of this book.

The full-page black-and-white illustrations throughout the book are from photographs by Kranzten Studios of Evanston, Illinois.

Several of the small black-and-white illustrations are from photographs by Alan Wallace of Glencoe, Illinois. These illustrations are individually credited to him.

The plates of hair bass bugs on pages 254 and 255 are from photographs by Dr. Charles B. Blake.

I would like to thank the following:

The late Dr. Norman A. Fleishman, one of my best pupils at Vaughan General Hospital during World War II, for mailing may flies and nymphs from Michigan.

J. G. Lesko for may flies and nymphs from the State of New York.

Lyman Barr for trying out my flies and bugs in Canada and Florida.

Art Besse for sending me natural flies and nymphs and material from Ashland, on Lake Superior.

Wilfred Blades, my son, for the many photographs he took of the natural insects and my artificials. He also reproduced several of my paintings as black-and-white photographs.

P. W. Oman, Head of the Insect Identification and Parasite Introduction Section, also Dr. B. D. Burks, for their assistance in identifying and giving me the scientific names of the insects, including nymphs and crustaceans, etc.

A note on this edition:

The following black and white plates appeared in color in the earlier editions: Plates IV, VI, XII, XXIII, LXVII, LXXXIV, and XCVI. Plate XCVI, Salmon Flies, was made from an oil painting by the author. The other original color photographs were taken by Carlos Photos of Evanston, Illinois.

The flies in the new color plates of this facsimile edition were tied from the author's original patterns by Poul Jorgensen.

TABLE OF CONTENTS

ILLUSTRATIONS

PLATES

DRAWINGS

INTRODUCTION

MY SOLE AIM in writing this book is to bring to the reader all that I have learned about the art of fly tying.

Fly tying is such a grand hobby and has given me so many hours of pleasure that I am anxious to share my experiences in this field with all who become interested.

It is by no means easy to describe by drawings and writing, the many things I would like to give my readers in the way of new methods and materials useful in modern fly tying. Seeing an expert fly tyer at work will save you many hours of constant study. Also, do not overlook the importance of knowing that after seeing this work performed, you must continually practice before mastering the work yourself. If you really want to tie flies there is no question in my mind of the outcome.

When you make any fly pattern try to secure a good sample and copy it; also use this sample every time; do not use the ones you have made or you will notice your flies will change a little in color and proportion each time you make a fly.

The material you use in making a fly is a very important factor. It is impossible to make a good fly if you are using the wrong or inferior material. To be able to pick out all the many fly tying materials and put them to their proper use will only be achieved after months of practice. If your flies do not come up to your expectations after they are tied, before putting the blame on yourself, check your materials. Some of my instructions may seem unnecessary to some tyers, yet I advise you to tie them well, as they will be more durable.

The professional fly tyer has accomplished a great deal to be able to make flies at a speed that enables them to be sold to the public at moderate prices. How often do we hear the fishermen say, "There is a lot of room for improvement in our artificial flies which are supposed to be copies of the natural nymphs and flies." I agree with this viewpoint and I made up my mind to try to improve this situation, although it took many hours of hard work at my fly tying table and drawing board. It is hoped that this book will both help and stimulate the beginner, and also be of some value to the expert.

I would like to thank my friends Charles B. Woehrle, Stuart S. Houston, J. Clark Salyer, II, Hal Bayliss, Don and Dick Olson and Clinton C. Bennett, who have assisted me greatly by sending me the natural flies and nymphs to copy.

This, to me, is a very interesting subject and I sincerely hope some of our young anglers will continue to make improvements on the copies of our natural insects. I have several friends who at one time were not interested in the natural insect imitations and who are now collecting them whenever they see the opportunity.

Every artificial fly that appears in this book has been made by the author; also the drawings and paintings. I have given credit to the originator of the flies when known.

Chapter I

FLY TYING
MATERIAL

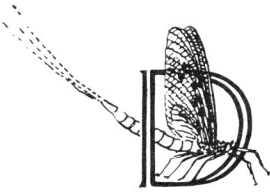

DO NOT OVERLOOK the fact that knowing what materials to purchase, and where they can be purchased is an important factor in tying the artificial fly. I have mentioned a few well-known material houses, but you can often get the material from your local fly tying material stores.

My material lists for making flies cover about everything that is used for fly making. Some of these materials are hard to obtain at the present time, which means you may have to take a substitute.

TYING SILKS. The tying silk should be fine and strong. Herter's of Waseca, Minnesota, carry a complete line of tying silk; the Belgium brand is very good and inexpensive.

For colored tying silk, Pearsall's No. 0000 is very good, and comes in many colors.

The Holland Manufacturing Company, New York, make very fine tying silk; I can highly recommend it. Pearsall's and the Holland can be obtained at most supply stores.

RAFFIA. This is excellent material for bodies of May Flies and can be dyed any color.

QUILLS. The most used quill is taken from the Peacock eyed tail feather; this is a two-toned quill.

A dark, solid colored quill comes from the fibres on the stem of the tail feather. These quills are also dyed orange, red, yellow, purple, and green for May Fly bodies. (See the dry fly instructions on Page 108 for instructions about stripping the herl from the quills).

A single strand can be taken from the flight feathers on the wings of several large birds, such as the Swan, Condor, Heron, Macaw, etc. These strands can also be taken from the Turkey tail and Pheasant tail. Take the fuzz off the Emu plume and you will have the whitest quill you have ever seen.

Take almost any wing feather, or tail feather, and cut off the top until the centre quill is large enough to handle. Now take a razor blade, or your thumb nail, and start to pull off (and tear downward) the quill from the top side of the feather. The Swan feathers make wonderful white quills for the Coffin Fly and can be dyed any color for other flies.

The purple blue white tipped feather on the Mallard wing makes a fine two-toned, transparent quill; this can be wound over colored floss bodies, making excellent-looking insect bodies.

Soaking the feathers in hot water makes the stripping of the quill much easier. Wetting the quills before tying them on prevents splitting, and they handle much better.

The trimmed centre stem of natural and dyed hackles makes an excellent quill body; this should be well-soaked in hot water before using.

WAX. This can be purchased in small cakes for a few cents each. I have a cake of Herter's soft wax that I rub on my finger tips when my fingers are rough. This prevents the rough fingers from tearing the silk floss and fine tying silk.

I have made some tacky wax, for making dubbing, from a recipe I obtained from an English fly tyer which is very good:

Take two ounces of the best resin, a half ounce of bees wax and simmer them together for ten minutes; then add a quarter of an ounce of tallow or deer fat, and simmer for about fifteen minutes. Now pour this in a bowl of cold water, then work it up with the fingers until it is pliable. Mold it in pieces suitable for use and keep it in a jar of water.

FUR FOR DUBBING. This fur can be purchased in small packets, and you can collect a great amount of it yourself. These are a few that you will need: Muskrat, Mink, Mole, Rabbit, Hare, Seal (natural and dyed in several colors), Grey Squirrel and Fox Squirrel, Opossum (buff flank), Mohair, white and

PLATE I. STARLING WINGS.

dyed, Fox, Water Rat skin, etc. You can buy a few colors of spun fur that can be used the same as wool.

Instructions for making dubbing can be found in the section describing "Tying the Dry Fly."

TINSEL. Buy tinsel from a reliable fly tying material store, and be sure it is tarnish-proof. This can be bought in many styles and sizes, such as Flats, Embossed, Ovals, Round Threads, Lace Twist, and wire for ribbing small flies. E. Veniard carry a very fine quality tinsel and a large selection.

WOOL. Any good wool will make a fine body; it floats well, and holds its color very well when in use.

For dry flies, I use one strand and wind it on with the hackle pliers, thus preventing possible breakage which might be caused by rough skin on your fingers.

You can shred wool and make a dubbing out of it on colored silk; this makes an ideal body for small flies. Buy the best grade wool you can. Secure it from a fly tying material store.

LACQUER. Herter's line of lacquer, head cement, bug cement, enamel, color fixative, etc. is very satisfactory. All this kind of material must be

[17]

thinned at times. The head cement should penetrate into the silk to make a good job. Without attention, all of these materials get stiff and sticky, and will not make a good finished job.

STARLING WINGS

In the photograph on p. 17 the left wing is the outside and the right wing is the inside of the wing. The first six largest feathers are called "primaries." The remaining quills are called "secondaries." Sections are taken from these quills to make small fly wings. The inside lower small feathers are used for wet fly hackles and are called the under coverts. The first row of small feathers on the outside are called the lesser coverts and the second row is called the greater coverts; these are darker than the inside coverts and are also used as hackle. If you open the wings as soon as they come off the birds and pin them on a board they will set as shown in the photograph, which makes them better to handle when taking off the feathers.

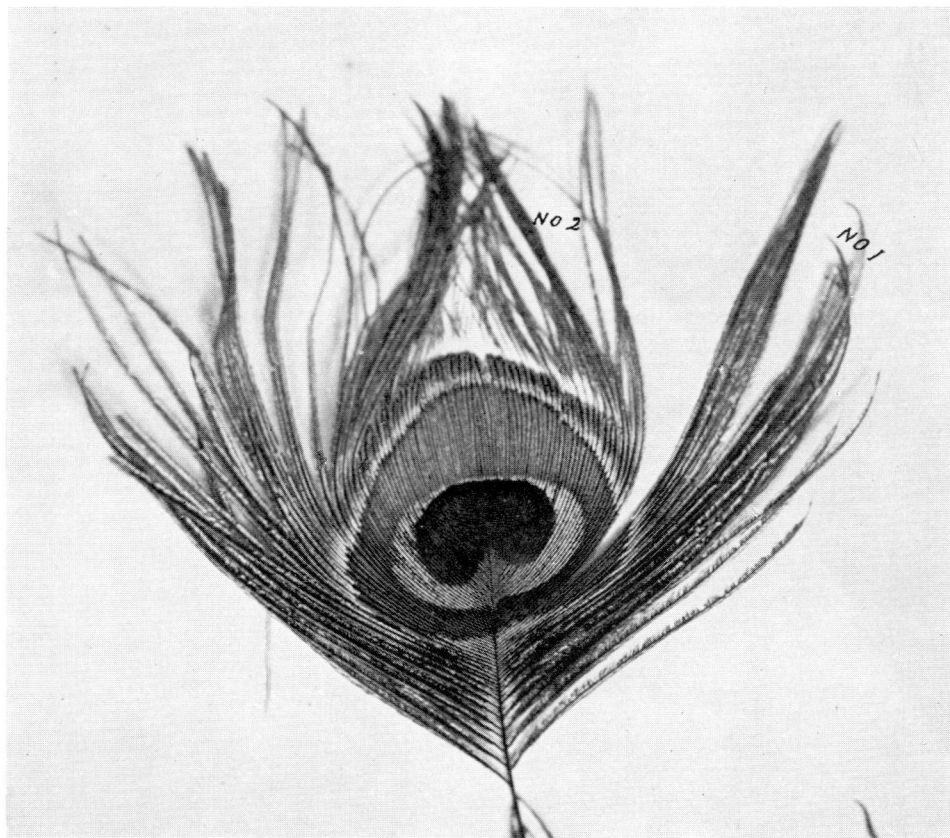

Alan Wallace

PLATE II. THE PEACOCK EYED TAIL FEATHER.

PEACOCK EYED TAIL FEATHER

In the accompanying photograph the first portion of the eye on the right side marked No. 1 is ideal for the bodies on such flies as the Coachman. When making these bodies try the following method; tie in three or four strands by the tips and twist them togther; also keep twisting them as you wind them on.

The second portion marked No. 2 has the fibres, or herl, that is stripped to make the two colored quill bodies; on such flies as the Quill Gordon, Cahill Quill, etc. When judging this quill, turn the feather over and look at the color and quality at the back.

DYEING FLY TYING MATERIALS

If you have the desire to dye your own fly tying materials, get a catalog from Herter's, Waseca, Minnesota, and E. Veniard, 138 Northwood Road, Thornton Heath, England. The following list of dyes are the colors stocked by E. Veniard:

Specially Prepared For Dyeing Feathers, Furs, Etc.

Recommended by Roger Woolley, T. J. Hanna, F. Napier-Sutton, etc.

Black	Magenta	Medium Olive
Purple	Brown Olive	Iron Blue
Golden Olive	Red Spinner	Naples Yellow
Ginger	Lemon Yellow	Blue (Teal & Blue)
Summer Duck	Hot Orange	Dark Blue
Scarlet	Bright Green	Grannom Green
Dark Green	Dun	Sienna
Mole	Flame	Light Claret
Claret	Green Olive	Blue Dun (Slate)
Beige	Bright Yellow	Yellow
Kingfisher	Lt. Blue (Cambridge)	Dark Olive
Green Drake	Olive Dun	Fiery Brown
Cinnamon	Red	Crimson
Insect Green	Green Highlander	Grey

*The above list of colors is also very
useful when ordering dyed goods.*

When dyeing materials, read the instructions and follow them.

Mix the dye in a cup with a small amount of boiling water; be sure all particles of dye are mixed thoroughly before putting it in the dyeing bath. I use a white enameled bath; it can be washed out easily, and the dye will not spoil the enamel.

The material must be washed, before dyeing, in strong, hot soap suds (Lux or its equivalent). If you soak some materials for a few minutes it will be sufficient, but waterfowl will take much longer, in order to take out the grease.

If you take a quart of boiling water for the bath, add the amount of dye that will stay on the point of a penknife. This will vary according to what you are dyeing; add a little more if you want darker colors.

Watch the quill of the feathers as you are dyeing; you can then get a good idea of the shade you are obtaining. I take them out before they are finished and dry them to be sure I am not getting them too dark. If they are too light when dried, I can always put them back for a few seconds more to darken them.

I mix the dyes to get different shades, the same as I mix oil color for painting. I use a tablespoonful of vinegar to fix the color.

When adding dye to the bath, take out the material or you will get it spotted.

After the feathers are dyed I wash them out in warm water, then press

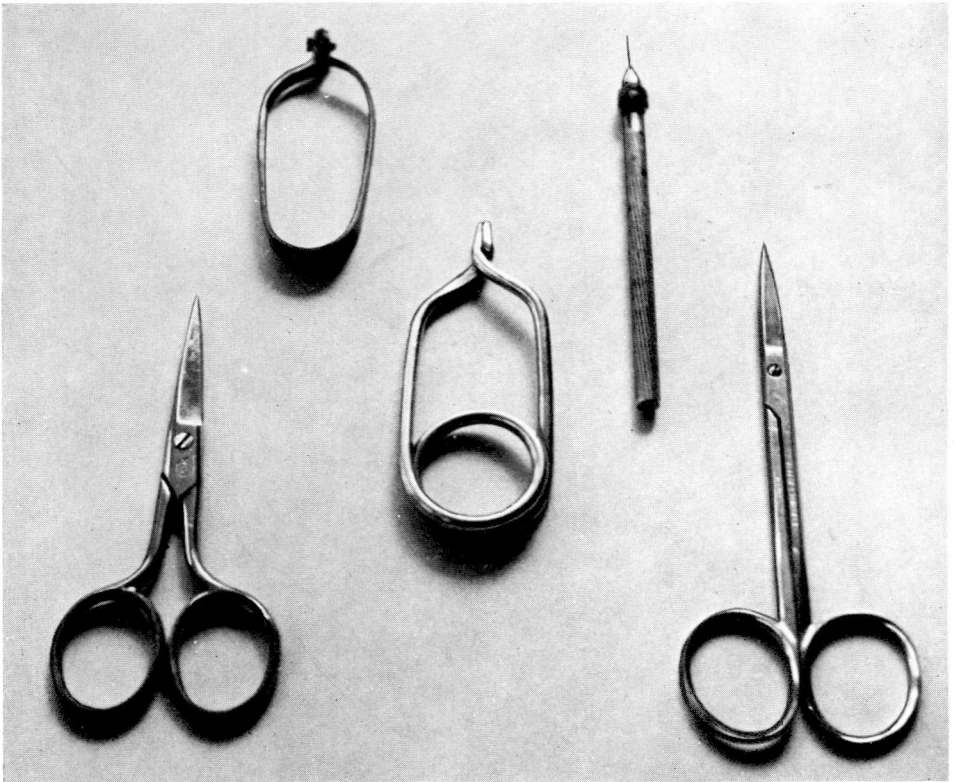

PLATE III. FLY TYING TOOLS.

out the moisture between newspaper, and allow them to dry. I also shake them a little to bring them back to their natural shape.

I also dye raffia and floss for May Fly bodies, and rabbit and seal fur for dubbing.

It is not easy to dye these special colors, as the color will change in one minute if you leave it in the bath too long.

By all means, get the natural insect or feather that you are trying to copy, if this is at all possible.

It is very easy to dye special colors of tying silk. Wrap a small amount of white tying silk on a piece of stiff paper. This dyes very quickly; just lower it in the dye and out, at first; then put it back in the dye, if you desire a darker shade.

FLY TYING TOOLS

Purchase a good vise—do not buy a cheap one at first, thinking it will be all right for a beginner, for this money will then be wasted. I have used the Thompson A lever-type vise with the clamp mount for years.

Vise for Fly Tying.

They will handle hooks from size 22 to 3-0. If you want to make a large quantity of large flies, purchase a larger vise.

These vises are made to hold a hook securely and in a position so that you can easily work around it when making a fly. Contrary to some tyers, I recommend placing the hook in the vise by gripping it with as small an amount of the bend as possible. This gives you more room to work your fingers when tying and you will soon learn to keep your thread away from the point and barb. Keep all the adjustments oiled at all times; many vises

I have used belonging to people that I have taught could not be adjusted as they had never been oiled. When your fly is in the vise, you should be able to turn the fly over to inspect the opposite side. Learn to operate your vise correctly or you will not get the best out of it.

Purchase a good pair of scissors with straight blades from 3½ to 4½ inches long. Some tyers like the curved blades and a pair of larger scissors is helpful when making large hair bugs. Hackle pliers, to me, are very important; they should be able to pick up the finest hair and also hold a large hackle. I use a pair of imported pliers from England, and also a pair of the light rubber jaw-type ones made by Thompson of Elgin, Illinois.

You can make a bodkin by putting a piece of plastic on any size needle you wish to use. I use a small pin vise as you can release the needle and change it at any time. I use this to put cement or lacquer on small fly heads, in fact, for many purposes.

I use razor blades to cut off the thread, etc.

The thread holder is necessary for holding the tying silk when it is not in use when tying flies. This can be purchased in many styles, and can be made with a couple of rubber washers and a screw. A pair of tweezers or forceps are also very helpful at times.

The bobbin is used by many professional tyers. It is also very helpful for one who has rought hands that break or wear the tying silk. I personally do not use one.

HOOKS

My advice is, do not waste your time tying flies on inferior hooks.

Most of my flies have been tied on Allcock's hooks imported from Redditch, England. I have also used Henning's hooks and Mustad's from Norway.

I prefer the model perfect bend, although I have no objections to the sproat bend, and also the limerick bend which is used on most salmon fly hooks.

The regular model perfect hook which I prefer for wet flies is marked No. 4991. The tapered-eye hook is marked No. 04991, which is an ideal dry fly hook.

The light wire hooks which are made to assist in floating dry flies are marked No. 04991 SF 1 X fine. When fishing with fine hooks of any make, use a light leader and a light rod.

I would like to explain why a hook is called 1 X long. The shank is one size longer than the regular length hook; a *No. 10 2 X long* hook has the same length shank as a No. 8 regular.

These hooks are made as long as 8 X long and are used for streamer flies.

Hooks marked *2 X, 3 X, 4 X or 5 X short* means they are two to five sizes shorter than the regular hook and are used for spiders and variants.

The words 1 X and 2 X *stout* mean that the hook is stronger and heavier than the regular weight hook and is used for steelhead trout; in sizes 2, 4, 6, and 8, the popular sizes are 6 and 4. Mustad make 4 X stout.

For salmon flies, use a loop-eyed hook with the limerick bend.

The hump shank hooks with either inside or outside kink are used for cork-bodied bass bugs; this hump prevents the cork from slipping around the hook. Herters make a double hump 3 X long.

William DeWitt of the Shoe Form Company carry a very fine line of nickel hooks.

Wright and McGill Company make very fine bait fishing hooks; they also have a line of gold plated hooks that are very good. They also make fly tying hooks.

Paul H. Young, 17701 W. 8 Mile Rd., Detroit 35, Michigan, carries a complete line of Mustad "Viking" Hooks.

Both Ernest Hille of Williamsport, Pennsylvania, and Herter's of Waseca, Minnesota, offer complete lines of fly tying materials and equipment and each issues an extensive annual catalog.

WING FORMER

The use of a wing former will greatly reduce the headaches of securing good quill section wings. This, generally, is a tedious task and by use of the wing former you can readily make, cut and store for future use any number of wings.

The new Thompson Fly Wing Former, recently perfected, provides the fly tyer with an excellent fly tying tool which will make a fine addition to the fly tyer's kit.

The Thompson Fly Wing Former may be purchased from D. H. Thompson, 335 Walnut Ave., Elgin, Illinois.

Machine-Made Fly Wings.

Chapter II

HACKLES

THIS IS A VERY important subject for the fly tyer, and I will try to handle it so that the beginner will receive the necessary help right from the start thus eliminating many hours of wasted time. This will prevent throwing away many hackles that you can use later when you have learned of their many uses. Most fishermen get a thrill by catching the fish on the surface, which means, if you are using a fly, it is called the dry fly, and the hackle for this fly is the most difficult to procure.

These hackles come from old roosters, two years or more, which are only kept for breeding purposes; also from bantam roosters that have been kept as pets.

Dry fly hackles should be stiff, practically free of web and they should be springy.

The best ones are long and narrow with glossy fibres and rather even in length. The underside of the hackle should be almost the same color as the topside, but they are generally much lighter. I use a lot of variant colored hackles for my dry flies; the trimmed stems of the multi-variant (which means a grizzly crossed with ginger to fiery brown) make very natural looking legs for the March Brown and several others which will be explained in the material descriptions of my May Flies. Freak badger necks are also valuable for this purpose.

The light grizzly and chinchilla necks are excellent when dyed blue dun. It is very hard to get a good, natural blue dun neck in the dry fly quality.

I think most people will agree with me that I favor natural colored hackles if I can procure them, but I have no objection to a perfectly dyed hackle of the shade I require. E. Veniard, 138 Northwood Road, Thornton Heath, England carry a good and large selection of dyes for fly tying material. When I test the quality of a dry fly hackle, I take hold of the tip and stroke the fibres down on each side separately and carefully; then stroke down the centre quill bringing both sides down at once. If the fibres stay almost at right angles to the stem, the hackle is of dry fly quality.

The only way to be able to judge hackles as to quality and name is to secure some of each.

The tips of spade hackles and some saddle hackles furnish the dry fly hackles for spiders and variants; also good neck hackles can be used.

Wet fly hackles are easy to obtain inasmuch as they come from young roosters. Chickens that are hatched around March 1st have fine wet fly hackles on them when killed in January and February the following year; this is the time to get good hackles, not in the summer. These are excellent for palmering wet salmon flies.

Many bird hackles are used for wet flies, especially in Europe, such as the Starling, Grouse, Partridge, Pheasant, Landrail, and many others.

Wet fly hackles are soft and have lots of web, which absorbs water and takes the fly down to the fish that are feeding under water.

Hackles on the wet flies have only to represent the legs, but on the dry fly they have to float the fly in addition to forming the legs.

The quantity of hackle to use cannot be stated, inasmuch as every fisherman has his own idea about what amount to use.

In calm water you can get along with a sparsely tied fly, but in fast water a heavily hackled fly floats much better.

You can get many good chicken heads from your poultry dealer, and some farmers have old roosters and bantams that have good necks.

If the neck is of very good dry fly quality, don't think you are going to enjoy eating the chicken. One method of preparing necks is to cut off the head and leave the neck long; you can always trim this off later.

To take off the skin, start to cut around the eyes and the top of the head, leaving on all of the small feathers; continue to cut on each side on the skin and under the neck; now come straight down to where you cut the head off. If you have cut this properly, it will be no trouble to gradually pull off the scalp.

The next step is to stretch this on a board and clean off any excess fat or blood and cover it with borax; I then lay it on a hot air duct for a few days. Now take off the borax and scrape off the fat, and if the fat has not been taken off or absorbed, put the borax back on and scrape it again in a few days.

I now trim the edges to shape and wash the neck with a mild soap; DO NOT wash the fat from the back into the feathers; lay it on the side of the washtubs and wash the feather side only. You can fix deer tails and small pieces of hide in this same manner. During the last eight years I have given a friend of mine two hundred rooster chicks of the following breeds: Andalusian, Grizzly, White and Buff, which have been mixed with Rhode Island Red and others, producing some very good variant necks.

Variant hackles in the light shades, such as the ginger variant and light tans and greys, can be dyed blue dun, making them into very effective hackles.

Many flies have mottled wings and legs which can be imitated by the variant hackles.

HACKLES

(See Plate IV. Read left to right and top to bottom.)

1. NATURAL RED: This is a brown or reddish brown. I have many different shades in these necks.
2. FIERY BROWN: A shade of fiery mahogany.
3. COACHMAN BROWN: A dark, flat brown.
4. LIGHT GINGER: This is a pale tan shade.
5. DARK GINGER: Same as above, only a darker shade.
6. BADGER: This has creamy white fibres, with a natural black centre marking.
7. YELLOW BADGER: These fibres are a yellow ginger, or pale gold color, with a natural black centre marking. I have a box marked "Badger variant" that has fifteen different colored Badger necks in it from white to a rich ginger, and several have mottled centre markings.
8. GRIZZLY: This is a pure-bred Plymouth Rock chicken, and the markings are barred black and white.
9. BLUE DUN: This is a light blue dun dyed hackle, which is pale grey and hard to procure in the natural feather in dry fly quality.
10. BLUE DUN: Natural hackle which is a little darker.
11. IRON BLUE DUN: This a similar hackle, much darker, and blue grey in color.
12. CHINCHILLA: Marked the same as the Plymouth Rock, only in dun grey and white.
13. FURNACE: This is a brown hackle with a black centre marking.
14. COCHY-BONDHU: This hackle is a furnace brown with black on the edge of the fibres, and has a black centre marking.

PLATE IV. HACKLES FOR FLY TYING.
(See page 26 for identification)

15. HONEY DUN: Pale honey color with brown or brownish grey centre markings, which can be broken or solid.

16. FIERY VARIANT: Fiery brown hackle with cream and grey markings.

17. MULTI-VARIANT: This hackle is barred in dark and light grey, ginger to fiery brown; in other words, a mixture of many colors.

18. GINGER VARIANT: This hackle is ginger, barred similar to the Plymouth Rock with cream and tan markings.

19. NAROBI: Brown with white tips, and also black with white tips. White hackles are found on the same neck.

20. FURNACE HEN HACKLE: Brown hackle with black centre. These are very soft feathers used for wet flies and nymphs.

21. ENGLISH GROUSE: Soft hackle for wet flies; the colors are dark grey, tan and brown, mottled.

22. BLUE DUN HEN: Soft, for wet flies.

23. GREY PARTRIDGE: Breast feather for wet flies. Grey with black markings; also grey with brown markings. Used on March Browns and Sedges.

24. BROWN SPADE: Excellent for spider and variant flies.

25. BADGER HEN: For wet flies. White on tips, dark centre markings.

26. ENGLISH BLUEJAY: Used on several English salmon flies.

27. BADGER SADDLE HACKLE: White to cream sides, with black centre.

BIRD HACKLES

LANDRAIL: This bird furnishes many hackles and wings for English flies. It is very hard to explain the color, but I would say, a cinnamon pink grey,—a very beautiful shade.

PLOVER: These hackles are dark grey, or an ash color with yellow speckles on them. Good for speckled legs, on wet flies.

DOTTEREL: The throat of the Dotterel has some very good blue dun, soft hackles on it, which can be substituted by the under coverts on the Starling wing, as the Dotterel is now protected.

WOODCOCK: The English Woodcock furnishes some brown and tan hackles for sedges, spiders, and March Brown flies.

Drawing No. 1   *Drawing No. 2*

Drawing No. 1 is the bird hackle. Drawing No. 2 is the same hackle prepared ready to tie in. The soft fibres have been cut from the base and the fibres have been stroked down. Tie in by the tip and hold the hackle vertical. Commence to wind and stroke the fibres back towards the bend of the hook with the thumb and finger of your left hand; in other words, you are doubling the hackle as you wind it.

[28]

TYING ON HAIR HACKLE

Place a hook in the vise, coat the hook with cement, and wrap it with tying silk. Select the hair, and pull out the short hairs; also, even up the tips.

First see that you are back far enough from the eye to put on the head after the hackle is turned back. You must also tie in the hair the proper length so as to make the hackle the right length when tied back.

Put a little cement on the hook and hair, and roll the hair evenly around the hook; then wind over the butts, as shown in Drawing No. 1.

Drawing No. 1   *Drawing No. 2*

Construct the body, as shown in Drawing No. 2, out of material for the fly you are tying, then pull back the hair and take the tying silk through it and form the head so as to hold the hair in the proper position.

Your fly will now appear the same as Drawing No. 2.

HAIR HACKLE

This is the method I used to put the hair hackle on the two streamer flies, Hair Coachman and Hair Professor.

First, make the Professor (as shown in Drawing No. 3), making a neat sloping base for the hair hackle. Now prepare a small bunch of hair by taking out the short hairs, making the tips uniform.

Drawing No. 3   *Drawing No. 4*

Take the hair between your thumb and first finger and flatten it out, then put a little cement on the base up to the place where you will make the tie; allow the cement to make its initial set, then wrap it around the front of the streamer (as shown in Drawing No. 4), and tie it firmly on.

Now trim off the butts and form the head, and you will have the finished streamer.

The accompanying drawing is of the skin and feathers from a rooster's neck, which is called a *cape* or neck. These necks vary in size a good deal, which makes it impossible to give the exact locations of hackle sizes. These figures are approximate locations on an average size neck.

Section No. 1 has hackles for hooks, size 18 to 22; also small hackle points and spent wings.

Section No. 2 has hackles for hooks, size 14 to 18; also small hackle points and spent wings.

Section No. 3 has hackles for hooks, size 12 to 16; also medium size hackle points, spent wings and spiders.

Section No. 4 has hackles for hooks, size 10 to 14; also hackle points and spent wings for hooks 10 to 14. On the side of Section No. 4 and No. 5 you will find some very good spider hackles, on some necks.

Section No. 5 has hackles for hooks sizes 10 to 8; also hackle points and spent wings for hook sizes 8 to 12; also spiders 8 to 12.

The remaining portion of the neck is useful for tail hackle fibres, bass flies, streamers, and any large fly.

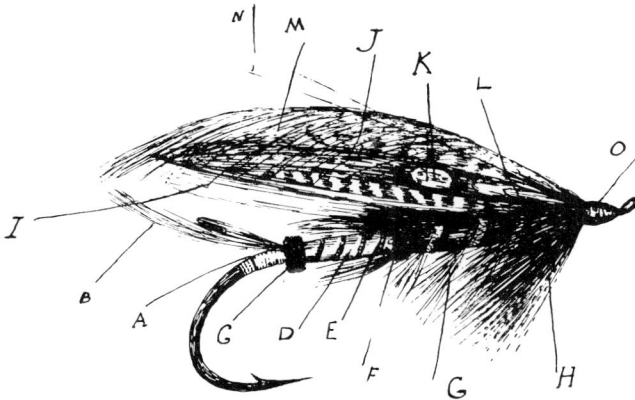

PARTS OF A FLY

A.—*The tag or tip,* composed of a few turns of tinsel and silk floss.

B.—*Tail,* topping and small colored feathers.

C.—*Butt,* made of Ostrich herl, Peacock herl, wool, or chenille.

D.—*Body,* sometimes made of floss, tinsel, wool, fur dubbing, etc.

E.—*Ribbing,* usually tinsel, but can be quill, horse hair, silk thread, hackle, etc.

F.—*"Joint"* is a term used to designate the portion between body sections which is usually made of Ostrich herl, or Peacock herl. Small feathers are often tied on the top and bottom.

G.—*Body* hackle (palmered).

H.—*Shoulder* hackle.

I.—*Underwing,* often formed of tippets and turkey wing quill sections.

J.—*Wing* proper.

K.—*Shoulder,* Jungle Cock.

L.—*Cheek,* usually made of Blue Chatterer.

M.—*Topping,* Golden Pheasant crest, Peacock herl, etc.

N.—*Horns,* Macaw tail feather fibres.

O.—*Head.*

TYING THE WHIP FINISHING KNOT

I suggest that you use a very heavy thread or light twine when you are learning to tie this knot.

Wind the thread to the position shown in Drawing No. 1, and hold the thread with the left hand up and out toward you; now put the top side of the first and second finger of the right hand under the thread about two inches from the hook; grasp the thread quickly, and turn the hand over to the right with the inside of the hand facing toward you, as shown in Drawing No. 1.

Open the first and second fingers on the right hand and raise them, as shown in Drawing No. 2; now bend your wrist and go to the back of the hook, keeping a slight tension on the thread with your right first finger, which is used to direct the position of the thread. Now slide the second finger to position, as shown in Drawing No. 3, and swing down to position shown in Drawing No. 4.

You now have completed one loop; repeat this three to six times, as you desire. To tighten this knot, I leave the second finger in the loop and grasp the two threads with my thumb and first finger, then pull tightly on the thread in my left hand. Drawings Nos. 5, 6, and 7 are made to show how the thread actually travels, and also shows how the knot can be tightened with a bodkin.

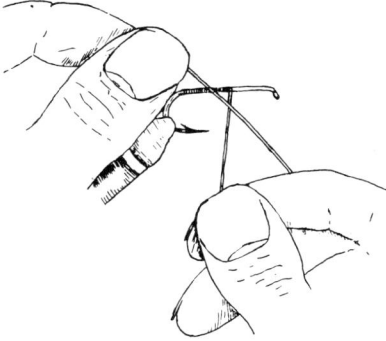

Drawing No. 1

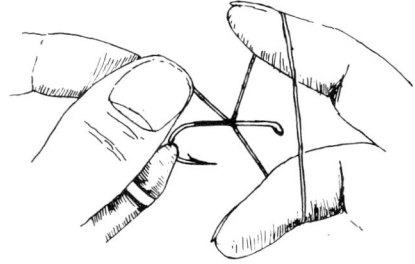

Drawing No. 2

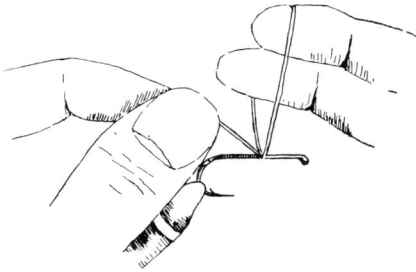

Drawing No. 3

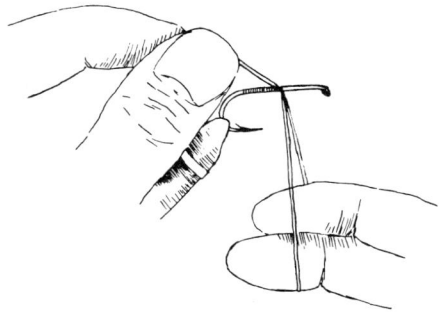

Drawing No. 4

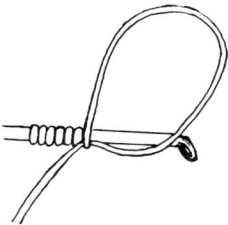

Drawing No. 5

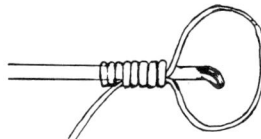

Drawing No. 6

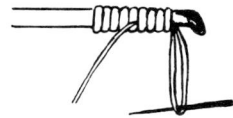

Drawing No. 7

STEPS IN TYING THE WHIP FINISHING KNOT.

Chapter III

TYING THE WET FLY

OST BEGINNERS ask the question, "What is a wet fly?"
This is a very good question, and I hope the following lines will assist the inexperienced fly tyer and fisherman.

The wet fly is simply a fly made to represent the many forms of underwater food, such as nymphs, grubs, minnows, etc. This undoubtedly forms a great part of the fish's food.

When you select a hook for a wet fly, it should be made of wire that is called "regular"; that means it is heavier than the dry fly wire which is called "fine."

The heavy wire sinks the fly quicker, taking it down to where the fish are feeding.

If a very heavy hook is used, it is much harder to set the hook, especially if you are using light tackle. I prefer a regular hook, and I weight my fly with soft copper wire when fishing deep.

[35]

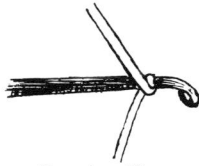

Drawing No. 1

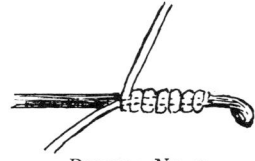

Drawing No. 2

Drawing No. 3

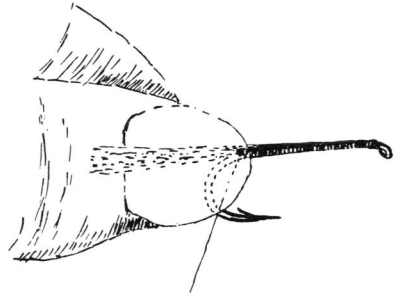

Drawing No. 4

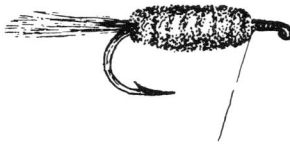

Drawing No. 5

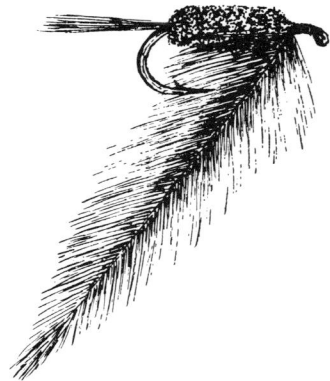

Drawing No. 6

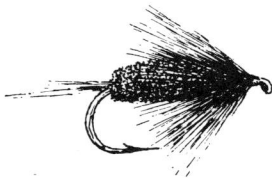

Drawing No. 7

TYING THE CHENILLE-BODIED FLY.

The wet fly tails are made of soft hackle fibres, both dyed and natural; also fibres of Wood Duck, Mallard, Turkey, Goose, Swan, Duck, Golden Pheasant topping and crest, Red Ibis, Pheasant, Partridge, and many others.

The bodies are made of floss, chenille, wool, mohair, tinsel, wire, plastic, etc.

The wings are made of sections of wing quill feathers from ducks, swan, geese, and many other birds; also hair from the squirrel, bear, badger, deer, etc.

For other information on wet flies, read the instructions for tying nymphs and streamers.

CHENILLE-BODIED WET FLY

This is an ideal fly for the beginner, it is easy to make, attractive when made in many color combinations, and will also take fish.

This fly will have scarlet hackle fibres for the tail, body, white chenille, hackle, scarlet. Excellent Crappie fly.

Secure the hook firmly in the vise with the shank about level. I do not bury a lot of the hook in the jaws of the vise—just use enough to secure the hook firmly. This gives you more space between the fly and the vise to manipulate your fingers.

Coat the hook with liquid cement, which I use in place of wax. Now take a piece of tying silk No. 000; commence near the eye of the hook, wrapping over itself for a few turns (as shown in the enlarged drawings No. 1 and No. 2), cut off the surplus short end and continue until you are in the position as shown in Drawing No. 3.

Place the tying silk in the thread holder which is at the right of the vise. Take a few scarlet hackle fibres between the thumb and first finger of the left hand and place them on top of the hook, as shown in Drawing No. 4.

Take a firm grip on the fibres and hook, then open the thumb and finger tips and bring the tying silk up between the thumb and hook and down between the finger and hook; close the tips and pull the silk straight down. Repeat this a second time, and add a few more turns of silk. If these fibres are not in the position, as shown, take them off and practice this until you can tie them in, as this is the key to many operations in fly tying.

Take a short piece of white chenille and pull off about ⅛th of an inch of the silk so as to expose the centre core; tie this in at the tail position with the core only and take the tying silk to the end of the body. When wrapping the chenille body, do not pull the chenille too hard. This will make it twist, and if your fingers perspire, grasp it with the hackle pliers. Wind each turn close together and continue up the body to position as shown in Drawing

No. 5. (Notice I have left plenty of space to tie in the hackle and finish off the head).

To prepare the hackle, which is a white hackle dyed scarlet, take hold of the tip with your first finger and thumb on your left hand and carefully stroke the fibres down until they are nearly at right angles to the stem. Now cut off the soft fibres at the base; this leaves the centre quill rough, which enables you to tie in the hackle more securely. Tie in the hackle on the under-side of the hook, almost at right angles to the hook, and cut off the surplus stem a little shorter than the end of the hook. Now take the tying silk to the eye, binding the stem very firmly, then secure the silk in the thread holder. (Drawing No. 6). Grasp the hackle by the tip, with the hackle pliers and commence to wind clockwise; avoid winding the fibres under the quill as much as possible. As you make each turn, stroke the fibres back pointing to the bend of the hook, with your left hand fingers; wet your fingers a little and hold the hackle up above the hook when pulling the fibres back.

When you have wound on the necessary amount of hackle, take a tight turn of tying silk over the hackle stem, then turn the surplus hackle forward to open up the fibres which will allow the next turn to go in between the fibres; this makes a smaller head. Now cut off the surplus hackle and form the head; finish off with the whip finish. Apply the head cement, and your fly is finished, the same as Drawing No. 7.

TYING THE HAIR-WING GRIZZLY KING

The fly I have selected is a Hair-Wing Grizzly King, a very good fly, and undoubtedly has been responsible for many fish finding the angler's creel. The hook is a No. 6 Model Perfect. After putting the hook in the vise, cover it with liquid cement, which I use in place of wax. Now take a piece of tying silk No. 000; start at the eye, wrapping over itself for a few turns, then cut off the surplus end and continue until you are in the position shown in Drawing No. 1.

Place your tying silk in the thread holder, which is at the right of the vise; I use two, one is placed about four inches from the vise and the other about eight inches. Take a narrow piece of gold, flat tinsel and place the end under the hook and take two or three turns of tying silk over it; then secure the silk in the thread holder; wind the tinsel to the left about five turns, and five turns over it to the right; tie off and put a little clear lacquer over the gold tag and cut off the short end of the tinsel; now let the long end hang down for ribbing later.

Select a piece of red feather section from a dyed wing feather and place it on the top of the hook between the thumb and first finger of the left hand (as shown in Drawing No. 2). Take a firm grip on the feather and hook, then open the thumb and finger tips and bring the tying silk up between the thumb and hook and down between the finger and hook; close the tips and pull the silk straight down; repeat this a second time, then put on a half hitch. Now trim off the surplus ends of the feather. Take the tying silk to the centre of the body and tie in a narrow piece of green silk floss; continue the tying silk to the position shown in Drawing No. 3, leaving plenty of room for the hair-wing and hackle.

After cutting off the surplus end of the floss, wind the floss tightly and as smoothly as possible (humps are hard to hide), and taper the body in front and rear, as shown in Drawing No. 3. Tie off the floss and cut away the surplus end, then wind the tinsel ribbing, being careful with the first turn; afterwards put on a good strain all the time you are making the spirals; tie off the tinsel with a half hitch and your fly will be the same as Drawing No. 3.

Cut off close to the skin a piece of grey Squirrel hair; grasp it tightly and pull out the short hairs and fuzz; then coat the butts with liquid cement. Make a smooth foundation for the hair-wing and put a little cement on it; use the same method to tie on the wing as I described in tying on the tail, and make a smooth foundation for tying on the hackle—and your fly will be the same as Drawing No. 4.

Drawing No. 1

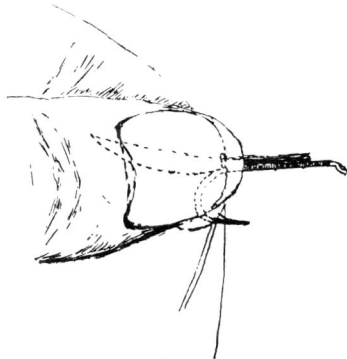

Drawing No. 2

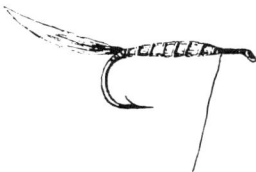

Drawing No. 3

Drawing No. 4

Drawing No. 5

TYING THE HAIR-WING GRIZZLY KING.

To prepare the hackle, which is a grizzly or barred rock, both being the same, take hold of the tip and carefully stroke the fibres down until they are nearly at right angles to the stem. Now cut off the soft fibres at the base; this leaves the quill rough, which enables you to tie in the hackle more securely. Tie in the hackle on the underside of the hook almost at right angles to the hook, and cut off surplus stem a little shorter than the end of the hook; now take the tying silk to the eye, binding the stems very firmly; then secure the silk in the thread holder. Grasp the hackle tip with the hackle pliers and commence to wind clockwise. Avoid winding the fibres under the quill as much as possible; as you make each turn, stroke the fibres back with your left hand fingers. When you have wound on the necessary amount of hackle, take a couple of turns over the hackle stem and cut off the surplus, and form the head, finishing with a whip finish. Apply the head cement, and your fly is finished, as shown in Drawing No. 5.

TYING THE WET GINGER QUILL

Before explaining how to tie the Ginger Quill, I would like to take up the subject of tying the quill section wings which are tied in several different ways.

Take a pair of Mallard wings and select a secondary or primary feather from each wing. Now cut or pull off the soft fibres at the root of the feather, then stroke the fibres gently up and out so that they are nearly at right angles to the stem. Do not split the fibres any more than you have to. Now take a razor blade and cut into the centre stem a little, then cut up, which will leave a little of the centre stem attached to the fibres, as shown in the drawing. You can split the centre quill from top to bottom with a little practice, then cut off any size wing you desire.

For the beginner I advise cutting the wing sections small at first, they will not split so easily.

If you are tying the flat downwing, which means the wings are close together, place the dull sides of the wing sections together and, if you desire the wings to be divided, place the glossy or underside of the feathers together.

Tying on the wings is not an easy task and will need a little practice. Place the wings on top of the hook, as shown in Drawing No. 5, gripping them tightly with the thumb and first finger tips on the left hand. To pass the tying silk over the wings, open up the tips of your fingers only. Take the silk up between the hook and your thumb, then over and down between the finger and hook. Grip the wings very tightly, then pull the tying silk straight down, compressing the wing fibres vertically; take about three tight turns around the wings, then trim off the surplus ends and form the head.

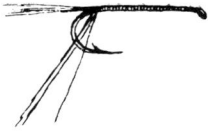

Drawing No. 1

Drawing No. 2

Drawing No. 3

Drawing No. 4

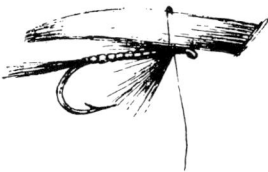

Drawing No. 5

Drawing No. 6

TYING THE WET GINGER QUILL.

A little wax on your thread will assist you in this operation; also, put a little cement on the wrapped hook in the wing position before tying them on.

To tie the Ginger Quill, place the hook in the vise, coat it with liquid cement, and wrap it with tying silk to the tail position.

Tie in a few ginger hackle fibres and a stripped quill from the Peacock-eye feather, as shown in Drawing No. 1. Before winding the quill body, form an underbody with a piece of fine floss, as it makes the body look much better.

Now wind the quill body to position shown in Drawing No. 2.

Tie in a wet fly hackle, which is soft. I tie the wet fly hackle in by the tip; I hold it vertical and stroke the fibres back as I am winding. The fibres should point to the bend of the hook. About three turns of hackle is generally enough for a wet fly. Your fly will now be the same as Drawing No. 3.

Take the wing sections, as shown in Drawing No. 4, which you will notice are the full length of the fibres; this prevents splitting. Place them on top of the hook and crowd them down carefully, taking a perfect turn over the wings by opening the finger tips and pull the thread straight down. Do this three times, then inspect the wings. If they are tied in correctly, cut off the surplus butts and put on a little cement, then form the head. Finish with the whip finish, and your fly will be the same as Drawing No. 6.

TYING THE ICE FISHING FLY

DIVER OLIVE

Tail: Olive Marabou; Ribbing, soft copper wire.
Body: Yellow floss.
Wings: Olive Marabou.
Head: Split Shot painted with yellow enamel. Eyes, red, black centre.

The size of the hook will vary according to the fish you are fishing for. A No. 12, 3X, or No. 10, 3X, is about right for pan fish, and the one I have used for the drawings is a No. 4, 3X.

Place the hook in the vise, coat it with liquid cement, and wrap it with tying silk to the tail position.

Take a split shot of the desired size, fill the slot with cement, and put a little cement on the hook and press it into position; then squeeze the slot tight with pliers, as shown in Drawing No. 1.

Paint the head with two coats of yellow enamel, and make the eyes red with a black centre. Allow this to dry before finishing the fly.

To make the eyes, first be sure the enamel is not too thick and not too thin, but just right. Now take a round stick about the size of the outside circle and place it in the enamel so that the end is just covered—do NOT dip in too far; place this straight down on the head of the fly, then lift straight up

Drawing No. 1

Drawing No. 2

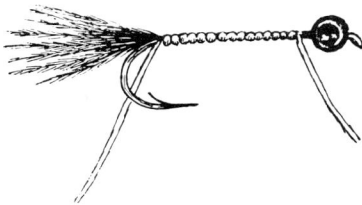

Drawing No. 3

Drawing No. 4

Drawing No. 5

TYING THE ICE-FISHING FLY.

and off. Allow this to dry a little, then put in the black centre with a smaller round stick, using the same method.

The next step is to tie in the olive Marabou tail and cut off the tying silk. You will now be the same as Drawing No. 2.

Now take a piece of soft copper wire and hold the short end with your right hand thumb and fingers, or a pair of pliers, and wind the long end carefully down the hook with your left hand to position shown in Drawing No. 3. Then cut off the front end of the wire.

Tie in a piece of yellow tying silk, and tie in a piece of yellow floss. Wrap the floss body and take the long end of the wire, make four close turns at

[43]

the tail and spiral the body, as shown in Drawing No. 4; then cut off the end.

In the space between the end of the body and the head, tie in the olive Marabou as shown, cut off the surplus ends, and tie off neatly with the yellow silk.

Put on a little head cement and your fly will be the same as Drawing No. 5.

Using the copper wire not only makes a more durable body, but also forms the segments and distributes the weight along the hook, taking it down in a more natural position—not head first.

PLATE V. ICE FISHING FLIES.

(See opposite page for identification, reading top to bottom, left to right)

ICE FISHING FLIES
(See opposite page)

Left column, reading down

No. 1   DIVER OLIVE

Tail: Olive marabou.
Body: Yellow floss; ribbing, soft copper wire.
Hackle: Olive marabou.
Head: B B Split shot painted yellow.
Eyes: Red, black centre.

No. 2   DIVER BLACK

Tail: Black marabou.
Body: Black floss; ribbing, soft copper wire gold plated.
Hackle: Black marabou.
Head: B B Split shot painted yellow.
Eyes: Red, Black centre.

No. 3   DIVER HERON

Tail: Heron hackle or substitute.
Body: Soft copper wire gold plated.
Hackle: Heron or substitute.
Head: B B Split shot painted yellow.
Eyes: Red, Black centre.

Centre column, reading down

No. 4

DIVER BLACK AND ORANGE

Tail: Black marabou.
Body: Soft copper wire gold plated.
Hackle: Orange hen hackle.
Head: B B Split shot painted yellow.
Eyes: White, black centre.

No. 5   DIVER GINGER

Tail: Ginger marabou.
Body: Yellow floss; ribbing, soft copper wire gold plated.
Hackle: Ginger marabou.
Head: B B Split shot painted yellow.
Eyes: Red, black centre.

No. 6   DIVER WOOD DUCK

Tail: Wood Duck fibres.
Body: Soft copper wire gold plated.
Hackle: Wood Duck; Thorax Peacock herl.
Head: B B Split shot painted yellow.
Eyes: Red, black centre.

Right column, reading down

No. 7

DIVER RED AND BLACK

Tail: Red marabou.
Body: Black marabou; ribbing, soft copper wire.
Hackle: Black hen hackle; tied forward.
Head: B B Split shot painted yellow.
Eyes: Red, black centre.

No. 8   DIVER ORANGE

Tail and Wing: Orange marabou.
Body: Black floss; ribbing, soft gold plated copper wire.
Head: B B Split shot painted yellow.
Eyes: Red, black centre.

No. 9   DIVER GREEN

Tail: Green marabou.
Body: Red floss; ribbing, soft copper wire gold plated.
Hackle: Green marabou.
Head: B B Split shot painted yellow.
Eyes: Red, black centre.

Chapter IV

SELECTED WET FLY
PATTERNS

THIS LIST of one hundred and forty-four wet fly patterns is only a small portion of the patterns that have been made to date. To me this is a large list of flies and I feel sure that you can select a few from it that will take fish in any part of the country.

The photographs that have been taken from the actual flies will greatly assist you in tying them if you will carefully read the material lists. The wet flies are made to be fished under the surface and represent minnows, nymphs, or any underwater larvae, and I try very hard to imitate the movements of the above mentioned food.

Every fisherman has his favorite flies which he uses continually and will never know the value of other flies if he lets them stay in the fly box.

When fishing a strange location, see the local sport store and purchase a few flies that have proved successful in this part of the country.

One of my first lessons given to me by an Indian guide was to get the flies in the water, they will not catch fish in the boat.

PLATE VI. SELECTED WET FLIES.
(See page 48 for description)

SELECTED WET FLY PATTERNS

(See Plate VI. Read top to bottom and left to right.)

No. 1 ABBEY
Tail: Golden Pheasant tippet.
Body: Red floss; ribbing and tip, gold tinsel.
Wings: Grey Mallard.
Hackle: Light brown.

No. 2 ADMIRAL
Tail: Scarlet.
Body: Red floss; tag and ribbing, gold tinsel.
Wings: White quill sections.
Hackle: Scarlet.

No. 3 ALDER
Body: Peacock herl.
Wings: Dark mottled brown Turkey or speckled game hen.
Hackle: Black or cochy-bondu.

No. 4 ALEXANDRIA
(Dr. Brunton)
Tail: Red Ibis and Peacock sword.
Body: Flat silver tinsel.
Wings: Peacock sword strands, red Ibis strip on each side. Jungle Cock Eye.
Hackle: Black.

No. 5 APPLE GREEN
Tail: Brown hackle fibres.
Body: Green floss.
Wings: Slate.
Hackle: Brown.

No. 6
ARMSTRONG FONTINALIS
Tail: White hackle fibres.
Body: Orange wool.
Wing: Dyed orange goose or duck quill section; edged with grey and white of the same.
Hackle: White saddle.

No. 7 ARTFUL DODGER
Body: Red floss; tag and ribbing, gold tinsel.
Wings: Pheasant, brown mottled.
Hackle: Claret.

No. 8 BABCOCK
Tail: Black stripe over yellow.
Body: Crimson floss, ribbing, gold.
Wings: Yellow, black stripe on each side.
Hackle: Black.

No. 9 BALDWIN
Tail: Grey Mallard.
Body: White floss.
Wings: Grey Mallard.
Hackle: Claret.

No. 10 BEAVERKILL
Tail: Grizzly hackle fibres.
Body: White floss.
Wings: Starling or Mallard.
Hackle: Brown tied palmer.

No. 11 BLACK GNAT
Body: Black Ostrich herl.
Wings: Dark slate.
Hackle: Black.

No. 12
BLACK AND ORANGE
Body: Tail half orange, front half black, fur dubbing of dyed seal or pigs wool.
Ribbing: Gold oval.
Wings: Brown Mallard.
Hackle: Black.

No. 13 BLACK O'LINDSAY
(Western Pattern)
Tail: 6 or 8 fibres ginger and Blue Jay mixed.
Body: Bright yellow wool; ribbing, gold.
Wings: Under wing, Peacock sword; over wing barred Mallard or Teal.
Hackle: Chestnut, with Blue Jay fibres over.

No. 14 BLACK PRINCE
Tail: Scarlet hackle fibres.
Body: Black floss; ribbing, silver.
Wings: Crow or black bear or squirrel.
Hackle: Black.

No. 15 BLOA POULT
Body: Yellow tying silk.
Hackle: Grouse.

No. 16 BLUE DUN
Tail: Blue dun hackle fibres.
Body: Blue grey fur from the Muskrat.
Wings: Mallard blue grey quill sections.
Hackle: Blue dun.

No. 17
  BLUE DUN HACKLED
Tail: Soft blue dun hackle fibres.
Body: Blue dun Mole fur dubbing. Ribbing, gold wire.
Hackle: Blue dun hen.

No. 18 BROUGHTON POINT
Body: Light blue silk.
Wing: Starling.
Hackle: First, reddish brown; then black.

No. 19 BROWN HACKLE
Body: Peacock herl; ribbing, fine gold.
Hackle: Brown.

No. 20 BUTCHER
Tail: Scarlet Ibis.
Body: Silver tinsel; ribbing, silver wire.
Wing: Purple feather from outside Mallard wing.
Hackle: Black.

No. 21
  BUSTARD AND ORANGE
Tail: Golden Pheasant tippets.
Body: Orange mohair ribbed with oval gold.
Wings: Bustard.
Hackle: Ginger.

No. 22
  BUSTARD AND YELLOW
Tail: Golden Pheasant tippets.
Body: Yellow mohair ribbed with oval gold.
Wings: Bustard.
Hackle: Ginger.

No. 23 CAHILL
Tail: Wood Duck or brown hackle fibres
Body: Grey Muskrat fur dubbing.
Wings: Wood Duck.
Hackle: Brown

No. 24 CAIRN'S FANCY
Tail: Black hackle fibres.
Body: Blue floss; ribbing, silver tinsel.
Wings: Starling.
Hackle: Black.

The end of the trail—The Little Thessalon River, Ontario Canada.

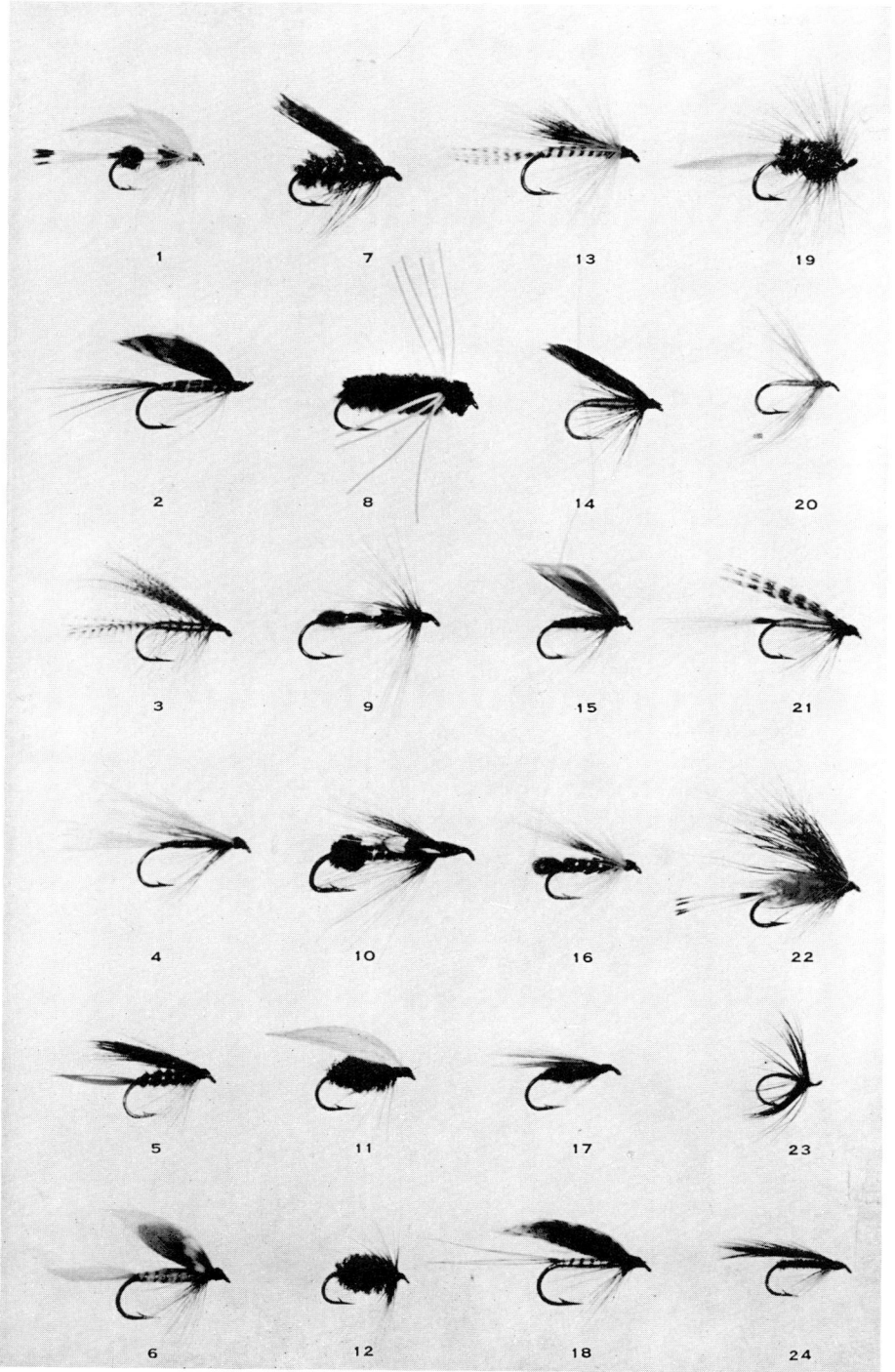

1   7   13   19

2   8   14   20

3   9   15   21

4   10   16   22

5   11   17   23

6   12   18   24

PLATE VII. WET FLIES.
(See opposite page for description)

SELECTED WET FLY PATTERNS

(See Plate VII)

No. 1
CALIFORNIA COACHMAN
Tail: Golden Pheasant tippet fibres.
Body: Peacock eyed tail fibres at each end, middle portion, yellow floss.
Wings: White duck quill section.
Hackle: Yellow.

No. 2   CALDWELL
Tail: Brown Mallard fibres.
Body: Brown floss; ribbing, yellow tying silk.
Wings: Woodcock wing sections.
Hackle: Brown.

No. 3.   CATSKILL
Tail: Wood Duck.
Body: Orange floss.
Wings: Wood Duck.
Hackle: Brown tied palmer.

No. 4
CARTER DIXIE HAIR WING
Tail: Yellow hackle fibres.
Body: Gold oval tinsel, or flat on small sizes.
Wings: White polar bear.
Hackle: Crimson.

No. 5   CARTER HARRISON
Tail: Red goose.
Body: Black seal fur; ribbing and tip, gold.
Wings: Brown Mallard.
Hackle: Brown.

No. 6   CHALLONER
Tail: Red Ibis.
Body: Yellow wool; ribbing, gold oval tinsel.
Wings: Hen Pheasant.
Hackle: Natural red.

No. 7   CHANTREY
Body: Bronze Peacock herl; ribbing, gold twist.
Wings: Brown hens feather sections, or Partridge.
Hackle: Black.

No. 8
CHENILLE SPIDER GREEN
Body: Green and black chenille.
Legs: Fine rubber.

No. 9   CLARE FLATT
(Paul H. Young)
Butt: Red seal or wool.
Body: Black floss; ribbing, silver.
Hackle: Brown (Jungle Cock eye).

No. 10   CLARE FLATT
Butt: Black chenille.
Body: Rear two thirds brown floss; ribbing, yellow tying silk and gold oval tinsel tied on together, front one third red floss, no ribbing.
Hackle: Stiff brown hackle length of the hook.
Shoulder: Jungle Cock.

No. 11   COACHMAN
Body: Peacock herl.
Wings: White duck section.
Hackle: Dark brown.

No. 12   COCHY-BONDHU
Body: Bronze Peacock herl tipped with flat gold.
Hackle: Cochy-bondhu cock, a red hackle with black centre and tips.

No. 13   COLE FLY
(Clarence Cole)
Tail: Teal section.
Body: Yellow quill; ribbing, dark Peacock quill.
Wings: Grey squirrel.
Hackle: Orange.

No. 14   COOPER
Tail: None.
Body: Orange floss.
Wings: Brown Turkey tail feather.
Hackle: Black.

No. 15   COWDUNG

Body: Olive green wool or seal fur.
Wings: Mallard or Starling primary wing
   quill section.
Hackle: Dark ginger.

No. 16   COSSEBOOM

(John C. Cosseboom)

Body: Dark green wool; ribbing, silver;
   eggsack, Dark green wool.
Wings: Grey squirrel, sparse.
Hackle: Yellow or golden olive.

No. 17   DEER FLY

Body: Tan and brown seal fur dubbing,
   ribbing, dark Peacock quill.
Wings: Hackle tips, mottled brown and
   grizzly, tied flat and divided.
Hackle: Ginger.

No. 18   DOLLY VARDEN

Tail: Brown hackle fibres.
Body: White floss; ribbing and tag, gold
   tinsel.
Wing: Mottled Turkey wing sections.
Hackle: Brown.

No. 19   DON'S FANCY

(Don Frame)

Tail: Yellow Duck quill section.
Body: Peacock herl tied thick; ribbing,
   gold oval tinsel.
Hackle: Brown.

No. 20
   DOTTEREL AND YELLOW

Body: Yellow tying silk.
Hackle: Gold tipped feather from dotterel
   wing, or a small feather from under
   Starling wing similar color.

No. 21   DORSET

Tail: Furnace hackle fibres.
Body: Green floss.
Wings: Teal body feather.
Hackle: Furnace.

No. 22   DUN CADDIS

(Wayne Buszek)

Tail: Golden pheasant tippet strands.
Body: Dark straw colored chenille.
Wing: Tuft of mule deer hair tied to
   flare at angle from hook.
Hackle: Natural red.

No. 23   DUN SPIDER

Body: Waxed yellow tying silk.
Hackle: Dun feather from underside of
   Starling's wing.

No. 24
   EARLY BROWN STONE
   (Art Flick)

Body: Rhode Island Red cocks hackle
   stem.
Wings: Two dun hackle tips tied flat
   over body.
Hackle: Blue dun hen's hackle.

SELECTED WET FLY PATTERNS

(See Plate VIII)

No. 1 FEMALE BEAVERKILL
Tail: Grey mottled Mallard.
Body: Grey floss; yellow chenille eggsack.
Wings: Grey duck.
Hackle: Brown.

No. 2   FIRE FLY
Body: Silver tinsel wound over with clear plastic.
Hackle: Brown deer tail hair.

No. 3 FLIGHT'S FANCY
Tail: Brown hackle fibres.
Body: Pale yellow floss.
Wings: Grey duck quill sections.
Hackle: Ginger.

No. 4 GINGER QUILL
Tail: Ginger hackle fibres.
Body: Peacock quill.
Wings: Grey duck quill.
Hackle: Ginger.

No. 5 GOLDEN OLIVE
Tail: Golden Pheasant crest; tag, orange floss.
Body: Golden olive seal fur; ribbing, gold oval.
Wings: Tippet fibres topped with brown Mallard.
Hackle: Golden olive.

No. 6
    GOLD RIBBED HARE'S EAR
Tail: Wood Duck, Mallard or grizzly hackle fibres.
Body: Hare's ear fur; ribbing, fine gold.
Wings: Grey duck or Woodcock.
Hackle: Pick hairs out of fur.

No. 7   GORDON
Tail: Wood Duck fibres.
Body: Yellow floss; ribbing, gold tinsel.
Wings: Wood Duck.
Hackle: Badger.

No. 8   GRANNOM MALE
Body: Brown mink fur dubbing.
Wings: Partridge wing feather.
Hackle: Brown.

No. 9   GRIZZLY KING
Tail: Section of red goose.
Body: Green silk floss; ribbing, gold.
Wings: Grey Mallard or squirrel tail.
Hackle: Grizzly.

No. 10 GREENWELL'S GLORY
(James Wright)
Body: Green silk floss with yellow tint, ribbing, gold.
Wings: Woodcock sections.
Hackle: Cochy-bondhu.

No. 11 GROUSE and PEACOCK
Body: Peacock herl.
Hackle: Grouse body feather.

No. 12 GROUSE and YELLOW
Tail: Red duck quill strands, or hackle, short.
Body: Yellow floss; ribbing, gold tinsel.
Wings: Grouse quill sections from tail feather.
Hackle: Brown.

No. 13   GUINEA HEN
Tail: Scarlet hackle fibres.
Tag: Gold tinsel.
Body: Red seal fur; ribbing, gold tinsel.
Wings: Guinea.
Hackle: Claret.

No. 14   GUNNISON
Tail: Grey Mallard fibres.
Body: Green floss; ribbing, white tying silk.
Wing: White tipped turkey.
Hackle: Brown.

[53]

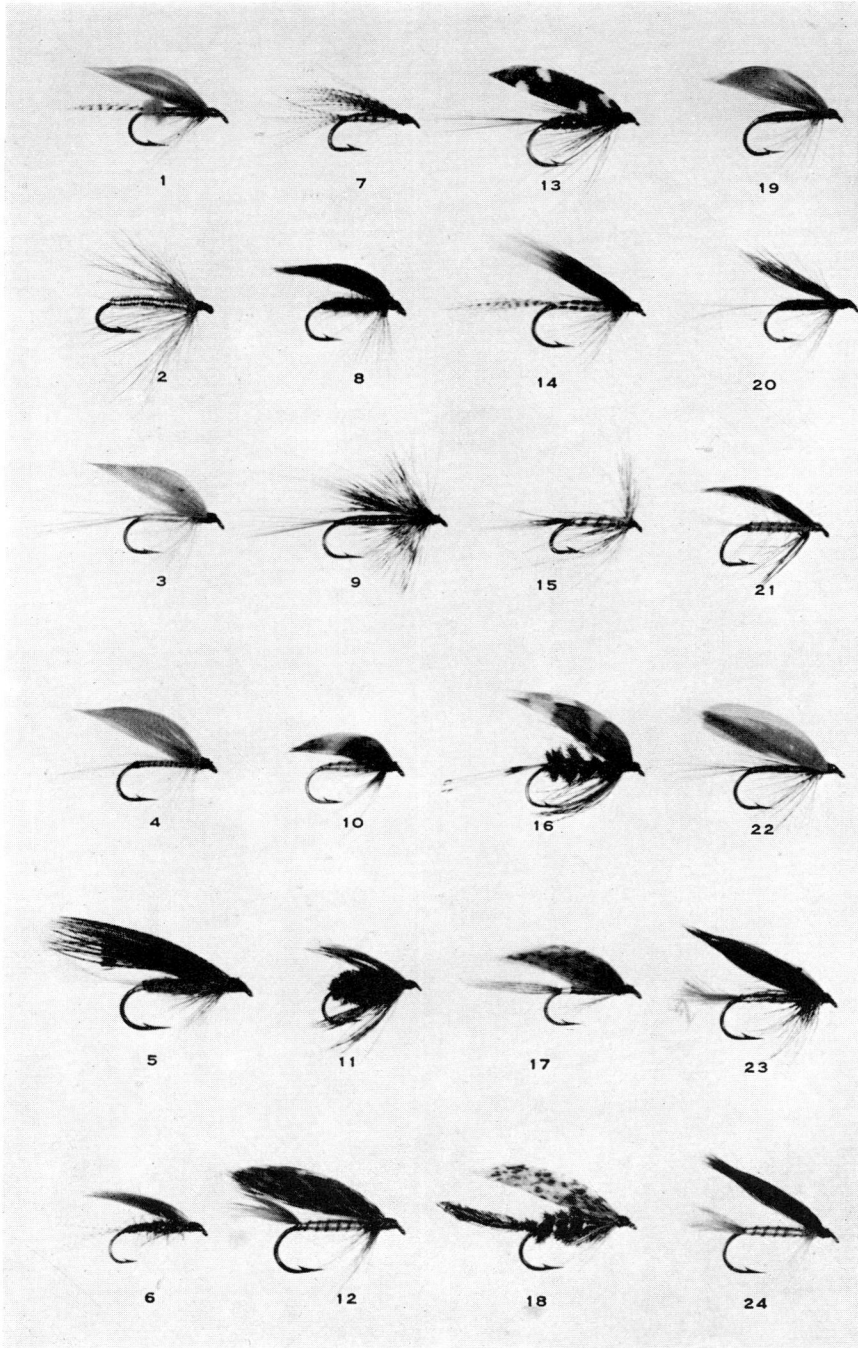

PLATE VIII. WET FLIES.
(See page 53 for description)

No. 15   GUZZLE
Tail: Badger.
Body: Yellow floss; ribbing, gold.
Hackle: Badger.

No. 16 HARDY'S FAVORITE
Tail: Golden Pheasant tippet fibres.
Body: Peacock herl; ribbing, red floss.
Wings: Woodcock, or brown Turkey.
Hackle: Brown.

No. 17   HECKHAM RED
Tail: Brown Turkey.
Body: Scarlet floss; *Tag* white
Wings: Brown mottled wild Turkey.
Hackle: Light brown.

No. 18   HENSHALL
Tail: Peacock sword.
Tag: Gold tinsel; ribbing, white tying
   silk.
Body: Peacock herl.
Wings: Light grey Turkey.
Hackle: Grey grizzly.

No. 19   HERMAN FLY
Body: Crimson floss; ribbing, gold.
Wings: Slate.
Hackle: Brown.

No. 20 HOFLAND'S FANCY
Tail: Two or three strands of red hackle.
Body: Reddish dark brown floss.
Legs: Red hackle.
Wings: Woodcock's tail section.
English fly originated by T. C. Hofland
   used in 1848.

No. 21   INVICTA
Tail: Golden Pheasant crest.
Body: Yellow mohair; ribbing, gold oval
   tinsel.
Wings: Tan and brown, Grouse, Partridge
   or Turkey.
Hackle: Ginger tied palmer.
Throat: English Blue Jay fibres.

No. 22   IRON BLUE QUILL
Tail: Iron blue dun hackle fibres.
Body: Dark Peacock quill.
Wings: Dark slate.
Hackle: Dark iron blue.

No. 23   JAY and BLUE
Tail: Red duck quill strands, or hackle,
   short.
Body: Blue floss; ribbing, silver tinsel.
Wings: English blue jay wing sections
   rolled and divided.
Hackle: Black.

No. 24   JAY and YELLOW
Tail: Red duck quill strands, or hackle,
   short.
Body: Yellow floss; ribbing, gold tinsel.
Wings: English blue jay wing sections
   rolled and divided.
Hackle: Brown.

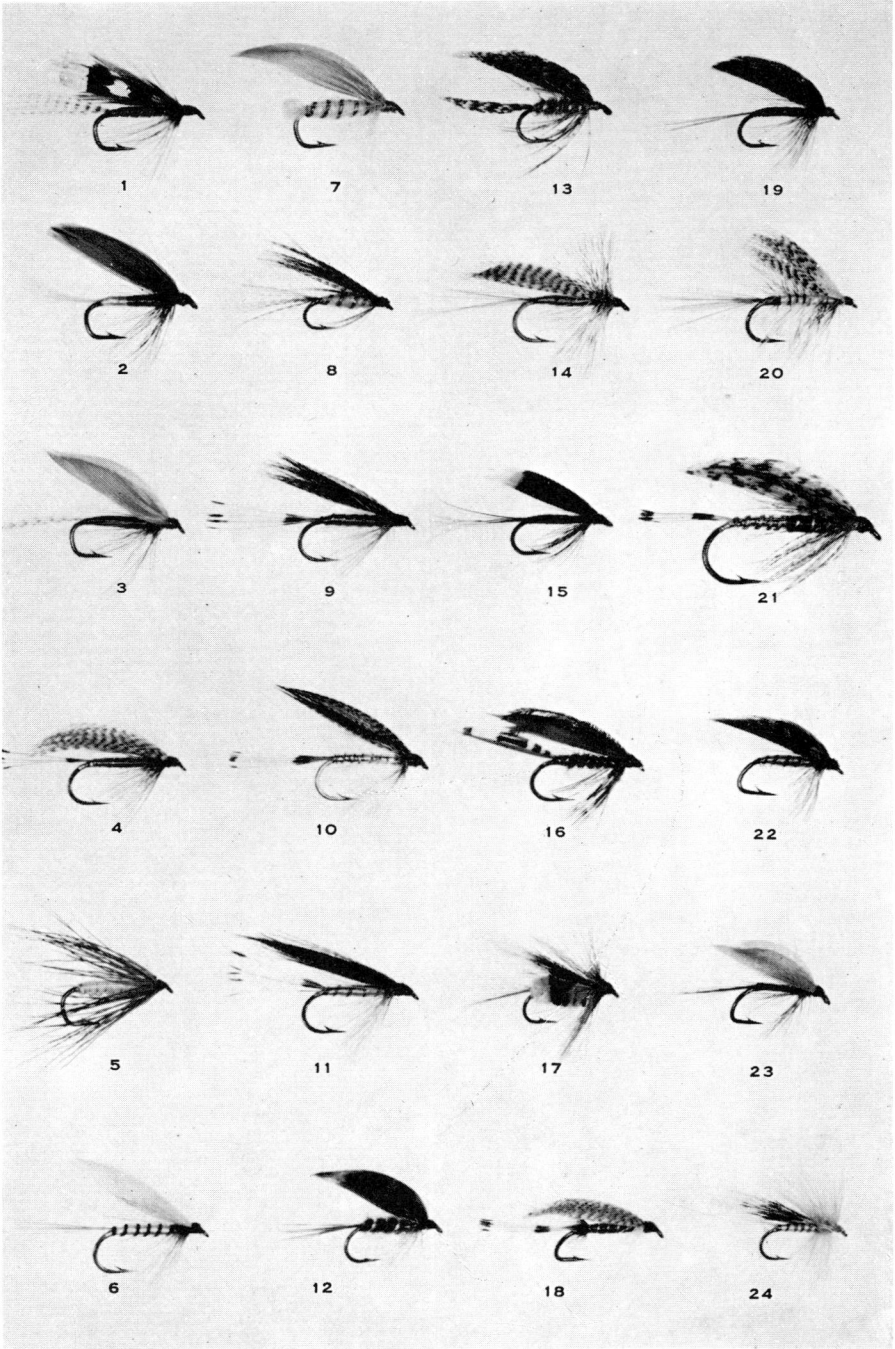

PLATE IX. WET FLIES.
(See opposite page for descriptions)

SELECTED WET FLY PATTERNS
(See Plate IX)

No. 1   JUNGLE COCK
Tail: Wood Duck fibres; tag, silver tinsel.
Body: Red floss; ribbing, silver tinsel.
Wing: Jungle Cock.
Hackle: Furnace.

No. 2   KATE
Tail: Golden Pheasant tippet.
Body: Yellow floss at tail; red floss front half.
Wings: Cinnamon.
Hackle: Black.

No. 3   KING OF WATERS
Tail: Grey Mallard.
Body: Crimson floss or wool.
Wings: Grey Mallard.
Hackle: Brown.

No. 4   KINGFISHER
Tail: Golden pheasant tippet.
Tag and ribbing: Gold tinsel.
Body: Scarlet floss.
Wings: Grey Mallard breast feather.
Hackle: Brown.

No. 5   LADY MITE
Body: White horse hair or polar bear woven with yellow floss, so as to form a yellow stripe on the underside.
Hackle: Hard deer body hair tied on as hackle.

No. 6   LAST CHANCE
Tail: Scarlet hackle fibres; tag, gold tinsel.
Body: Yellow floss; ribbing, black tying silk.
Wings: Starling or Mallard wing sections.
Hackle: Brown.

No. 7   LIGHT FOX
Tail: Yellow wool tag.
Body: White wool, ribbing, gold.
Wings: Slate.
Hackle: Yellow.

No. 8   MALLARD
Tail: Brown Mallard.
Body: Yellow wool, ribbing, gold.
Wings: Brown Mallard.
Hackle: Brown.

No. 9   MALLARD and RED
Tail: Strands of Golden Pheasant tippet.
Body: Red floss; ribbing, gold tinsel.
Wings: Brown Mallard.
Hackle: Brown.

No. 10
MALLARD and SILVER
Tail: Golden Pheasant tippets.
Body: Silver tinsel; ribbing, silver oval.
Wings: Brown Mallard.
Hackle: Badger.

No. 11
MALLARD and YELLOW
Tail: Strands of Golden Pheasant tippet.
Body: Yellow floss; ribbing, gold tinsel.
Wings: Brown Mallard.
Hackle: Brown.

No. 12   MARCH BROWN
(American)
Tail: Brown hackle fibres.
Body: Brown fur, ribbing, gold or yellow silk.
Wings: Dark mottled Partridge or **Turkey**.
Hackle: Brown and grizzly.

No. 13   MARCH BROWN
(English Male)
Tail: Partridge tail fibres.
Body: Medium Hare's ear fur picked out to form legs.
Ribbing: Unwaxed yellow tying silk.
Wings: Partridge tail feather sections.

No. 14   McKENZIE
Tail: Brown hackle.
Body: Olive green floss; ribbing, gold tinsel.
Wings: Mallard breast.
Hackle: Grizzly.

No. 15 MERSHON
Tail: Black hackle fibres.
Body: Black silk floss.
Wings: Dark blue, white tipped.
Hackle: Black.

No. 16 McALPIN
Tail: Barred Mandarin and scarlet wing section.
Tag: Gold tinsel.
Body: Claret seal fur; ribbing, gold tinsel.
Wings: Scarlet wing sections; topping, peacock herl.
Hackle: Guinea fowl.

No. 17
MC GINTY HAIR WING
Tail: Mallard and red hackle fibres.
Body: Black and yellow chenille (alternated).
Wings: Grey squirrel.
Hackle: Brown.

No. 18 MILL'S No. 1
Tail: Fibres of Golden Pheasant tippet.
Body: Crimson floss; ribbing, gold, black tag, tip, gold.
Wings: Mallard, dyed yellow.
Hackle: White.

No. 19 MONTREAL
Tail: Scarlet hackle fibres.
Body: Wine floss; ribbing, gold.
Wings: Brown mottled Turkey.
Hackle: Claret.

No. 20 MORMAN GIRL
Tail: Scarlet hackle fibres.
Tag: Scarlet silk floss or tying silk.
Body: Yellow floss.
Wings: Grey mottled Mallard breast.
Hackle: Grizzly tied palmer.

No. 21 NATIONS SHINER TIP
Tail: Golden Pheasant tippets, tag, silver tinsel.
Body: First half silver, second half black floss, ribbing, silver oval.
Wings: Brown mottled Turkey, and a strip of red goose on top.
Hackle: Guinea fowl.

No. 22 OAK
Tail: Brown Turkey, (optional).
Body: Orange floss or wool; ribbing, dark Peacock Quill.
Wings: Brown Turkey, or Pheasant.
Hackle: Brown.

No. 23 OLIVE QUILL
Tail: Olive hackle fibres.
Body: Olive quill.
Wings: Slate.
Hackle: Olive.

No. 24 ORANGE COLE
Tail: Golden Pheasant crest.
Body: Yellow floss; ribbing, gold.
Wings: Woodchuck.
Hackle: Orange.

SELECTED WET FLY PATTERNS
(See Plate X)

No. 1 ORANGE FISH HAWK
Body: Orange floss; gold ribbing and tip (optional).
Hackle: Badger.

No. 2 ORANGE QUILL
Tail: Orange hackle fibres.
Body: Stripped Condor quill, dyed orange.
Wings: Starling secondary, or Mallard quill sections.
Hackle: Orange.

No. 3 PARMACHENE BELLE
Tail: Red and white hackle fibres.
Body: Yellow floss; ribbing, silver.
Wings: White goose, Scarlet strip on each side.
Hackle: Red and white.

No. 4 PARTRIDGE and GREEN
Body: Green floss.
Hackle: Partridge.

No. 5 PARTRIDGE and ORANGE
Body: Orange floss.
Hackle: Partridge.

No. 6 PETER ROSS
Tail: Golden Pheasant.
Body: One third silver, remainder red seal; ribbing, silver.
Wings: Teal or Widgeon.
Hackle: Black.

No. 7 PHEASANT TAIL
Tail: Three strands purple Pheasant tail.
Body: Four strands purple Pheasant tail wrapped around body, ribbing, gold wire.
Hackle: Blue dun.

No. 8 PRIEST
Tail: Scarlet hackle fibres.
Body: Silver tinsel, ribbing, silver oval.
Hackle: Badger.

No. 9 PROFESSOR HAIR WING
Tail: Red hackle fibres.
Body: Yellow floss: ribbing, gold tinsel.
Wings: Grey squirrel hair.
Hackle: Brown.

No. 10 PULASKI
(Dr. Ernest Ovitz)
Tail: Yellow and red hackle fibres; tag, gold.
Body: Red floss; ribbing, gold tinsel.
Wing: Fox squirrel tail.
Hackle: Orange.

No. 11 QUEEN OF WATERS
Body: Orange floss.
Wings: Grey Mallard, mottled.
Hackle: Brown tied palmer.

No. 12 RED ANT
Body: Red floss, with Peacock herl butt.
Wings: Grey Mallard quill sections.
Hackle: Brown.

No. 13 RED FOX
Tail: Grey Mallard.
Body: Light red fox under-fur.
Wings: Slate.
Hackle: Brown.

No. 14 RED QUILL
Tail: Brown Hackle fibres.
Body: Peacock quill, or red hackle stem.
Wings: Slate.
Hackle: Brown.

No. 15 RED SPINNER
Tail: Brown hackle fibres.
Body: Red seal or wool; ribbing, gold wire.
Wings: Dark grey.
Hackle: Brown.

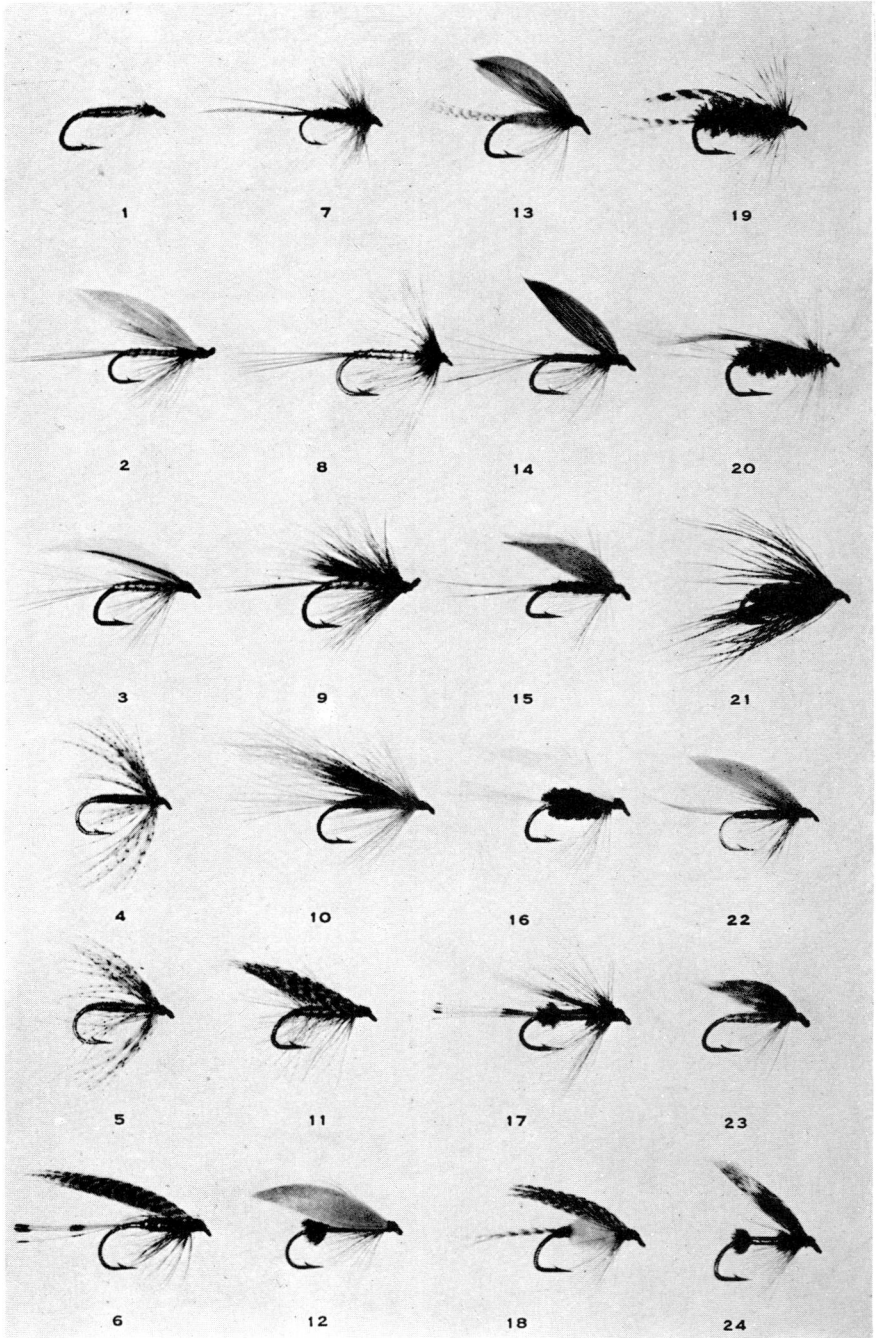

PLATE X. WET FLIES.

(See page 59 for descriptions)

No. 16   RIO GRAND KING
Tail: Yellow hackle fibres; gold tip.
Body: Black chenille.
Wings: White quill section.
Hackle: Brown.

No. 17   ROYAL COACHMAN
Tail: Golden Pheasant tippets.
Body: Red floss; Peacock herl butts at each end.
Wings: White goose or grey squirrel.
Hackle: Reddish dark brown.

No. 18   RUBE WOOD
Tail: Teal.
Body: Red floss, tip, white chenille.
Wings: Grey Mallard, mottled.
Hackle: Brown.

No. 19
SALYER'S GENERALIZED
STONE FLY
(Grey)
Tail: Two sections of barred teal.
Body: Peacock herl; ribbing, gold oval tinsel.
Wing: Scaup black and white barred back feather; or a well barred flank feather, tied flat.
Hackle: Grizzly.

No. 20
SALYER'S GENERALIZED
STONE FLY
(Brown)
Tail: Grizzly hackle fibres.
Body: Peacock herl; ribbing and tag, gold wire.
Wing: Honey dun hackle tips, tied flat.
Hackle: Furnace.

No. 21   SANDY MITE
Body: Brown and white cow hair or horse hair woven with red floss to form a red stripe on the underside.
Hackle: Hard deer body hair tied on as hackle.

No. 22   SCARLET IBIS
Tail: Scarlet quill section.
Body: Scarlet floss; ribbing, gold.
Wings: Scarlet quill section.
Hackle: Scarlet.

No. 23   SETH GREEN
Body: Green floss; ribbing, yellow silk.
Wings: Dark mottled Turkey tail.
Hackle: Brown.

No. 24   SHAD FLY
Body: Peacock herl, gold centre.
Wings: Brown Turkey wing.
Hackle: Brown.

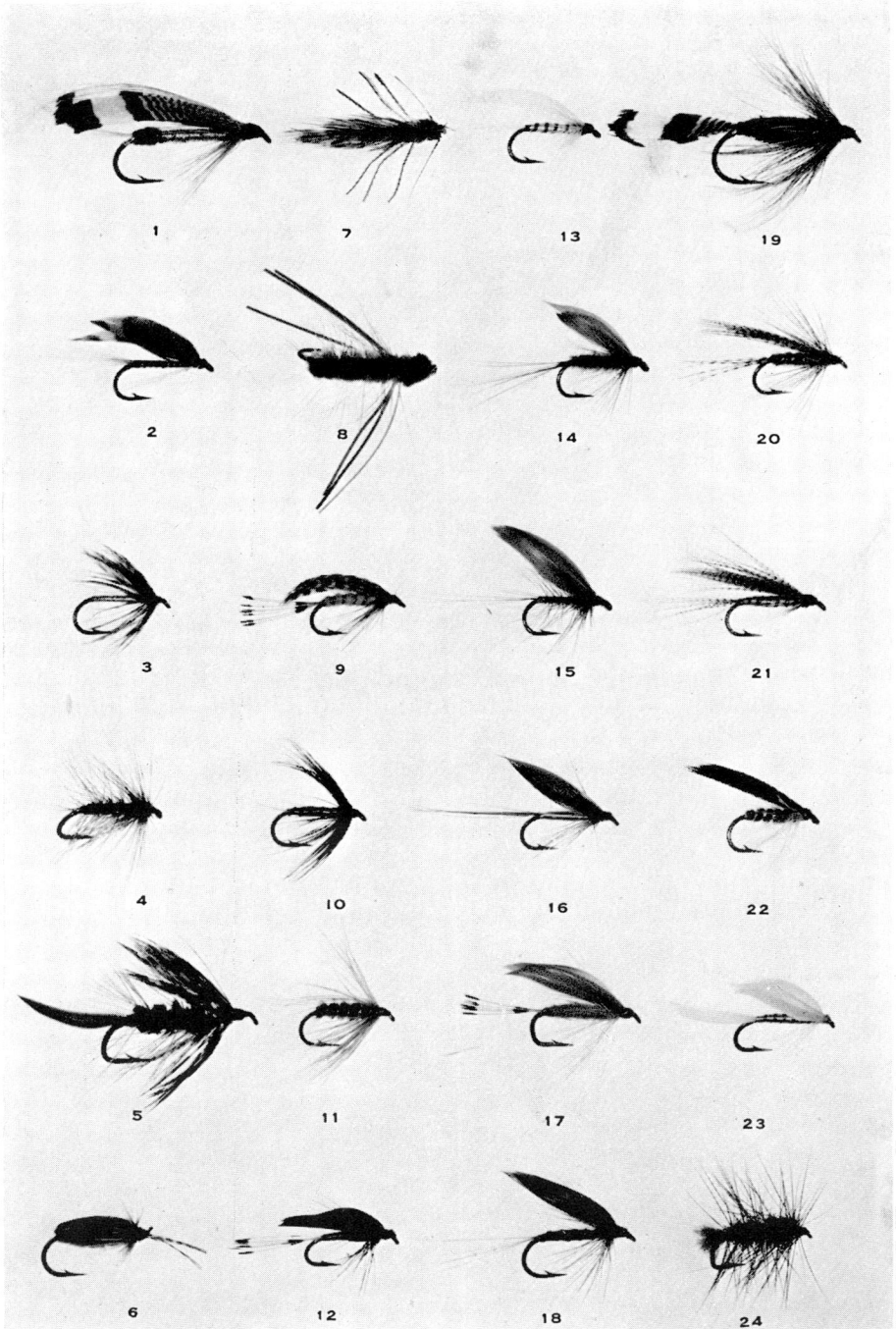

PLATE XI.   WET FLIES.

(See opposite page for descriptions)

SELECTED WET FLY PATTERNS
(See Plate XI)

No. 1   SILVER DOCTOR
Tail: Golden Pheasant crest, tag, silver tinsel.
Butt: Red wool.
Body: Silver oval tinsel.
Wings: Golden Pheasant tail sections, topped with barred Wood Duck; Golden Pheasant topping.
Hackle: Silver doctor blue.

No. 2   SKINNUM
Tail: Blue dun cock hackle fibres; tag, flat silver.
Body: Peacock quill.
Hackle: Blue dun.
Wings: Woodcock.

No. 3   SNIPE AND YELLOW
Body: Primrose buttonhole silk.
Hackle: Snipe under covert feather; ribbing, gold wire, (optional)

No. 4   SOLDIER PALMER
Body: Scarlet wool; ribbing, gold; gold tip.
Hackle: Brown tied palmer.

No. 5   SPITFIRE
(Don Gapen)
Tail: Red (dyed Turkey)
Body: Black silk floss on chenille.
Hackle: Brown tied palmer Guinea hen at head, all hackle fibres tilt toward tail.
Shoulder: Jungle cock (optional)

No. 6   SQUASH BUG
Body: Orange wool overlapped with a grey or brown goose feather.
Hackle: Soft badger or grizzly.
Antennae: Two grey feather fibres.

No. 7   STONE FLY
(Wm. F. Blades)
Tail: Legs and antennae; Brown hackle trimmed.
Body: Tan raffia; ribbing, Peacock quill; markings, brown enamel.
Wings: Four variant tan grizzly hackle tips tied flat.

No. 8
STRIDER YELLOW AND GREEN
Body: Yellow chenille, palmered with brown hackle.
The back is one strand of green chenille.
Head: Green chenille.
Legs: Six fine rubber strands.

No. 9   TEAL AND YELLOW
Tail: Golden Pheasant tippet.
Body: Yellow seal fur; ribbing, gold oval tinsel.
Wings: Teal.
Hackle: Brown.
Different colored bodies are used for this fly; such as red, orange, green, etc.

No. 10   WATER CRICKET
Body: Orange floss; ribbing, black silk.
Hackle: Black hen.

No. 11   WATER HEN BLOA
Body: Mole fur on yellow silk; ribbing, yellow silk.
Hackle: Water hen wing feather or blue grey hen hackle.

No. 12   WATSON'S FANCY
Tail: Golden Pheasant tippet.
Body: First half red floss, remaining half black floss.
Wings: Black quill section.
Hackle: Black.

[63]

No. 13   WHITE MILLER
Tail: White hackle fibres.
Body: White floss; ribbing, gold.
Wings: White goose.
Hackle: White.

No. 14   WHIRLING DUN
Tail: Brown hackle fibres.
Body: Blue grey fur.
Wings: Slate quill section.
Hackle: Brown.

No. 15 WICKHAM'S FANCY
Tail: Brown hackle fibres.
Body: Gold tinsel.
Wings: Slate quill section.
Hackle: Brown tied palmer.

No. 16   WILLOW
Tail: Brown hackle fibres.
Body: Olive grey floss.
Wings: Dark slate quill section.
Hackle: Brown.

No. 17   WILSON
Tail: Golden Pheasant tippet.
Body: Orange wool, gold tip.
Wings: Grey Mallard.
Hackle: Orange.

No. 18 WOODCOCK and RED
Tail: Natural red hackle fibres.
Body: Red floss; ribbing, silver twist.
Hackle: Natural red.
Wings: Woodcock, rolled and divided.

No. 19
      WOOD DUCK AND BLACK
Tag: Silver tinsel.
Tail: Barred Wood Duck.
Body: Black fur dubbing. Weighted with
   a wrapping of soft copper wire for fast
   water, or early fishing.
Hackle: Natural black.

No. 20
      WOOD DUCK AND ORANGE
Tail: Wood Duck fibres.
Body: Orange seal fur; ribbing, gold oval
   tinsel.
Wings: Wood Duck.
Hackle: Orange.

No. 21
      WOOD DUCK AND YELLOW
Tail: Wood Duck fibres.
Body: Yellow floss; ribbing, gold tinsel.
Wings: Wood Duck body feather.
Hackle: Badger.

No. 22   YELLOW DUN
Body: Grey fur; ribbing, yellow silk.
Wings: Brown Mallard.
Hackle: Yellow.

No. 23   YELLOW SALLY
Tail: Yellow quill section.
Body: Yellow floss; ribbing, gold, gold
   tip.
Wings: Yellow quill section.
Hackle: Yellow.

No. 24   ZULU
Tail: Scarlet wool tag.
Body: Peacock herl.
Hackle: Black tied palmer.

Clare Flatt, Jungle Cock, Nations Shiner Tip, Squash Bug, Golden Olive, Wood Duck and Black,
Royal Coachman, Watson's Fancy

Description refers to flies in Color Plate C.

above are (read left to right) Blades weighted Bucktail Streamer No 3, ginger Furnace Frey, Plate A
Thors Red optic fly. D o F, Paint Brush Two wing, Cains River Silver grey, New Trier,
Roaring Rapids, Supervisor, Furnace grey, Blades weighted Bucktail Streamer No 2.

In Appreciation of a Fly Tyer

Notes on Bill Blades's Work by Poul Jorgensen

The first edition of FISHING FLIES AND FLY TYING was written in the late 1940s, published in 1951, and followed early in 1962 by an updated edition. It's not surprising, then, to find that it is somewhat different in style and technique from the books that have been published in the last fifteen years. Fly tying has come a long way since Bill Blades's day of silk thread and Allcock hooks. What *is* surprising is how fresh and appealing the patterns themselves remain to the fly tyer's eye.

While many of Bill's flies, particularly the realistic interpretations of mayflies and nymphs, were far superior to the standard patterns of his time, it's his tying methods, tools, and materials that hold the most fascinating lessons for today's angler—*especially* for those who have learned the basics of fly tying from recent books. In Bill's day there were no Matarelli tools, no fine prewaxed thread, no Seal-Ex or other synthetics, not very many instruction books, and very few suppliers of materials. The fine nymph bodies, the delicate legs on his dry flies, the exact proportions of his wets and streamers become even more impressive when one realizes that they are completely original—an expression of one tyer's determination and dedication to the art of fly tying.

It is a dedication that still has lessons for us today. As I have looked at my well-worn copy of *Fishing Flies and Fly Tying* over the years, I have always been reminded that fly tying is a school from which we never graduate. Thank heaven! For the accomplished tyer who can experiment with a battery of new tools and patterns, learning Blades's style offers the opportunity to add to the spectrum of his tying enjoyment. And it is more than nostalgia: there are practical tips and techniques here that confirm that fly tying is essentially a process of discovery—and discoveries come to us from the past as well as from synthetic materials and new tools. Bill's simple technique for anchoring feather wings, for example, by trimming the fibers and leaving stumps instead of tearing them, can be applied to many modern dry fly and fully dressed salmon patterns. It is techniques like this that have kept his work alive for hundreds of tyers.

But Bill Blades was of the old school. He used very few tools other than his vise, scissors, bodkin, and an assorted variety of hackle pliers. "That's all you need," I remember him saying in one of his usual pronouncements. "I know there are a lot of professional tyers who use a bobbin to hold the silk spool, but I personally don't use one." Since I learned tying from Bill, it was natural for me to use only what he suggested, and it was not until the early 1970s that I realized the practicality of a bobbin, not only to hold the thread spool, but also as a weight to eliminate the half hitch Bill had taught me to use to tie off materials.

Bill was well aware of the uniqueness of his realistic insect imitations ("natural imitations," as he preferred to call them). I remember one operation that often brought Bill to the point of talking to the fly in a very "inappropriate" manner. The small section of nylon he used as a core for the extension body on may flies (Chapter XI, "Natural May Flies and Imitations") would often get out of alignment when he was tying in the tails, or when winding the silk floss and raffia grass. He solved it simply by using flat-nosed pliers to flatten the small portion of nylon that is fastened on the shank. I was amazed. That small touch made a world of difference.

Although he was at heart a practical and economic tyer, Bill was willing to experiment to get the effect he wanted, as shown in a number of new techniques he used for tying realistic nymph imitations. In Chapter XIII, "Nymphs and Nymph Fishing," you will find several flies requiring an underbody of plastic which is pressed on the hook-shank and later filed to shape when completely dry. This, I am sure, will be difficult to understand at first. I remember having a lot of trouble with it, and it wasn't until I read the instructions for tying the Hexagenia Mayfly Nymph that I found out that the plastic he was referring to when tying the dragon fly and stone fly nymphs was ordinary Duco household cement which he squeezed out of a tube onto a small glass plate. He was never completely satisfied with this rather messy procedure. When he finally came up with a different idea, I thought it was the funniest thing I had ever seen. Tying a stone fly nymph, Bill would tie in the tails and antennae on a long shank Allcock hook in the usual manner, and start the underbody by attaching some size 3/0 cotton thread, which came off a large cone placed on the floor directly under the small tying table where his vise was located. When this was done he poured a generous amount of Duco on top of the entire length of the shank. Before it had time to drip he quickly started to wind the thread back and forth, leading the cement around the hook-shank, often blowing on it until he was dizzy in an effort to set it a little faster. He continued to pour cement on the shank and wind thread around like crazy until the underbody was the size he wanted. He hung it to dry near the heat coming from the metal shade on the small gooseneck lamp on his tying table. As it dried it would shrink a great deal, and he kept adding more cement from the tube. After it was completely dry he could file it to the desired shape. A laborious process to be sure, but it illustrates well the determination and invention that shine through on the cross section of Blades's patterns shown on the color plates.

As I look at them and recall how Bill worked to bring them to life on his vise, I often think of how it would be if he were with us today. What a picnic he would have with all the materials and tying techniques that have evolved since his days, when being a fly tyer was a very lonely endeavor. If he could see the thousands of young and old who have developed an interest in fly tying since then, and if he could see this new edition of his book, I am sure he would smile and feel satisfaction because he somehow had helped lay the foundation for the continuation of this wonderful angling art. Who knows, he might even have gone so far as to suggest that you use your own imagination and try to tie some of his flies with the new material available, saying, "There's got to be something better than Duco cement."

REALISTIC DRY FLIES AND NYMPHS

Clockwise from top

(Read ~~top to bottom, left to right~~)

Dragon Fly Nymph, Damsel Fly Nymph, Blades' Ephemera Simulans, Blades' Crane Fly Parachute, Blades' Stone Fly Nymph, Blades' Stenonema Vicarium

Plate B

STREAMER AND STEELHEAD FLIES

Wet Flies

(Read ~~top to bottom~~, left to right)

Blades' Weighted Bucktail Streamer No. 3, Ginger Furnace Frey, Thor, Red Optic Fly, Dot, Paint Brush Two Wing, Cains River Silver Grey, New Trier, Roaring Rapids, Supervisor, Furnace Frey, Blades' Weighted Bucktail Streamer No. 2

Correct names given on Plate A in error, above names refer to flies on plate a But read left to right)

Plate C.

STREAMER FLIES

Alaskan Mary Ann, Aleck's Wonder, Algoma, Ambrose Bucktail, A. S. Trude, Badger H O B Streamer, Barnes Special, Black Dog, Black Demon Cains River, Black-Nose Dace

√ see page 81 for patterns

Plate D

(Read left to Right)

LARGE BASS FLIES

Badger Furnace, Cockatouch Fly, Cowdung, Fox Squirrel Bug, Hackle Bass Fly, Johnson's Fancy, March Brown, Mc Ginty, "Readheads" Squirrel Tail Fly—Yellow, Bucktail Bass Fly, Mississippi Bug

Plate E.
Patterns on Page 256

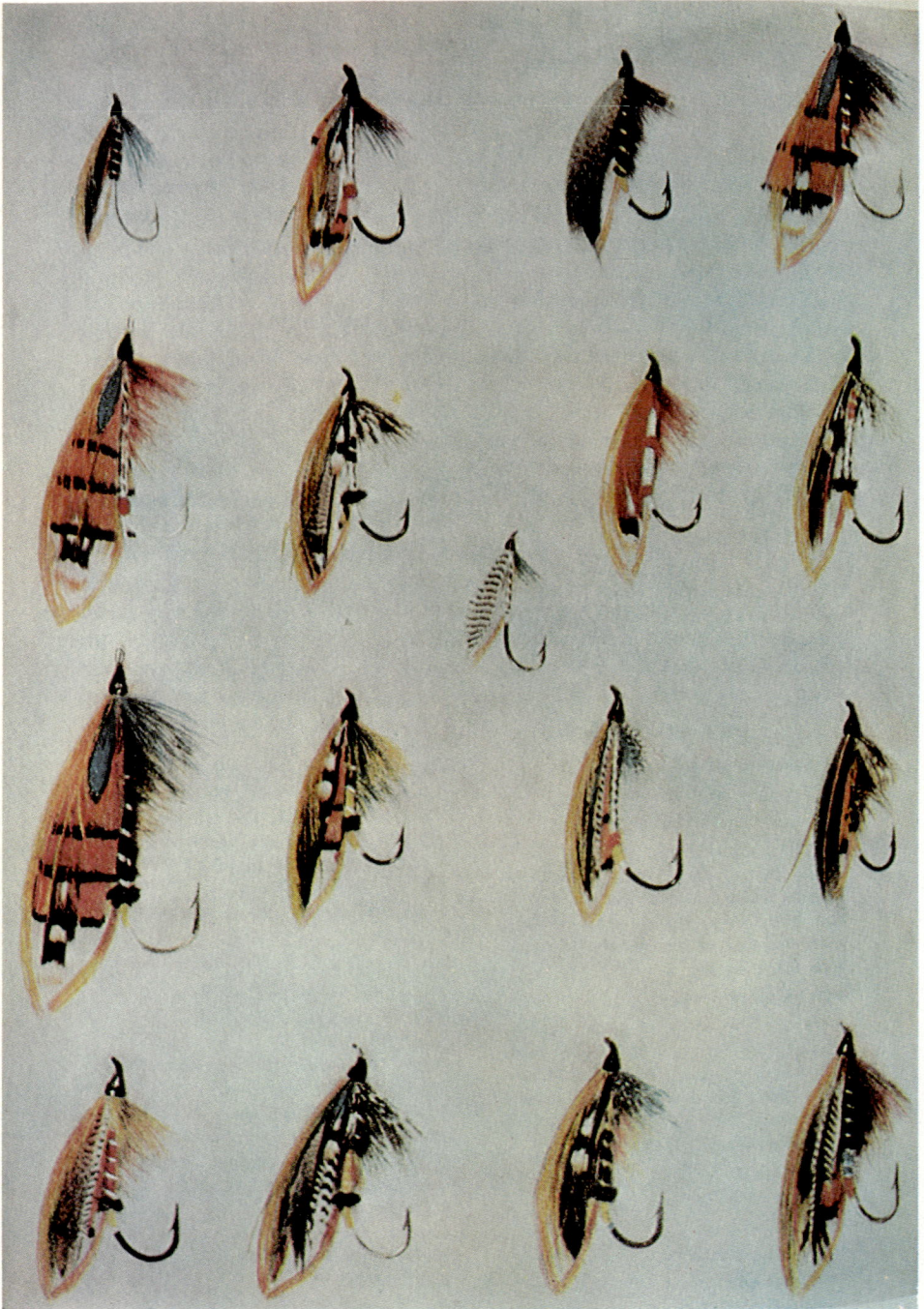

SALMON FLIES

Kate, Jock Scott, Thunder and Lightning, Black Dose, Black Ranger, Green Highlander, Silver Doctor, Butcher, Durham Ranger, Mar Lodge, Red Sandy, Dusty Miller, Logie, Silver Wilkinson, Black Fairy, Durham Ranger, Silver and Blue (center fly)

Plate F

Patterns on Page 281, 282, 283.

Chapter V

METHODS OF WINGING
THE ARTIFICIAL FLY

TYING ON WINGS is the most difficult operation for the beginner and I am asked to demonstrate this everywhere I go. The following drawings and writing will greatly assist the beginner in solving his winging troubles. Read the instructions several times and study the drawings before tying on the wings; also tie on the wings only, at first, and cut them off if they are not satisfactory.

The Hair Wing. This is explained in "Tying the Hair-wing Grizzly King" on pages 38 and 39.

The Bucktail Wing. This is explained in "Tying the Black and White Bucktail Streamer" on page 74.

Wood Duck Fibre Wing. This is explained in "Tying the Dry Fly, Hendrickson" and also tied spent in the "Cahill Parachute Fly" on pages 109 and 111.

The Flat Downwing and Divided Downwing. These are explained in "Tying the Wet Ginger Quill" on page 40.

Upright Dry Fly Wings, Single and Double. These are explained in "Tying the Dry Fly" on page 108.

Tying large, wet Turkey quill wings is explained in "Tying the New Trier Steelhead Fly"

Tying the Deerhair Moth Wing is explained in "Tying the Hair Moth"

TYING THE FAN-WING

Select two matched breast feathers from the Wood Duck, Mallard, or Teal; cut off the fibres close to the stem at the base until you have the proper size wing—as shown in Drawing No. 1; leaving the stem rough assists in holding the wings in place.

Now put the wings together (glossy side inside) and straddle the hook with the butts; put a little cement on the covered hook and butts, then take

Drawing No. 1

Drawing No. 2

Drawing No. 3

Drawing No. 4

several turns of tying silk around the butts, also in front and in behind, and in between, to bring them in the proper position, as shown in Drawing No. 2.

Cut off the butts and conceal the ends with a few turns of thread.

Tie the wings on securely and straight; crooked wings make the fly spin when it is cast.

TYING THE SPENT WINGS

Read instructions for tying on the wings in "Tying the Crane Fly," and follow Drawings No. 4 and No. 5. Page 178.

[66]

TYING THE HACKLE FIBRE WING

To tie this wing, select a good dry fly hackle of the size and color desired. Then wrap the hook with tying silk; now tie in the hackle by the butt, and wind on a few turns, as shown in Drawing No. 5.

For this type of wing, use colored tying silk about the same color as the hackle, as the base will form the thorax. Now evenly divide the hackle fibres and work them into a spent wing position, as shown in Drawing No. 6.

Drawing No. 5

Drawing No. 6

Drawing No. 7

Drawing No. 8

Take a few criss cross turns of silk to hold them in position; then stroke the fibres to an upright position.

Now take a few turns around the base and in between to hold them in the position as shown in Drawing No. 7.

For the spent wing, make your turns of silk so that the wings hold firmly and horizontally, as shown in Drawing No. 8.

This is a very durable wing which allows the light to filter through. I strongly advise trying this on your favorite dry flies.

HACKLE TIP WINGS

I feel very confident when I say hackle tips make some of our best fly wings. First, they are easy to tie on, and they also allow the light to filter through them, making them most effective.

A dry fly that is made with these wings can be made to float with a small amount of good hackles, making it ideal for the Eastern fly fishermen.

[67]

To tie on this wing, wrap the hook with tying silk and take the thread to the wing position. Trim the stems of two perfectly matched hackle tips to the size required; then put a little cement on the butts and hook, and take a few turns of thread tightly around and in between the butts, as shown in Drawing No. 9.

Pull the butt ends back, as shown in Drawing No. 2; wind over them, and cut off the ends.

Keeping a strong tension on your tying thread at all times, and putting the first few turns of thread in the proper place, is the secret of tying on good wings.

Drawing No. 9

Drawing No. 10

Drawing No. 10 shows a double hackle tip wing that I use on some May Flies and Flying Ants.

HACKLE TIP UNDIVIDED FLAT WING

These wings are used for Stone Flies. Simply prepare them as before described and prepare a base with tying silk that is about level with the body. Now put a little cement on the two pairs of wing butts and base, and tie them, as shown in Drawing No. 11.

Drawing No. 11

DOWN WINGED FLY
(*Drawing No. 12 is my Caddis Fly*)

You can select this shaped hackle from some rooster necks; the best are generally found on the outside.

Prepare four hackles as previously described and tie them on the side of the fly so as to form a "roof"; this is not easy, but a little practice will overcome this.

This type of wing is used on the Alder Fly also.

Drawing No. 12

TYING THE DEER BODY HAIR WING
AS USED ON THE "IRRESISTIBLE FLY"

Selecting the proper hair is half the battle when tying this dry fly hair wing. For your first wing, use a small amount of hair; it will be much easier to conceal the base of the wings.

Select fine, stiff hair; this can be obtained from the deer leg, and also from the face. *Don't* use thick hair.

Put a little cement on the hook in the wing position and take a few turns of tying silk. Now lay the hair on top of the hook and take two turns of

Drawing No. 13

Drawing No. 14

thread around the hook and hair—*not too tightly,* or you will make the hair flare up too much. Now take several tight turns around the butts, then divide the wing into two equal parts and criss-cross the thread in between and in front, bringing the wings to an upright position, as shown in Drawings No. 13 and No. 14.

[69]

Follow the previous instructions when tying the Wulff flies, but use deer tail hair for the wings and tail.

ROLLED WING

Take a secondary wing feather and cut off about one inch of the fibres on the wide side.

Now work the fibres with your fingers and thumbs until you get the tips level, and cut the bottom off level, as shown in Drawing No. 15.

The usual method of rolling these fibres is to roll them over every quarter of an inch so that you have four strips. They will now be same as Drawing No. 16.

Drawing No. 15

Drawing No. 16

I fold the fibres in half with the best side out; then make a second fold. This is an ideal wing when made of large Mallard and Wood Duck breast feathers.

I have used an English Woodcock feather for these drawings.

Drawing No. 17 is the finished rolled wing wet fly.

Drawing No. 17

TYING THE MARABOU WING

When winging flies such as the White and Yellow Marabou, take a feather that is a little larger than you require and split the centre quill, leaving the Marabou fibres attached to the quill. Cut the amount you need from a right and left feather so that they will match, and tie them in the length you require. If you have trouble when tying on the wings, you can take them off, straighten the fibres and tie them in again. Be sure to use this method on Peacock sword and herl wings, and toppings.

Drawing No. 18 shows the Marabou wing prepared ready to tie in.

Drawing No. 19 shows the wing tied in position.

Drawing No. 18

Drawing No. 19

Many of my readers have trouble making wings that are made from the quills taken from many different bird wings.

First you must have a pair of wings taken from the same bird. Cut off a piece the size you desire from each wing with the fibres attached to the centre quill, as shown in drawing.

Place a wing in the vise projecting up a little longer than the length you wish and do not tighten the vise too much or you will cut the wing; now put a little liquid cement on the fibres where you will tie the knot.

Take a piece of strong fine tying thread and tie a water-knot in the middle of it; place the loop over the wing; trap the thread in your left hand and place your first finger and thumb on each side of the wing; pull the right hand thread to the right; this will compress the fibres down and make a perfect wing. Tie on the wings below the knot, not above, or you will split the wings.

Chapter VI

STREAMER FLIES

TREAMER FLIES are simply flies that have long wings and are mostly made on long shank hooks. They are made to represent our many different minnows which form a large part of the food for all the fishes.

The wings are made of long hair from the Deer Tail, Polar Bear, Calf, Squirrel, Skunk, Black Bear, and many others. Hackles, both natural and dyed from the neck and saddle, are used in many flies.

When finished off with cheeks of Pheasant body feathers, Red Ibis, and Jungle Cock eye feathers, they make a very fine appearing fly. Painted heads and eyes have also added to their beauty and effectiveness.

The bodies are made of gold and silver tinsel, chenille, colored floss ribbed with tinsel, Peacock herl, wire, plastic, kapok, etc.

To get fish with the streamer fly you must cast it properly.

Try casting the fly at the edge of fast water, then work your fly to resemble a minnow swimming in the calm water, at the edge of the fast water. This will often bring good results.

If you follow the in-coming tide up an inlet and cast your streamer where you see the different colored water, you will nearly always take your share of fish.

The hook is a Model Perfect No. 2, 3X. Place the hook in the vise and cover same with liquid cement; start the No. 00 tying silk near the eye of the hook by winding a few turns over itself, and wind the hook down to position shown in Drawing No. 1; this is done to make a foundation for the rest of the materials.

Cut off a piece of oval tinsel No. 16 or 17 and grasp it ⅛th of an inch from the end between your thumb and fingernails; unwind the silver ⅛th of an inch and cut it off; tie this in by the centre core only, in position shown, which is the end of the body; this eliminates making a hump on the body.

Drawing No. 1

Now tie in a narrow piece of white floss and wind your tying silk to the front, allowing plenty of room for the hair wing. Wind your floss body tightly and perfectly, and to the size you desire; cut off the surplus floss and tie in a long piece of fine silver tinsel (as in Drawing No. 2); wind the tinsel perfectly down the body to the oval tinsel and take a few turns past the oval to form a tag. Now carefully wind the tinsel back over the first winding to the wing position, and tie off. Put the hackle pliers on the oval tinsel and wind

Drawing No. 2

Drawing No. 3

it spirally up the body; keep the strain on the tinsel to the right; tie off and trim off the surplus ends. Now coat the silver body with clear lacquer. I apply this with a brush on the top of the body and allow the surplus to drain to the underside. I take this off with my thumbnail, which makes a smooth body (Drawing No. 3).

The hair wing is made of black and white bucktail, using the black as the centre layer. I also make it, omitting the top white layer.

I will now explain how I prepare the hair before tying it in on the fly.

First of all, cut off, close to the hide, a little more than you think you will require; grasp the hair with your thumb and first finger in the middle and pull out the short hairs and fuzz at the base. I then turn my hand and pull out the long hairs from the top and put them back in the bunch in a position that will make the bunch almost level at the top. If this is not done, you will have too much bulk at the base where you tie in, and the wing tip will be too thin.

My next step is to decide the length of the wing, then saturate the butts with liquid cement from the position where I tie in to the end of the butts.

Drawing No. 4

Prepare all three layers in this manner and lay them on top of each other as shown in Drawing No. 4; tie them in before the cement is thoroughly set. To tie them in, grasp the hair very firmly between the thumb and first finger, which has been placed on the top of the hook. I immediately start to crowd the hair down and open up the tips of the thumb and finger quickly to allow the tying thread to pass over the hair; close the tips, keeping the firm grip, and pull the thread straight down; repeat this three times, then slide your thumb and finger back and put on several very tight turns; finish off the head to your desired size, tying off with the whip finish. Now apply the black head cement.

These three layers of hair can be put on separately in the same manner described, which would be easier for the beginner.

Many different color combinations can be made with the colored bucktail, and most of them are very effective.

Drawing No. 5 is the finished Streamer.

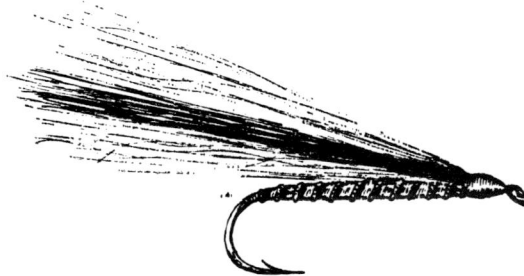

Drawing No. 5

TYING THE COCHY-BONDHU CREEPER WFB

The hook is an Allcock No. 6 2X Stout, loop-eyed, long shank.

Place the hook in the vise and cover it with liquid cement; tie in a No. 000 tying silk and wind down the hook from the eye to the position of the narrow gold tinsel tag. Tie in the tinsel and make a few turns down the hook, then double back to the tying silk and tie off. Then lacquer the tag. (Drawing No. 1).

Select a Golden Pheasant crest of the proper size and trim the butts with your scissors; put a little cement on the butt and tie in on top of the hook;

Drawing No. 1

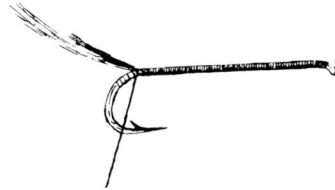

Drawing No. 2

on the top of this, tie in a small piece of red Ibis or substitute. (Drawing No. 2). Now select a soft cochy-bondhu hackle, long enough to palmer the body; the soft hackle gives more life to the streamer, and makes it easier to tie on the feather and hair wing. Tie the hackle in by the tip, also tie in the yellow floss and take your tying silk to the front of the body; now form a tight, smooth body of yellow floss and tie off. (Drawing No. 3). Take your hackle pliers and grasp the hackle by the butt bringing it to a vertical position above the hook; wet the finger tips, and very carefully, at first, start to

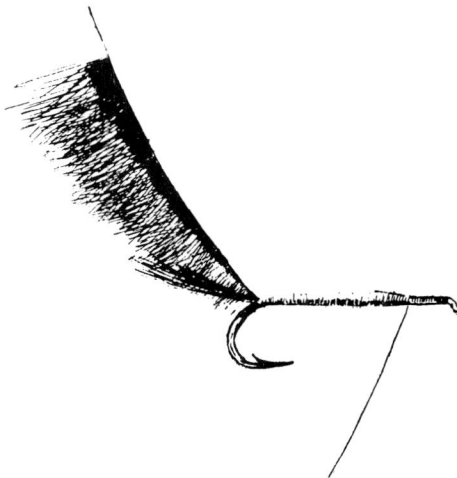

Drawing No. 3

stroke the fibres back so that both sides are pointing to the rear of the fly, and commence to wind the hackle continually stroking the fibres back until you have palmered the body. (Drawing No. 4).

For the wing, tie in 15 to 20 bucktail hairs, red, yellow, green and brown, mixed. This under wing will extend back to the tip of the tail. (Drawing No. 5). Tie in, over the hair wing, four cochy-bondhu neck hackles, two on each side. To get these hackles to stay in the proper position they should be

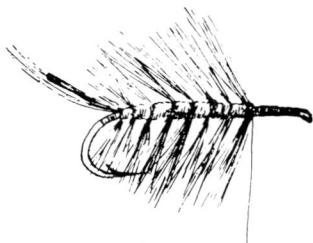

Drawing No. 4

Drawing No. 5

taken from a complete neck so the proper curve is on both feathers for each side; cut off the fibres from the butts. This rough stem helps to hold them from slipping; also, use a little cement on the butts and base which you are tying over.

Over the wing hackles tie in the two Jungle Cock cheeks. Now tie in the throat hackle, which has been doubled and tied in by the tip. Your fly should be the same as Drawing No. 6.

Drawing No. 6

Carefully wind the cochy-bondhu throat hackle and apply the whip finish.

The head is black, and the painted eyes are white with black centres.

Drawing No. 7 is the finished fly.

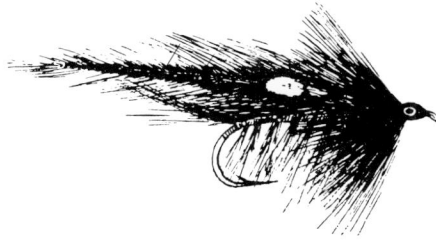

Drawing No. 7

The Author Instructing a Class in Fly Tying at the Vaughan General Hospital.

Bill Blades was elected to THE FISHING HALL OF
FAME and wins DOLPHIN AWARD. Only 100 sports-
men of the world will be the recipients of this award,
the highest in sport fishing.

Chapter VII

STREAMER FLY PATTERNS

HAVE carefully selected the streamer fly list that I believe will take game fish wherever they abound. The wire and plastic bodied flies are excellent for early fishing for rainbow trout in Michigan. I have given the name of the originator when known.

Try some of these out for small Tarpon, Snook, Salmon, Steelhead, etc. When these streamers are made up on small 3X hooks they are excellent for brook trout and many game fish.

My friend Joe Trainor, Jr. of the South Bend Bait Company used the wire and plastic bodied streamers on opening day two years in succession on the Pere Marquette, taking a few fish when all other flies failed. This to me, means the flies were taken down deep where the fish were feeding.

Victor Brown of Everglades City, Forida, one of the most artistic taxidermists I ever met, was the first I saw catching small tarpon on small streamers around the shallow inlets of the Everglades.

No. 1 ALASKAN MARY ANN
(Original by a Kobuk Indian, made
        practical by Frank Dufresne)
Tail: Scarlet hackle fibres.
Body: Light tan floss, ivory colored.
Wings: White polar bear.

No. 2   ALECK'S WONDER
Tail: Barred Mandarin, Blue Chatterer.
Body: Gold tinsel.
Wing: Blue, yellow, and claret hackle.
Eye: Jungle Cock.
Hackle: Blue and scarlet.

No. 3   ALGOMA
Tail: Amherst Pheasant tail section.
Body: Grey deer body hair.
Wings: Grey, brown and white bucktail.
Hackle: Brown.

No. 4 AMBROSE BUCKTAIL
        (Thomas Ambrose)
Tail: Scarlet and white bucktail.
Body: Yellow chenille; ribbing, gold
    tinsel.
Wings: White bucktail, top layer brown
    bucktail.
Hackle: First scarlet, then black.

No. 5   A. S. TRUDE
Body: Red wool; ribbing, silver tinsel.
Wings: Red squirrel, tied long.
Hackle: Reddish brown.

No. 6
    BADGER H O B STREAMER
            (Weber)
Body: Flat silver tinsel.
Wings: Six badger saddle hackles.
Hackle: Badger—not blue as shown.

No. 7   BARNES SPECIAL
            (Gardner Percy)
Tail: Jungle cock.
Body: Flat silver tinsel.
Wings: Mixed red and white bucktail
    below, then two yellow hackles, out-
    side of these, two grizzly hackles.
Hackle: White tied full.

No. 8   BLACK DOG
Tail: Black and yellow hackle fibres.
Ribbing: Silver tinsel.
Body: Black floss.
Throat: Yellow wing feather (short).
Wing: Dun hackle, Jungle Cock eye.

No. 9
    BLACK DEMON CAINS RIVER
Tail: Barred Wood Duck.
Body: Gold tinsel.
Wings: Black hackle.
Hackle: Orange.
Shoulders: Jungle Cock.

No. 10 BLACK-NOSE DACE
Tag: Red yarn, short.
Body: Silver.
Hair: Polar Bear, Black Bear in the
    middle, Brown bucktail on top.

see 4ᵗʰ color plate D.

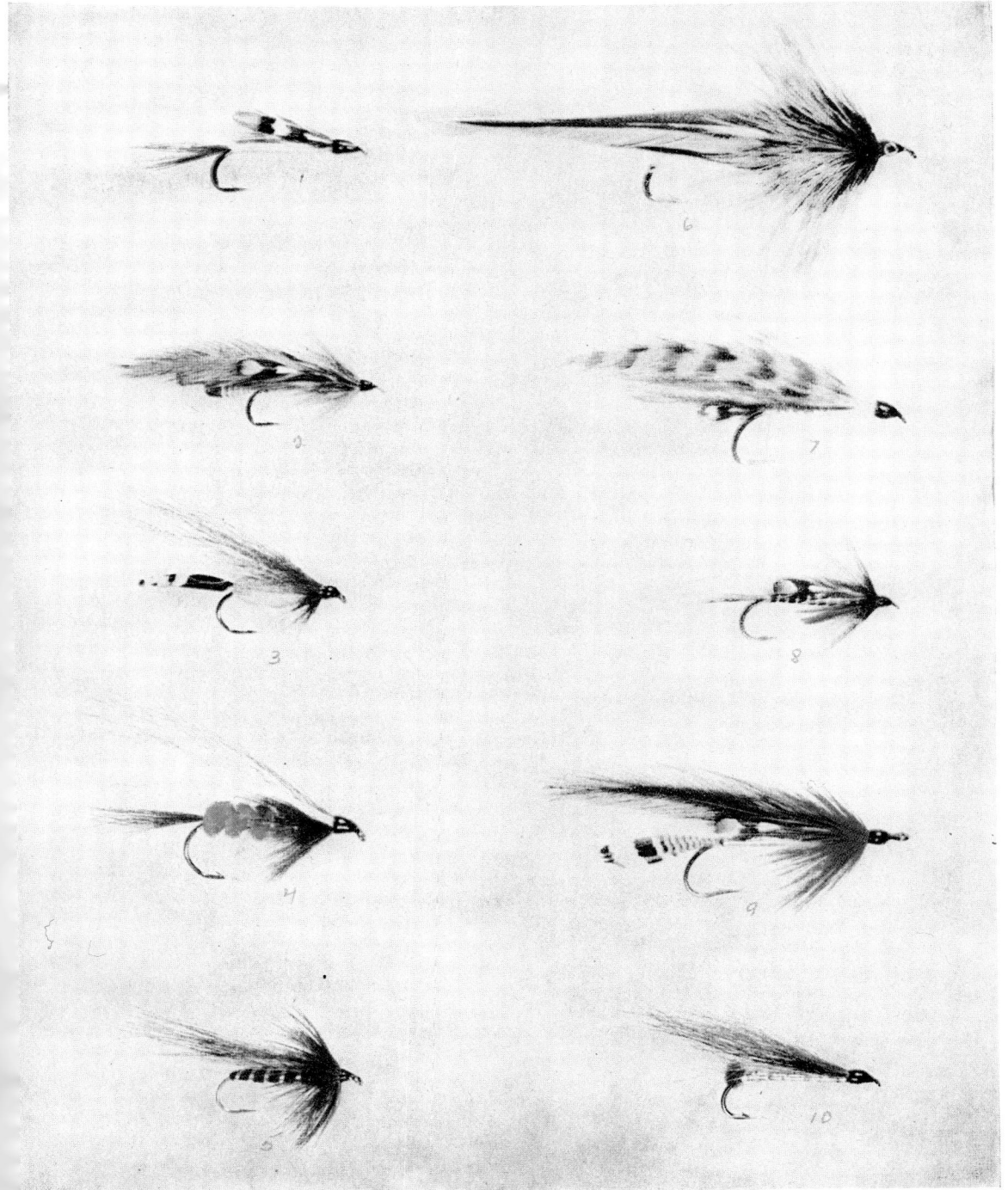

PLATE XII. STREAMER FLIES.
(*See opposite page for descriptions*)

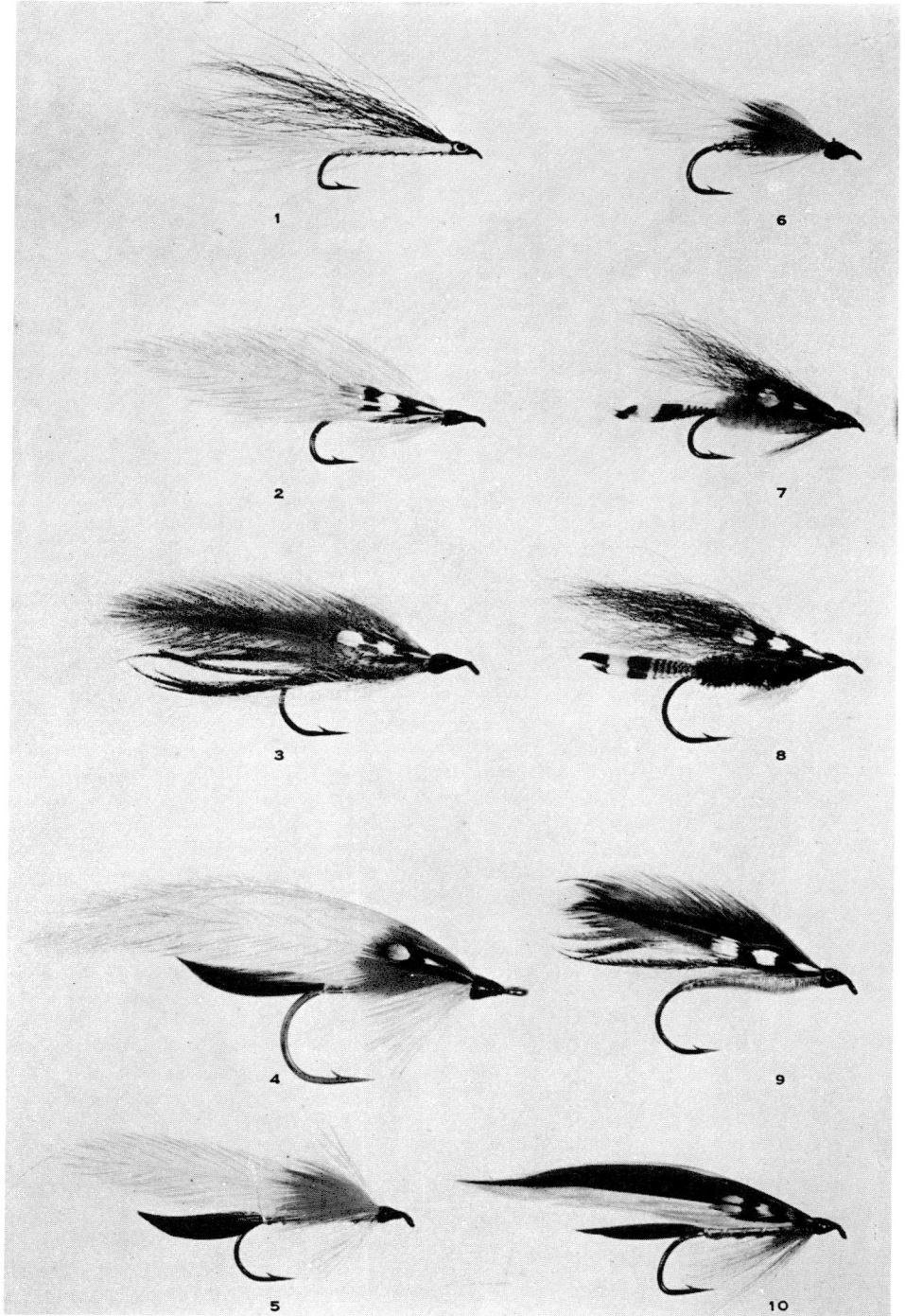

PLATE XIII.   STREAMER FLIES.
(See opposite page for descriptions)

SELECTED STREAMER FLY PATTERNS

(See Plate XIII)

No. 1
BLACK AND WHITE STREAMER
Body: Silver; ribbing and tag, silver oval.
Wings: White bucktail, top layer, black bucktail.

No. 2   BLACK GHOST
Tail: Yellow hackle fibres.
Body: Black floss; ribbing, silver.
Wings: White hackle; Jungle Cock eye.
Hackle: Yellow.

No. 3   BLUE DEVIL
Body: Black floss; ribbing, silver.
Wings: Four blue neck hackles overlapped with two orange.
Hackle: Peacock herl and white bucktail tied streamer.
Shoulder: Partridge barred body feathers, Jungle Cock.

No. 4   BONBRIGHT
          (Tarpon Fly)
Tail: Red goose quill section.
Body: Silver tinsel; ribbing, silver, tag, silver.
Wings: Four white hackles; topping, Golden Pheasant.
Cheek: Red goose or Ibis body feather; Jungle Cock eye.
Hackle: White.

No. 5   COLONEL FULLER
Tail: Black Goose quill section.
Body: Gold tinsel; ribbing, gold oval tinsel.
Wings: Yellow hackle.
Shoulder: Scarlet Ibis or Goose.
Hackle: Yellow.

No. 6   COLONEL WHITE
Body: Silver; ribbing, silver oval.
Wings: Four white hackles.
Shoulder: Red Ibis body feather or dyed goose.

No. 7   DARK TIGER
          (Bill Edson)
Tail: Barred Wood Duck.
Body: Yellow chenille.
Wings: Natural brown bucktail.
Hackle: Scarlet.
Head: Black.

No. 8   EDSON LIGHT TIGER
          (Bill Edson)
Tail: Barred Wood Duck or Silver Pheasant breast feather.
Body: Peacock herl.
Wings: Natural brown deer tail dyed yellow or yellow deer tail.
Shoulder: Jungle Cock.
Gill: Scarlet hen's neck feather.

No. 9   FURNACE MINNOW
          (W. F. Blades)
Body: Moulded plastic; covered with silver scale finish, wrap over this clear nylon or similar material, and finish with clear enamel.
Wings: First, white bucktail, then six strands of Peacock herl, and four furnace neck hackles.
Shoulders: Jungle Cock.

No. 10 GALLOPING GHOST
          (Bert Quimby)
Tail: Red quill feather.
Body: Orange floss; ribbing, silver oval.
Wing: Bali duck feathers.
Shoulder: Jungle Cock.

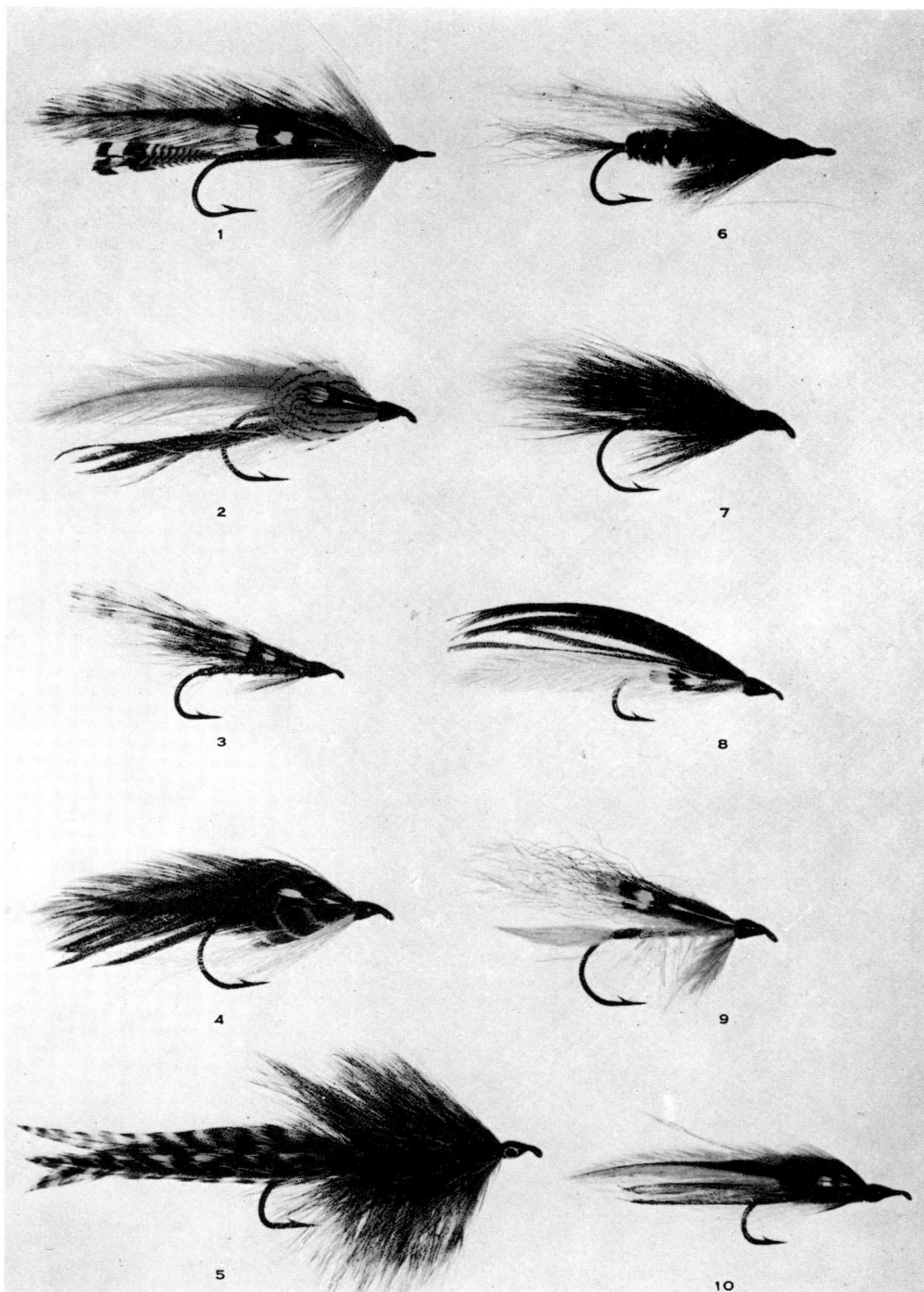

PLATE XIV.   STREAMER FLIES.
(See opposite page for descriptions)

SELECTED STREAMER FLY PATTERNS

(See Plate XIV)

No. 1
GOLD DEMON CAINS RIVER
Body: Gold tinsel.
Wing: Brown hackle in centre, plymouth rock outside.
Hackle: Orange.

No. 2   GREY GHOST
(Carrie G. Stevens)
Body: Orange floss; ribbing, silver.
Wings: Ten or twelve yellow polar bear hairs or Golden Pheasant crest, and four blue dun neck hackles.
Shoulder: Silver Pheasant body feathers, Jungle Cock.
Hackle: Six Peacock tail strands, and a little white bucktail, tied streamer, length of wing.

No. 3
GREY SQUIRREL SILVER
(Ray Bergman)
Body: Silver tinsel; ribbing, silver.
Wings: Grey squirrel hair; Grizzly hackle; Jungle Cock.
Hackle: Red, tied in whole, not wound on.

No. 4   GREEN GHOST
Body: Red floss; ribbing, silver tinsel.
Wings: Six Peacock tail fibres and four green neck hackles.
Shoulder: Widgeon throat feather and Jungle Cock.
Hackle: White polar bear tied under body; length of wing, yellow polar tied shorter.

No. 5
GRIZZLY HACKLE STREAMER
Tail: Six grizzly hackles.
Tag: Silver tinsel.
Body: Grizzly hackle tied palmer the length of body.

No. 6   HAIR COACHMAN
Tail: Red bucktail.
Body: Peacock herl; ribbing and tag, silver tinsel.
Wings: White polar bear.
Hackle: Brown squirrel tail.

No. 7   HAIR PROFESSOR
Tail: Red bucktail.
Body: Yellow floss; ribbing, gold tinsel.
Wings: Fox squirrel.
Hackle: Brown squirrel tail.

No. 8   JANE CRAIG
Body: Silver tinsel.
Wings: Four white hackles; topping, Peacock herl.
Hackle: White bucktail, tied under the head, Jungle Cock.

No. 9   LADY DOCTOR
Tail: Yellow goose feather section.
Body: First quarter, red floss; remainder, silver tinsel palmered with yellow hackle.
Wings: White deer tail; grey on top, Jungle Cock.
Throat: Hen's neck hackle whole; scarlet and yellow.

No. 10   LADY GHOST
Body: Silver tinsel.
Wings: Golden Pheasant crest or yellow polar bear hairs; next, four badger hackles.
Cheek: Copper Pheasant body feather; Jungle Cock.
Throat: Four Peacock tail fibres and white bucktail, as long as the wing.
Head: Black.

SELECTED STREAMER FLY PATTERNS

(See Plate XV)

No. 1 MALLARD STREAMER
(W. F. Blades)

Tag: Fine copper wire.
Butt: Red seal or wool.
Tail: Red goose feather section.
Body: Copper wire; ribbing, fine reddish brown enameled copper wire.
Hackle: Magenta.
Wings: Grey Mallard.

No. 2 MATUKA
(New Zealand Fly)

Body: Silver; ribbing, silver oval, passed through wing fibres.
Wing and Tail: Canadian Bittern wing feather, or Badger hackle.

No. 3 MICKEY FINN
(John Alden Knight)

Body: Silver tinsel; ribbing, silver oval.
Wings: Bucktail; yellow first layer, red second; yellow on top about twice the amount of the first yellow layer.

No. 4 MITCHELL

Tail: Red goose quill section; tag, scarlet floss.
Body: Black floss; ribbing, silver tinsel.
Wings: Yellow polar bear; black bear on top.
Shoulder: Jungle Cock.

No. 5 MUDDLER STREAMER
(S. S. Thomson)

Tail: Grizzly hackle tip, red duck feather section.
Body: Gold oval tinsel.
Wings: Two dark brown hackle and two dark grizzly.
Hackle: Brown and grizzly, tied on together.

No. 6 MOOSE RIVER

Body: Silver tinsel.
Wing: White bucktail topped with Peacock eyed tail strands.
Cheek: Golden Pheasant tippet.

No. 7 NEW TRIER
(W. F. Blades)

Tag: Fine copper wire and yellow floss.
Tail: Golden Pheasant crest.
Butt: Peacock herl.
Body: First half silver coated copper wire; butted with peacock herl. Second half copper wire.
Hackle: Blue dun.
Wings: Mottled grey brown Turkey.

No. 8 NINE-THREE
(Dr. Herbert Sanborn)

Body: Silver tinsel.
Wings: White bucktail topped with four olive green hackle feathers and two dark green or black on top.
Shoulder: Jungle Cock.

No. 9 ORANGE FURNACE
(W. F. Blades)

Body: Plastic over copper wire, wrapped over with orange nylon or similar material, and covered with clear enamel.
Wings: Brown bucktail, then six strands of Peacock herl, and four furnace hackles.
Shoulder: Jungle Cock.

No. 10 PARMACHENE BELLE

Tail: Red and white hackle fibres.
Tag and Ribbing: Gold tinsel.
Body: Yellow wool.
Wing: Scarlet and white hackles, scarlet on top.
Hackle: Scarlet and white.

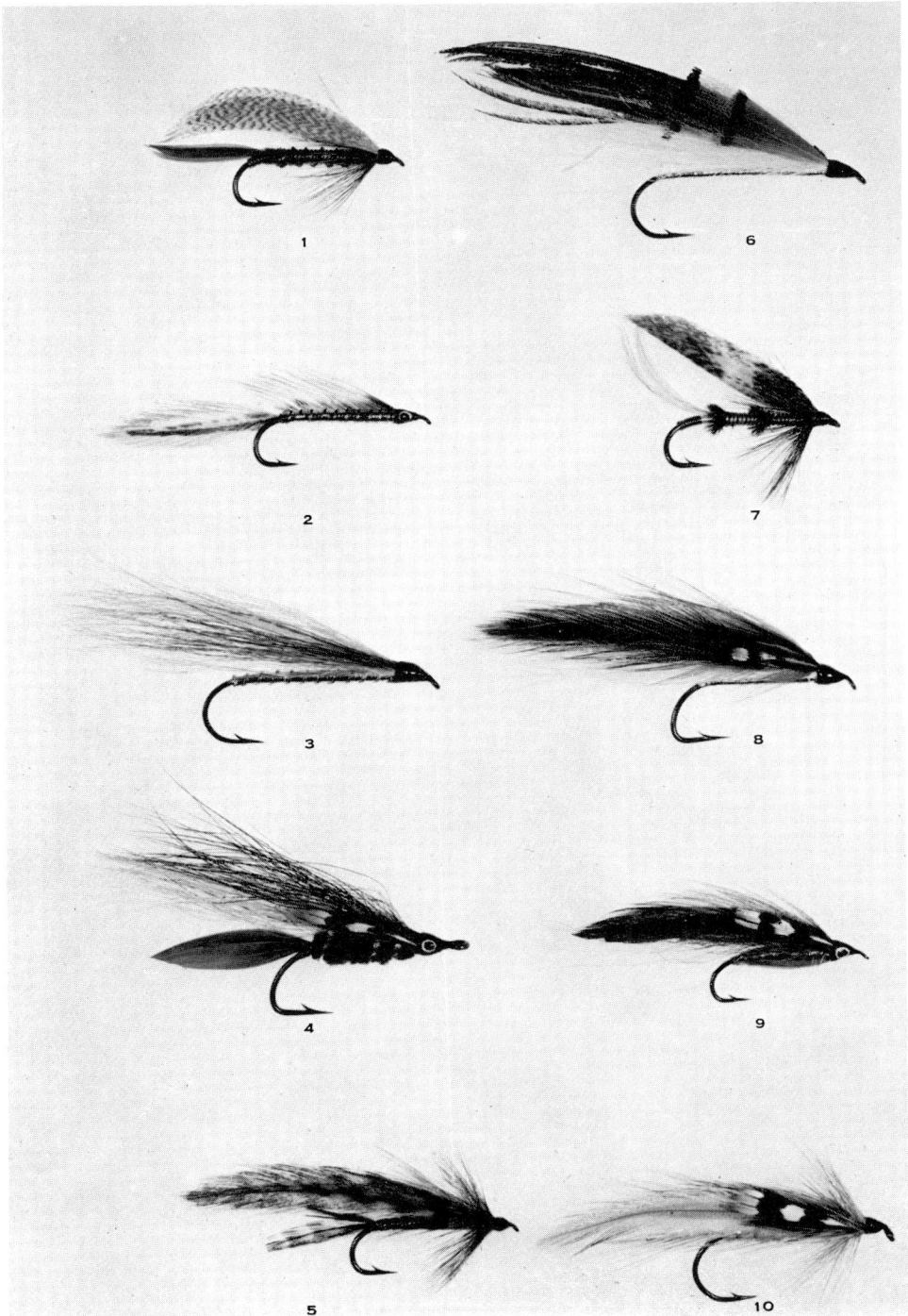

PLATE XV. STREAMER FLIES.
(*See opposite page for descriptions*)

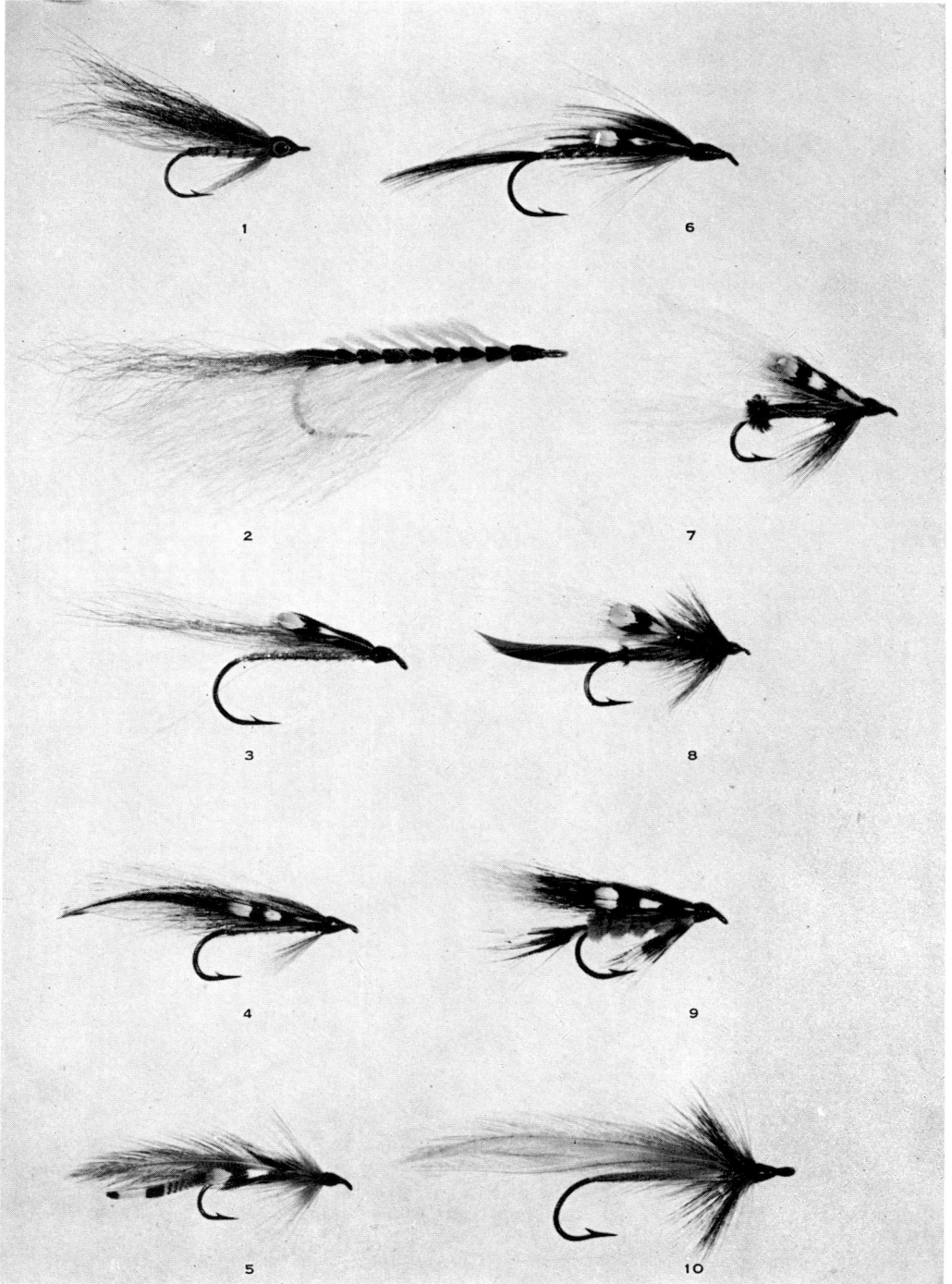

PLATE XVI. STREAMER FLIES.
(*See opposite page for descriptions*)

SELECTED STREAMER FLY PATTERNS

(See Plate XVI)

No. 1 SILVER SIDES
(Paul H. Stroud)

Tail: Golden Pheasant crest.

Body: Pale yellow floss; ribbing, silver oval; a few close turns, then spiral up the body. Shape body thin at the tail and thick at the thorax.

Wings: Mixed bucktail; White, Red, Green, Brown.

Hackle: Blue dun hen.

No. 2 RED and WHITE OZARK
(Miss Westwood)

Tail: Red bucktail.

Body: White bucktail.

No. 3
RED and WHITE POLAR BEAR

Body: Silver tinsel, ribbing, silver oval.

Wings: Polar bear, white, red centre, white on top.

Shoulder: Jungle Cock.

No. 4 RED SQUIRREL GOLD
(Ray Bergman)

Body: Gold tinsel; ribbing, gold.

Wings: Fox Squirrel hair; honey Badger hackles, Jungle Cock eye.

Hackle: Red, tied in whole, not wound on.

No. 5 ROARING RAPIDS

Tail: Barred Mandarin, red hackle fibres.

Body: Silver tinsel.

Wing: Yellow and scarlet hackle.

Shoulder: Jungle Cock.

Hackle: Blue.

No. 6 ROSS MC KENNEY

Tail: Golden Pheasant red breast fibres.

Body: Silver tinsel; ribbing, silver oval.

Wings: Golden Pheasant crest under four white hackles.

Cheek: Golden Pheasant red breast feather.

Shoulder: Jungle Cock.

No. 7
ROYAL COACHMAN STREAMER

Tail: White bucktail.

Body: Red floss, Peacock herl butts at each end.

Wing: White bucktail.

Hackle: Brown.

Cheeks: Jungle cock.

No. 8 ROYAL

Tag: Scarlet floss.

Tail: Scarlet goose.

Butt: Peacock herl.

Body: Scarlet silk floss.

Hackle: Brown.

Wing: White polar bear, or bucktail.

Shoulder: Jungle Cock.

No. 9 SAWTOOTH

Tail: Guinea fowl.

Body: Orange chenille, ribbing, gold tinsel.

Wings: Fox Squirrel; Jungle Cock eye.

Hackle: Guinea fowl.

No. 10
CAINS RIVER SCOTCH LASSIE

Body: Silver tinsel.

Wings: Neck hackles, two blue inside overlapped with two yellow.

Hackle: Magenta first, then blue.

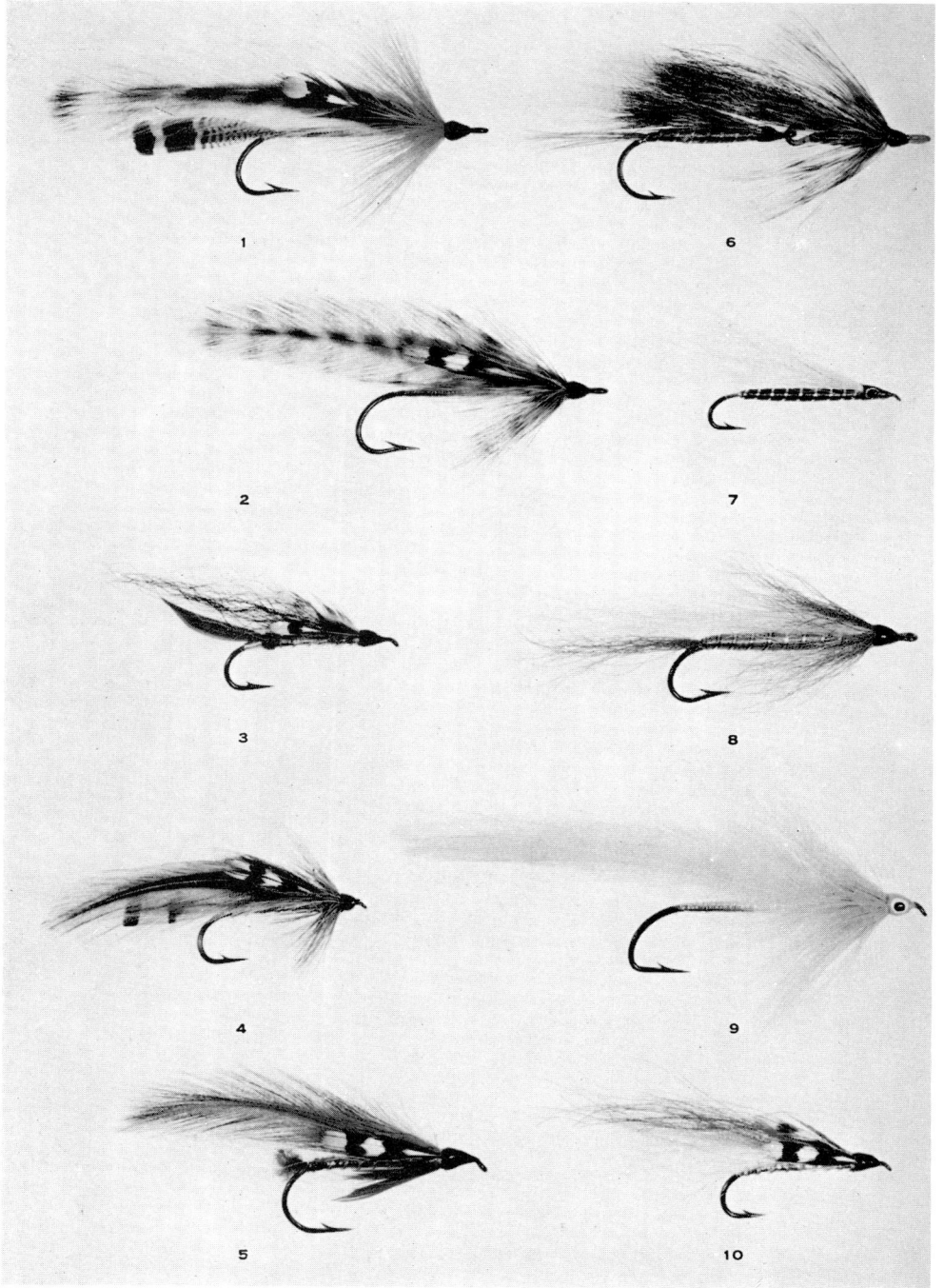

PLATE XVII. STREAMER FLIES.
(*See opposite page for descriptions*)

SELECTED STREAMER FLY PATTERNS

(See Plate XVII)

No. 1   SILVER DEMON
Cains River
Tail: Barred Wood Duck. (optional)
Body: Silver tinsel.
Wing: Four light plymouth rock hackles.
Hackle: Orange. Jungle Cock.

No. 2   CAINS RIVER
Silver Grey
Body: Silver tinsel.
Wing: Orange hackle inside, Grizzly out-side.
Hackle: Grizzly.
Shoulder: Jungle Cock.

No. 3   SILVER PLUME
Tail: Scarlet goose, tag, yellow floss.
Butt: Scarlet wool.
Body: Silver tinsel; ribbing, silver oval laquered.
Wing: White polar bear, or bucktail, on top and bottom with brown or black in between.
Shoulder: Jungle Cock.

No. 4   SPENCER BAY
Tail: Golden Pheasant tippet.
Body: Silver tinsel; ribbing, silver.
Wings: Blue inside; Badger outside; Jungle Cock eye.
Hackle: Green and yellow.

No. 5   SUPERVISOR
(Joe Stickney)
Tail: Red yarn.
Body: Silver; silver oval ribbing (op-tional).
Wings: White bucktail; next, two olive hackles; then two silver doctor blue.
Shoulder: Jungle Cock.
Throat: Sections of red goose.

No. 6   TANDEM STREAMER
(Grizzly King)
Tail: Scarlet hackle fibres, tag, gold tinsel-
Body: Green floss, ribbing, embossed gold tinsel.
Wing: Grey squirrel tail.
Hackle: Grizzly.

No. 7
WHITE BUCKTAIL STREAMER
Body: Red floss; ribbing and tag, silver tinsel.
Wings: White bucktail.
Eyes: White, black centre.

No. 8
WHITE POLAR BEAR and
ORANGE STREAMER
Tail: Red and white bucktail.
Body: Orange floss; ribbing and tag, gold tinsel.
Wings: White polar bear.
Hackle: White and red bucktail.

No. 9
YELLOW H O B STREAMER
(Weber)
Body: Flat silver tinsel.
Wings: Six yellow saddle hackles.
Hackle: Yellow.

No. 10
YELLOW and RED POLAR BEAR
Body: Silver tinsel; ribbing, silver oval.
Wings: Yellow polar bear; red on top. Jungle Cock.

FURNACE FREY
(Blades)

Tag: Gold tinsel.

Tail: Barred Wood Duck.

Body: Gold tinsel; ribbing, oval tinsel.

Throat: Yellow bucktail tied streamer.

Wing: A few strands of natural brown bucktail dyed yellow; tie over this four furnace hackles.

Shoulder: Jungle Cock.

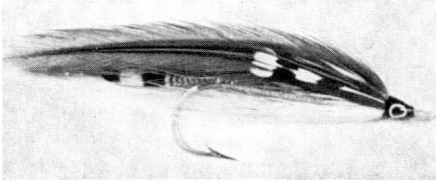

Alan Wallace

PLATE XVIII. FURNACE FREY.

GINGER FURNACE FREY
(W. F. Blades)

Same as the furnace frey except use ginger furnace hackles for the wings.

BADGER FREY
(W. F. Blades)

Same as the furnace frey except use silver for body, white bucktail and badger hackle wings.

PLATE XIX. BLADES' BUCKTAIL No. 1 and No. 2.

(Blades') WEIGHTED
No. 1 BUCKTAIL STREAMERS

Body: Underbody formed with soft copper wire or lead. Covered with soft copper wire silver-coated and maroon colored enamel coated, wound on together.

Wing: First, white bucktail topped with scarlet bucktail.

Hackle: Scarlet bucktail tied streamer.

Shoulder: Jungle Cock.

No. 2

Tail: Scarlet bucktail.

Body: Same as No. 1.

Wing: First, white bucktail, topped with yellow bucktail.

Hackle: Yellow bucktail tied streamer.

No. 3

Body: Underbody formed with soft copper wire or lead. Cover the underbody with cement and yellow floss, then wrap it with nylon.

Wing: First, white bucktail, then black, topped with natural brown.

Throat or Gill: Red goose or two red hen hackle tips.

Shoulder: Jungle Cock.

Excellent Spinning Flies especially for Tarpon, Snook, Jacks, Bluefish, etc., in Florida.

PLATE XX. BLADES' BUCKTAIL No. 3.

Chapter VIII

LARGE TROUT FLIES

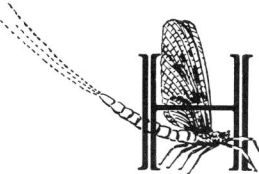

ERE IS A list of large trout flies that have been used successfully in many of our states; some were originated in England and British Columbia.

The Western Salmon Fly (No. 18, Plate XXII) and the Salmon Fly (No. 9, Plate XXII) should be fished when the large Stone Fly is on the water.

The McQueen Special (No. 5, Plate XXII) is an excellent trout fly for rough water because of its floating qualities.

The Crane Fly Parachute is very good for dry fly fishing. I have also taken fish on the Crane Fly (No. 11, Plate XXI) just under the surface.

Try out the wire bodied flies (No. 8, Plate XXI) and (No. 12, Plate XXII) when the fish are feeding below the surface.

Many of these Large Trout Flies are western patterns, designed and fished by expert fishermen, but by all means try them on your favorite stream.

The Hairy Crane Spinner (No. 18, Plate XXI), has been tested in Michigan by Paul H. Young. This is an excellent Large Trout Fly.

[93]

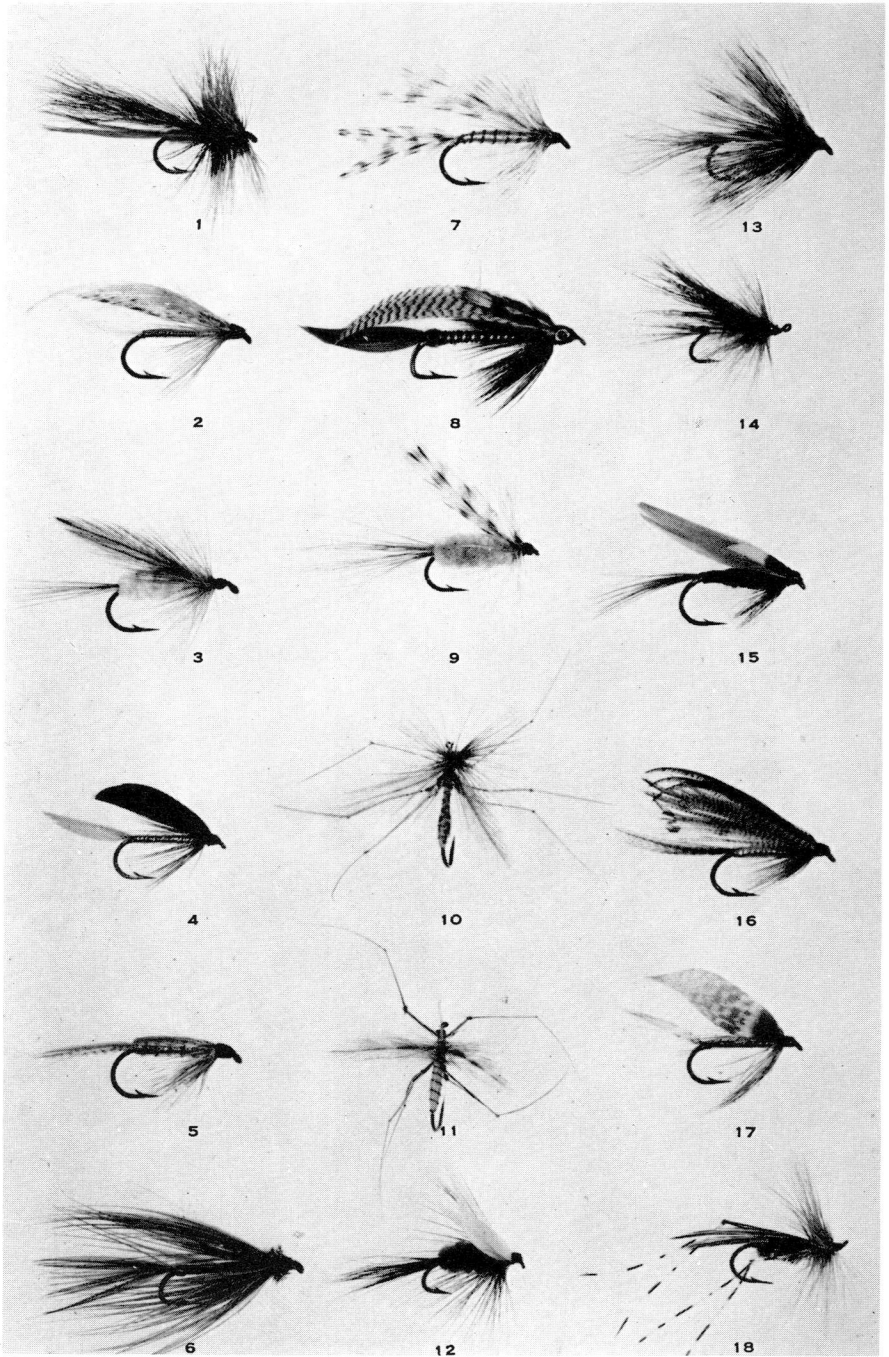

PLATE XXI.   LARGE TROUT FLIES.
(See opposite page for descriptions)

SELECTED LARGE TROUT FLIES
(See Plate XXI)

No. 1
ACKMAN'S SOFA PILLOW
Tail: Red quill feather section.
Body: Red wool.
Wings: Grey squirrel.
Hackle: Brown furnace, tied upright and full.

No. 2   AEMMY'S FANCY
Tail: Golden Pheasant topping.
Body: Silver tinsel.
Wing: Grey and tan mottled Turkey wing section.
Topping: Golden Pheasant.
Hackle: Brown.

No. 3   ALLEN'S CHOICE
Tail: Scarlet hackle fibres.
Body: White chenille.
Wings: Black hackle tips.
Hackle: Scarlet and yellow, tied on together.

No. 4   BLOODY BUTCHER
Tail: Red Ibis.
Body: Silver tinsel; ribbing, silver wire.
Wings: Purple Mallard wing quill sections.
Hackle: Scarlet.

No. 5 BLUE BACK MINNOW
Tail and back of minnow is made of a section of grey mottled Mallard body feather, and a section of blue goose wing feather on top.
Body: Silver tinsel; ribbing, silver oval.
Hackle: Grizzly.

No. 6   CAREY SPECIAL
Tail: Badger hair.
Body: Peacock quill.
Hackle: Chinese cock rump feather.
Head: Peacock herl.

No. 7 CHAPMAN'S CHAPPIE
Tail: Grizzly hackle tips.
Body: Yellow floss; ribbing and tag, gold oval tinsel.
Wings: Grizzly hackle tips.
Hackle: Grizzly.

No. 8   CLARET MALLARD
(Wm. F. Blades)
Tag: Silver tinsel; butt, scarlet seal fur.
Tail: Scarlet goose.
Body: Silver and maroon enameled soft copper wire wound on together.
Wing: Grey Mallard breast feather.
Cheeks: Jungle Cock.
Hackle: Claret.
Eyes: White, black centre.

No. 9   COWLITZ SPECIAL
Tail: Grizzly hackle fibres.
Body: Yellow chenille.
Wings: Grizzly hackle tips.
Hackle: Grizzly.

No. 10
BLADES' CRANE FLY PARACHUTE
Body: Raffia; ribbing, gold wire.
Legs: Pheasant tail fibres, knotted twice to form joints.
Wings: Blue dun hackle tips.
Hackle: Natural red, tied on horizontal.

No. 11   CRANE FLY
Body: Raffia; ribbing, gold wire.
Legs: Pheasant tail fibres, knotted twice to form joints.
Wings: Brown speckled hackle tips.
Hackle: Rusty blue dun.

No. 12
CUTTHROAT SPECIAL
Tail: Black hackle fibres.
Body: Red chenille.
Wings: White goose wing sections.
Hackle: Black.

No. 13   DRIDGE

Tail: Scarlet bucktail.

Body: Scarlet horse hair.

Hackle: Brown and grizzly tied on together.

No. 14   FLYING CADDIS

Tail: Brown hackle fibres.

Body: Yellow wool; palmered with
brown hackle.

Wings: Brown speckled deer body hair.

Hackle: Brown.

No. 15   GENERAL MONEY

Tail: Fibres from Golden Pheasant breast
feather.

Tag: Silver tinsel, flat.

Body: Black floss; ribbing, silver oval with
six close turns at the tail, then open
spirals to the head.

Wings: Goose wing feather sections, dyed
reddish orange.

Hackle: Claret.

No. 16   GOLDEN RANGER

Tail: Brown Mallard fibres.

Body: Gold oval tinsel.

Wings: Tippet fibres, Wood Duck flank;
topped with green Peacock herl.

Hackle: Badger dyed scarlet.

No. 17

     GOLD MARCH BROWN

Tag: Gold tinsel.

Tail: Brown Partridge body feather fibres.

Body: Gold tinsel; ribbing, gold wire.

Wings: Hen Pheasant wing sections.

Hackle: Brown Partridge.

No. 18

    HAIRY CRANE SPINNER
      (Paul H. Young)

Body: Peacock herl, slender legs of Lady
Amherst tail fibres, knotted to form
joints.

Wings: Brown hackle tips.

Hackle: Brown.

SELECTED LARGE TROUT FLIES
(See Plate XXII)

No. 1   LIONESS

Tail: Yellow and red hackle fibres.

Body: Black chenille.

Wing: White quill section.

Hackle: Yellow and red.

No. 2

    MALLARD and MAGENTA

Tag: Gold tinsel.

Tail: Golden Pheasant tippets.

Body: Magenta seal fur dubbing; ribbing, gold tinsel.

Wings: Brown Mallard.

Hackle: Magenta.

No. 3

    MICHIGAN NIGHT CADDIS

Tail: Grey Turkey.

Body: Yellow wool palmered with grizzly
and brown hackle, trimmed; egg sack,
yellow wool.

Wings: Four grizzly hackle tips, tied
spent.

Hackle: Brown and grizzly tied on together.

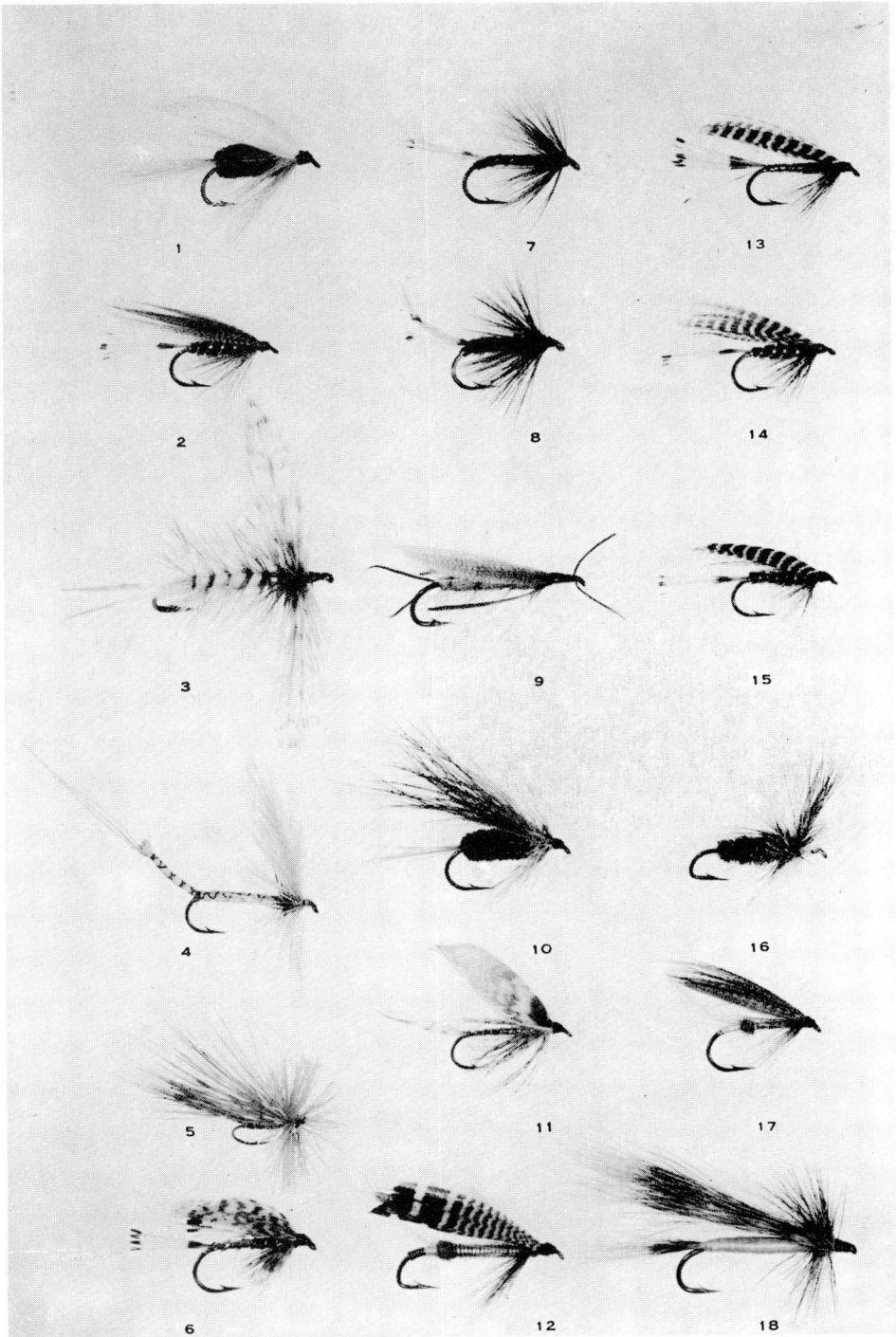

PLATE XXII.   LARGE TROUT FLIES.
(See page 96 for descriptions)

No. 4

MOOSE MANE MAY FLY
(S. S. Thomson)

Tail: Moose mane; two or three hairs.

Body: Moose mane; ribbing, heavy green silk.

Wings: Grizzly hackle tips.

Hackle: Grizzly hackle.

No. 5   McQUEEN SPECIAL

Entire fly constructed of natural deer body hair; ribbing, black silk.

No. 6 NATION'S SHINER TIP

Tag: Silver tinsel.

Tail: Golden Pheasant tippet.

Body: Rear half silver tinsel; front black floss, ribbing, silver oval.

Wings: Underwing tippet strands; wing grey mottled Turkey wing sections and a strip of scarlet Goose on each side.

Hackle: Guinea Fowl.

No. 7

PENNELL'S BLACK and SILVER

Tail: Golden Pheasant crest and tippet fibres.

Tag: Silver oval tinsel.

Body: Black floss; ribbing, silver oval.

Hackle: Black.

No. 8   RED and BLACK

Tag: Silver.

Tail: Golden Pheasant crest and tippet fibres.

Body: Red seal fur dubbing; ribbing, silver oval.

Hackle: Black.

No. 9   SALMON FLY

Tail: Two strands of Turkey wing feather, (outer feather) dyed brown. Antennae and horns of the same material.

Body: Orange wool; one strand of red wool on the underside entire length of body. Body palmered with furnace hackle tied sparse.

Wings: Transparent veined wing material tied on flat, a little longer than the body.

No. 10 SHOFF'S BUCKTAIL

Tail: Scarlet hackle fibres.

Body: Black chenille.

Wings: Brown speckled deer body hair.

Hackle: Grizzly.

No. 11 SILVER MARCH BROWN

Tag: Silver tinsel.

Tail: Brown Partridge body feather fibres.

Body: Silver tinsel; ribbing, silver wire.

Wings: Hen Pheasant wing sections.

Hackle: Brown Pheasant.

No. 12   SILVER WOOD DUCK
(Wm. F. Blades)

Tag: Copper wire, fine, also pale yellow floss.

Tail: Golden Pheasant topping.

Butt: Scarlet seal fur.

Body: Soft silver wire.

Wing: Barred Wood Duck.

Hackle: Blue dun.

No. 13

TEAL GOLD and ORANGE

Tag: Gold tinsel.

Tail: Golden Pheasant fibres.

Body: Tail half gold tinsel; front half orange seal dubbing; ribbing, gold oval tinsel.

Wings: Teal.

Hackle: Black.

No. 14   TEAL and MAGENTA

Tag: Silver tinsel.

Tail: Golden Pheasant tippets.

Body: Seal fur dubbing dyed magenta; ribbing, silver.

Wings: Teal.

Hackle: Black.

No. 15 TEAL RED and GREEN

Tail: Golden Pheasant tippet fibres.

Body: Tail half red seal fur dubbing; front half green; ribbing, gold oval tinsel.

Wings: Teal.

Hackle: Black.

No. 16   THE BLACK RAT
(Alex Rogan)
(Wet Atlantic Salmon)

Tag: Gold tinsel.

Body: Peacock herl.

Wings: Mixed polar bear and skunk hair.

Hackle: Badger.

No. 17   THE WINSUM

Tag: Silver twist and yellow floss.

Tail: Small topping, butt, red wool.

Body: Silver tinsel; ribbing, silver wire.

Wings: Golden Pheasant tippet fibres, green and red Parrot, Teal and brown Mallard topping.

Hackle: Badger dyed scarlet.

No. 18
WESTERN SALMON FLY
(Don Harger)

Tail: Fox squirrel tail, length of wing.

Body: Natural raffia over thick padding of kapok, lacquered.

Wing: Fox squirrel.

Hackle: Mixed ginger and black.

Tunnel on the Missisaga River, Ontario, Canada; excellent Walleyed Pike water.

STEELHEAD FLIES

The following list of flies have been designed and proved to be excellent patterns for steelhead by some of our well-known western fishermen.

You will notice steelhead flies are tied with brilliant colored material which enables them to be seen by the fish when the water is murky.

The hook is very important; it should be made with stout wire. The most popular size is a No. 1 short shank, which means the shank is the same length as a No. 6 hook. This makes the fly ride better in fast water.

For the streamer type flies I have used a loop-eyed stout salmon fly hook. Follow the material lists and photographs when making these flies.

SELECTED STEELHEAD FLIES

(See Plate XXIII. Read top to bottom, left to right.)

No. 1
ALASKA MARY ANN (Original by a
   Kobuk Indian Made Practical by
     Frank Dufresne)
Tail: Scarlet hackle fibres.
Body: White chenille; ribbing, silver oval.
Wings: White Polar Bear; Jungle-Cock eye.

No. 2
   BELLAMY, THREE WINGED
     (Peter J. Schwab)
Tail: Yellow bucktail.
Body: Yellow brass wire in two sections.
Wings: Rear wing, tied in centre of the body, is white bucktail, the front wings are yellow bucktail, topped with yellowish brown.
Spike: Yellow bucktail ends of yellow front wing.

No. 3   BLACK DEMON
Tail: Golden Pheasant crest.
Body: Gold tinsel.
Wings: Black bucktail.
Hackle: Orange.

No. 4 BLAIR'S BLACK JOE
Tail: Scarlet hackle fibres; tag, scarlet floss.
Body: Black chenille.
Wings: Scarlet hackle tip, with white goose on each side.
Hackle: Black.
Shoulder: Jungle Cock.

No. 5   BLAIR'S DEMON
     (Bodiless)
Tail: White Polar Bear.
Hackle: Orange.
Wings: Guinea Hen (bunched)

No. 6   BLAIR'S RAILBIRD
     (Bodiless)
Tail: Claret hackle tips.
Wings: Teal flank feather.
Hackle: Yellow.

No. 7   BOBBIE DUN
     (Peter J. Schwab)
Tail: Red goose or red bucktail, broad and long.
Body: Copper wire.
Wing: Lower section white bucktail, topping, red. A small section of reddish brown is sometimes added on top.

No. 8   BRASS HAT
     (Peter J. Schwab)
Tail: Yellow goose quill section.
Body: Yellow brass wire.
Wings: White bucktail topped with yellow bucktail.

No. 9   CARTER'S DIXIE
Tail: Yellow hackle fibres.
Body: Round gold tinsel (Tag, seven turns also).
Wings: White goose.
Hackle: Scarlet.

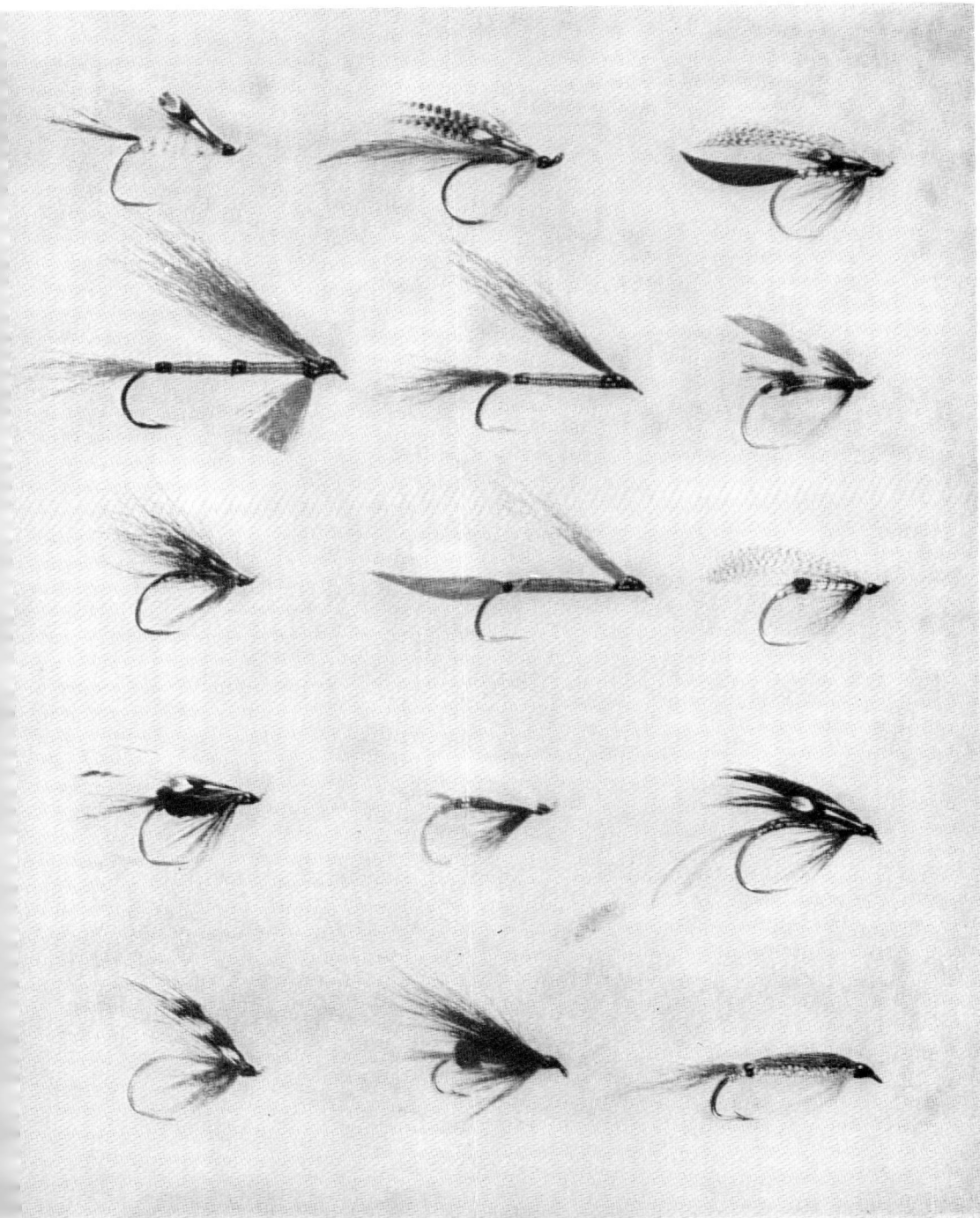

PLATE XXIII. STEELHEAD FLIES.
(See opposite page for descriptions)

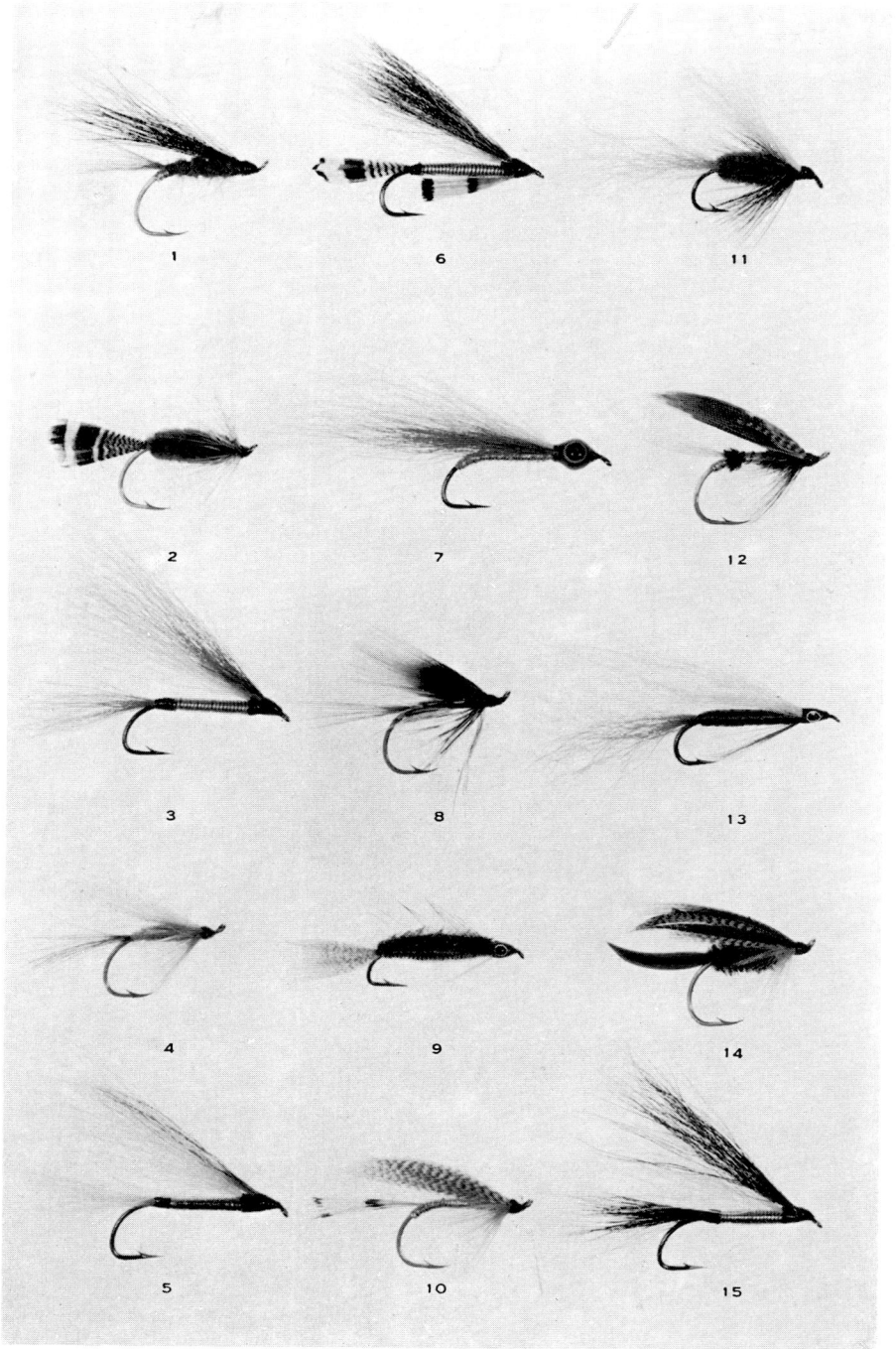

PLATE XXIV. STEELHEAD FLIES.

(See page 103 for descriptions)

No. 10   CARTER FLY
(C. Jim Pray)

Tail: Yellow polar bear; tag, scarlet chenille.
Body: Silver oval.
Wings: Black bucktail.
Hackle: Scarlet.

No. 11   CORRIE FLY

Tail: Scarlet Ibis, or goose.
Body: Silver tinsel; ribbing, silver oval.
Wings: Grey Mallard. Shoulders: Jungle Cock.
Hackle: Bright claret.

No. 12   DOT
(Wm. F. Blades)

Tail: Topping and Golden Pheasant red breast feather.
Tag: Fine maroon colored copper wire, and yellow floss.
Butt: Peacock herl.
Body: Tail, half silver wire; front half maroon enameled copper wire.
Wings: Grey mottled Turkey.
Hackle: Dark blue dun.

No. 13
GENERAL EAGLES FAIRY

Tail: Topping; tag, silver oval, yellow floss.
Butt: Scarlet wool.
Body: Silver tinsel; ribbing, silver oval.
Wings: Grey Mallard.
Hackle: Black.

No. 14   GOLDEN DEMON

Tail: Golden Pheasant crest.
Body: Flat gold tinsel.
Wings: Brown M a l l a r d naushua or brown bucktail.
Hackle: Orange.

No. 15
JACK HORNER'S SILVER SHRIMP

Body: Silver oval tinsel.
Hackle: Ashy dun at throat.
Tail and back are dark brown bucktail. Tie this in at the fourth turn of oval tinsel, and take it over to the front to form the back, tie down at the head.

SELECTED STEELHEAD FLIES
(See Plate XXIV)

No. 1   KILLER

Tail: Scarlet hackle fibres.
Body: Scarlet seal fur; ribbing and tag, silver tinsel.
Wing: Black bucktail or bear.

No. 2   ORLEANS BARBER

Tail: Barred Wood Duck strip.
Body: Scarlet chenille.
Hackle: Grizzly.

No. 3
PAINT BRUSH, TWO WING
(Peter J. Schwab)

Tail: Red goose or red bucktail, broad and long.
Body: Brass (or silver) wire.
Wing: First section yellow bucktail, second red, topped with a small amount of reddish brown.

No. 4   POLAR SHRIMP

Tail: Scarlet hackle fibres.
Body: Orange wool.
Wings: White polar bear.
Hackle: Orange.

No. 5 PRINCESS, TWO WING
(Peter J. Schwab)
Tail: Orange bucktail.
Body: Flat gold tinsel over a thin wire core body.
Wing: First section yellow bucktail, second orange, also a small topping of grey squirrel.

No. 6 QUEEN BESS
(Peter J. Schwab)
Tail: Grey squirrel or barred Wood Duck.
Body: Silver or copper wire.
Wings: Yellow bucktail topped with grey squirrel.
Spike: Golden Pheasant tippet.

No. 7 RED OPTIC FLY
(C. Jim Pray)
Body: Silver oval.
Wings: Scarlet bucktail; yellow polar bear on top.
Head: Large round red enamel head, with yellow and black eyes.

No. 8
ROGUE RIVER JOCK SCOTT
Tail: Red hackle fibres.
Body: Rear half, yellow floss; front, black floss.
Wings: White tipped Turkey.
Hackle: Guinea hen.

No. 9 SHINERAKLE
(Weber)
Tail: Grey Mallard body feather (shaping optional).
Body: Silver oval tinsel over padding; strip of red goose on each side overlapped with Peacock herl.
Fins: One red, one white hackle, trimmed.
Throat: White hackle.

No. 10 SILVER DEMON
(C. Jim Pray)
Tail: Golden Pheasant tippet.
Body: Silver oval tinsel; five turns below tail forming a tag.
Wings: Barred Mallard breast.
Hackle: Orange.

No. 11 THOR
(C. Jim Pray)
Tail: Orange bucktail.
Body: Scarlet chenille.
Wings: White bucktail.
Hackle: Mahogany.

No. 12 THE DON
Tail: Topping and Indian Crow.
Tag: Silver oval and yellow floss; butt, Peacock herl.
Body: One third at tail, yellow floss; remainder claret seal fur.
Ribbing: Gold oval tinsel.
Wings: Dun Turkey, strip of Teal on each side.
Hackle: Black.

No. 13 VAN LUVAN
(Peter J. Schwab)
Tail: Red goose.
Body: First, copper wire, then cover with red floss.
Ribbing: Silver oval tinsel
Wings: White bucktail.
Hackle: Brown.

No. 14 WELLS' SPECIAL
Tail: Scarlet duck quill section.
Body: Peacock herl, thick.
Wings: Teal overlaid with brown Mallard, also narrow strips of goose, yellow, red and blue.
Hackle: Yellow.

No. 15
WOOD PUSSY, TWO WING
(Peter J. Schwab)
Tail: Black bucktail.
Body: Silver wire.
Wing: Bucktail, lower section white, topping, black.

NEW TRIER
(W. F. Blades)

Tag: Fine copper wire, size .0142, and yellow floss.

Tail: Golden Pheasant crest.

Butt: Peacock herl.

Body: First half—silver-coated copper wire, size No. .023, butted with Peacock herl. *Second half*—copper wire, same size.

Hackle: Blue dun.

Wings: Mottled-grey brown Turkey.

The above wire sizes are given for a fly tied on a No. 6.4X long Allcock No. 2811, 2X stout hook.

Drawing No. 1

Drawing No. 2

Drawing No. 3

Place the hook in the vise, coat it with cement, then wrap it with tying silk to the beginning of the tag.

Put a little cement on the hook, then take hold of the short end of the wire and wind on the tag very tightly with the right hand, keeping a firm hold of the short end with the left hand. Cut off the surplus ends with nail clippers and file the ends if they are sharp or rough. Now give it a coat of cement. I use the copper wire that is coated with maroon-colored enamel for this fly.

Wind the yellow floss part of the tag and tie in the Golden Pheasant crest tail, and your fly will be the same as Drawing No. 1.

Wind the two wire body segments, using the same method as you did for winding the tag, and your fly will be same as Drawing No. 2.

Now wind on the two Peacock herl butts in the spaces which you left open. Wind on the blue dun hackle and either double it or pull the fibres back as you are winding, and your fly will now be the same as Drawing No. 3.

Select the mottled Turkey wing sections from right and left feathers,

Drawing No. 4

and leave the quill on them until they are tied on—this will keep them from splitting. Now cut off the surplus ends and form the head. Your fly will now be the same as Drawing No. 4.

This type of body could be used on many of our streamer flies and the English salmon flies. It is not only attractive, but very durable.

The Snowshoe River, Ontario, Canada.

Chapter IX

TYING THE DRY FLY

RTIFICIAL DRY FLIES are made to imitate the winged flies found floating on the water, and that means buoyancy is an important factor.

Select a light-weight hook with a tapered eye, of a size suitable for the fly you are tying. To float a heavy hook necessitates using far too much hackle, and inasmuch as the hackle represents the legs and wings of a fly, one can easily see this does not assist in imitating the natural fly.

Select your hackles from an old rooster; the hackle on a good neck is long and thin. The fibres are stiff and glossy, and run pretty evenly in length. If the color on the underside is about the same as the topside, it is a very rare neck. Hackle fibres are best for the tails of dry flies as they are very durable and if put on in the proper place will assist greatly in floating your fly.

Select a strong, fine tying silk; and use No. 4-0 on your first flies; tie them on a No. 10 to No. 14 hook. When you are tying the very small flies, use fine silk from 6-0 to 10-0. Quill bodies are used on many of our well-known flies, such as the Ginger Quill, Olive Quill, Quill Gordon, etc. The Peacock eye feather furnishes us with this quill; we also use fibres from large wing feathers from the Condor, Heron, Swan, etc. Moose Mane is also very good, also the hackle stem, and horse hair.

To remove the fibres from the Peacock herl, lay it on a level surface, and place a razor blade on the top of it at an angle of about 45 degrees away from you; carefully pull the herl towards you. Use an eraser to take off the fine fibres. This can also be done with the thumb and finger nails. Before winding on the quill, I make the under body smooth and to shape with fine floss or tying silk; then wind the quill so that each edge touches the other; *do not overlap them.*

Wings; Single and double upright wings are cut from the wing quills of many of our ducks and birds, such as the Mallard, Coot, Swan, Goose, Starling, etc. Before cutting out the sections, follow these simple rules. Use a pair of wings from the same bird, and take a feather from the same position on each wing—they match up better for size and color. The lower portion is usually the best. Be sure your sections are cut the same width, and a little over one-eighth of an inch for a fly tied on a No. 14 hook. Cut your sections as long as possible and they will not split so easily. Take two sections of feather and place them together on the top of the hook with the underside of the feathers together, and the tips projecting over the eye of the hook with the tips pointing down; bring the silk up between your thumb and hook, over the wings and down between your first finger and hook. The secret is to grip the sections and hook very tightly, and only release the tips of your fingers to pass the tying silk around, and when you pull the silk straight down increase your grip on the sections; repeat this two or three times, then cut off the surplus butts tapered; take a few turns of silk over them. Now raise the wings upright and take a few turns of silk in front of them to hold them in position.

Drawing No. 1

The dry fly I have selected is the Dark Hendrickson, a well-known fly, especially in the East. Secure a No. 12 or No. 14 light wire hook in the vise, coat it with cement and wrap it from the eye to where the tail is to be tied in. Select a few fibres of stiff Wood Duck flank feathers and place them in between the thumb and first finger tips of your left hand, seeing that the tips are closed; in fact, the nails should practically be together. Next put the

[108]

fibres down on the hook and bring the tying silk up in between the finger tips, which are opened momentarily, to allow the silk to pass between them; then continue over the fibres and around the hook and pull the silk straight down; repeat this two or three times, then slide your fingers back, put on a couple more turns of silk and a half hitch; then trim off the surplus ends. (See Drawing No. 1).

Drawing No. 2

I now tie in a piece of dubbing made from the fawn colored fur from the red fox belly. To make this, I place a fine piece of tying silk about one foot long, waxed with tacky wax, on my knee; then cut off the fur and mix it by pulling it apart with your fingers; then sparsely spread the fur onto the silk with a bodkin; now double the silk directly on top of the lower silk and press them together; put the thumb of your left hand on the nearest end to you, and the first finger on the other end. Commence to twist with your right hand thumb and first finger, gradually releasing the twists under the finger, and you will have a piece of fine yarn.

Then roll the dubbing between the palm of the hands, one way only; this makes it thinner and easier to handle on the small bodies. Take the tying silk to the wing position and place the tip of a Wood Duck flank feather on the top of the hook with the best side down. I now raise the tying silk almost vertically and tilt the tip to about 45 degrees, and with one quick turn of the silk I roll it over on top of the hook; take a few more turns around the butt; trim off the surplus ends and take a few turns in front of the wings, and your fly will be as shown in Drawing No. 2.

Now take the dubbing in the hackle pliers and wind on the body. Select two light blue dun neck hackles; stroke the fibres carefully down so that they are at right angles to the stem, and cut off the soft base, leaving a small amount on the stem; this stops them from slipping after they are tied on. I tie both hackles on at once with the best sides towards the eye. Your fly will be the same as Drawing No. 3.

[109]

Take two or three turns behind the wings, and the desired amount in front; finish off the head with the whip finish and head cement, and your fly will be the same as Drawing No. 4.

You will notice, when winding on two hackles at the same time, that they do not wind the same as each other; one becomes shorter than the other. You can overcome this by releasing the pliers and taking a new grip.

Drawing No. 3 shows one hackle which is often sufficient if the hackle is good.

Drawing No. 3

Drawing No. 4

TYING THE DARK CAHILL PARACHUTE DRY FLY

The Dark Cahill Parachute is simply a Cahill tied with the hackle tied on horizontally, and the legs of hen Pheasant neck feathers. The length of the hackle is the thing that has to be studied to make the fly float properly. If the hook is heavy, you require longer hackle and more of it. The legs have been used by the British for many years; they are easy to put on, and surely improve the fish-taking qualities of your fly.

To make this fly: Coat the hook with liquid cement and wind it with tying silk to the tail location, then tie in the tail which is brown hackle fibres. (Drawing No. 1).

Drawing No. 1

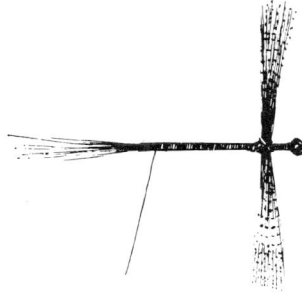

Drawing No. 2

Now take the tying silk to the wing location and tie in the tip or strands of Wood Duck breast feather. Divide the fibres equally and crisscross the tying silk, bringing them back and at right angles to the hook (as shown in Drawing No. 2).

The body is grey Muskrat fur dubbing or grey spun fur yarn can also be used.

For the legs, take three or four turns of hen Pheasant neck feathers. Bind them down and cut off any fibres that are above the hook, as they will inter-

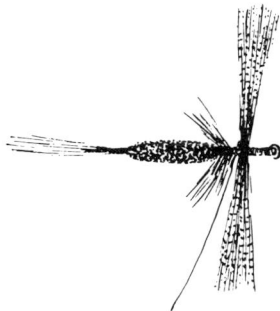

Drawing No. 3

fere with the winding of the parachute-type hackle. Be sure you have left plenty of space to tie in the hackle. (Drawing No. 3).

I prefer a good saddle hackle which is brown; prepare the hackle by stroking the fibres so that they are at right angles to the stem; cut off the fibres at the base leaving the centre stem long, and tie it in very securely (as shown in Drawing No. 4).

 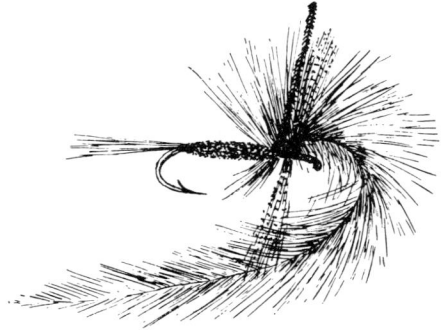

Drawing No. 4   *Drawing No. 5*

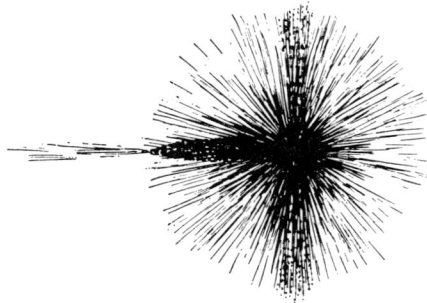

Drawing No. 6

To wind the hackle, take hold of the trimmed stem with the left hand first finger and thumb, and hold it straight up; now wind the hackle around the stem with the right hand; put a pair of hackle pliers on the tip and keep winding under the previous windings until you have the amount you desire, releasing the fibres as you wind. (Drawing No. 5).

Now, carefully place the hackle on the far side of the hook and the weight of the pliers will keep it in place; raise the horizontal hackle up with your first finger and thumb on the left hand, and take a few turns of tying silk over it with the right hand. Place a pair of hackle pliers on the centre stem and bring it carefully through the horizontal hackle, placing it on the near side of the hook; now secure it the same way as you did the tip end. Clip off the surplus ends, and put on the whip finish.

To put on the whip finish, I lift up the front portion of the hackle with my left hand finger and thumb, and I also hold the end of the tying silk in the left hand (under the second, third, and little finger); then put on about three turns of the whip finish with the right hand. This requires a little practice, but it will be very useful in the tying of many other flies.

Drawing No. 6 is the finished fly.

Edgar Evensen

Chapter X

IMPORTANT DRY FLY PATTERNS

OLLOWING is a list of dry flies which when tied on several different sized hooks, will take fish in almost any location. The position of some of the flies in the photographs are not as I would like them to be; this is caused by the stiff hackles that are used on dry flies. Many of these flies are copies of flies that were sent to me by noted fly tyers; namely, Dan Bailey, Don Martinez and F. B. and H. A. Darbee. I included the Green Drakes by F. M. Halford which appear in his book, dated 1886; this was about the beginning of the dry fly in England.

If you study my instructions on making the dry flies, you will be able to make most of these flies by reading the material list and examining the photographs. These flies should be presented to the fish to represent a winged fly dropping on the water, which is not a simple task. Care should also be taken to avoid dragging your fly, or it will immediately go under the surface.

When making these dry flies, by all means make your fly the size of the fly that is being taken on the stream you're fishing, or any hatch you are copying.

No. 1 ADAMS (Leonard Halladay)
Tail: Two strands Golden Pheasant tippet or grizzly hackle fibres.
Body: Grey wool or Muskrat fur; grey wool egg sack.
Wings: Grizzly hackle tips tied spent.
Hackle: Brown and grizzly, tied together.

No. 2 APPLE GREEN DUN
Tail: Ginger hackle fibres.
Body: Apple green floss.
Wings: Starling.
Hackle: Ginger.

No. 3 ASH DUN
Tail: Medium blue dun.
Body: Cream silk thread, waxed.
Wings: Starling.
Hackle: Medium blue dun.

No. 4 AUGUST DUN
Tail: Ginger hackle fibres.
Body: Brownish red quill or hackle stem; ribbing, gold wire.
Wings: Pale blue hackle tips.
Hackle: Ginger.

No. 5 BAIGENT'S VARIANT
Tail: Black hackle fibres.
Body: Red floss; ribbing, Peacock herl.
Hackle: Black, large saddle or spade.

No. 6 BADGER QUILL (Parachute)
Tail: Badger hackle fibres.
Tag: Gold tinsel.
Body: Peacock quill.
Hackle: Badger tied on horizontal.

No. 7 BADGER QUILL
Tail: Badger hackle fibres.
Body: Peacock quill.
Wings: Pale Starling quill sections.
Hackle: Badger.

No. 8 BEAVERKILL FEMALE
Tail: Dark ginger hackle fibres.
Body: Blue grey Muskrat fur; egg sack, yellow chenille.
Wings: Grizzly hackle tips; tied spent.
Hackle: Dark ginger.

No. 9 BEEDLE COACHMAN (Western)
Tail: Black bucktail.
Body: Scarlet floss.
Wings: White polar bear or bucktail, tied upright and divided.
Hackle: Brown.

No. 10 BEEFSTEAK
Tag: Ibis body feather fibres.
Body: Strand of Red Macaw tail feather.
Hackle: Two natural red hackles.

No. 11 BLACK ANT (W. F. B.)
Tail: None.
Body: Black tying silk, use cement on silk to form two humps for ants body.
Wings: Four pale blue dun hackle tips.
Legs: Brown moose mane.
Hackle: Cochy-bondhu.

No. 12 BLACK GNAT
Tail: Black hackle fibres.
Body: Black Ostrich herl or chenille.
Wings: Slate quill sections.
Hackle: Black.

No. 13 BLACK WULFF (Dan Bailey)
Tail: Black Moose hair.
Body: Pink silk floss lacquered.
Wings: Black Moose hair.
Hackle: Furnace.

No. 14 BLADES' FURNACE VARIANT
Body: Strands of the ruddy tail feather of the Cock Pheasant wound as a herl.
Ribbing: Gold wire.
Wings: Small jungle cock.
Hackle: Brown furnace.

No. 15 BLONDIE (Peter J. Schwab)
Tail: Pale barred orange baboon.
Body: Cream dubbing, red fox with a mixture of cream mole.
Wing: Pale barred orange baboon.
Hackle: Pale yellowish ginger.

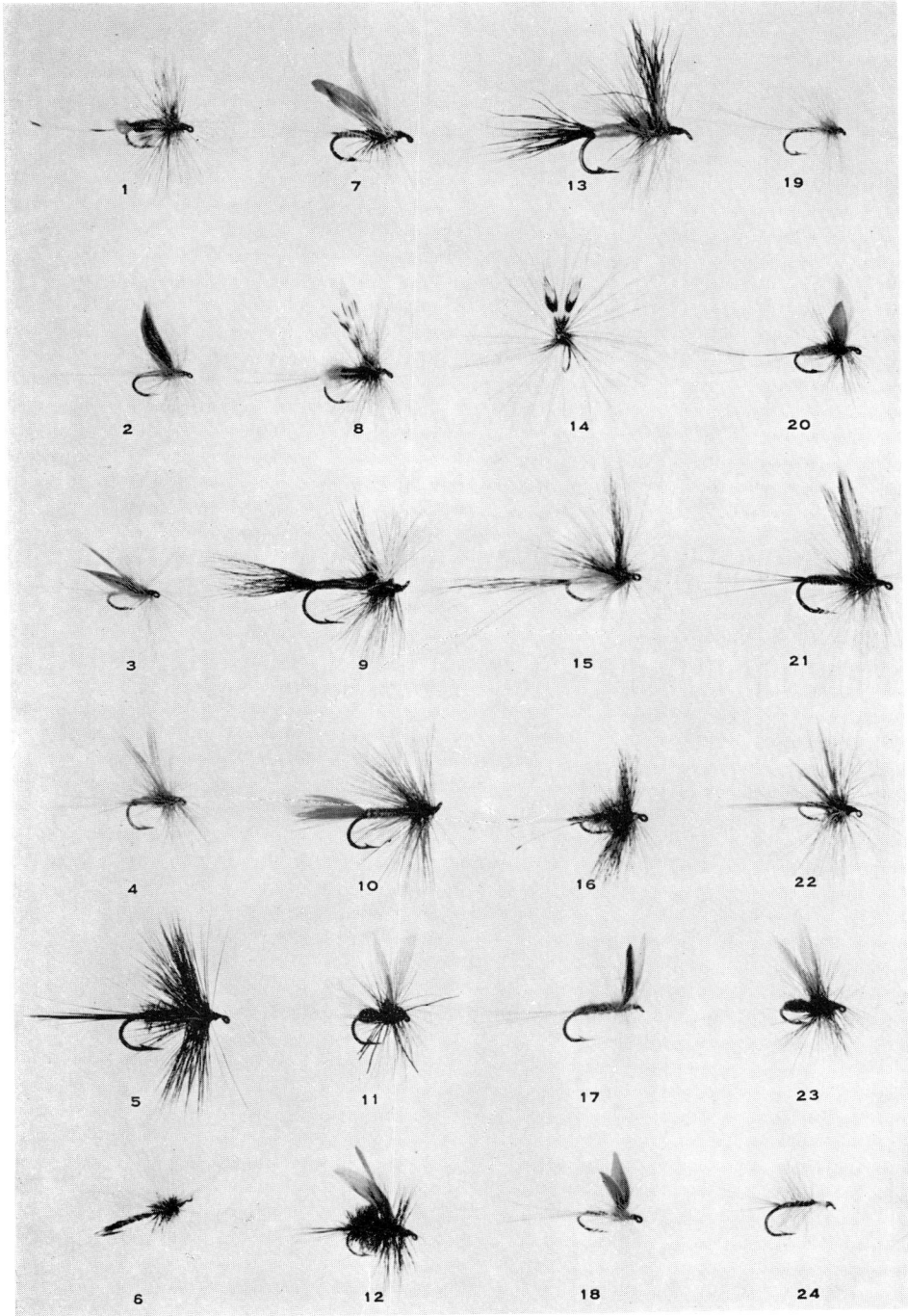

PLATE XXV.   DRY FLIES.

(See opposite page for descriptions)

No. 16   BOB LINCOLN
Tail: Golden Pheasant tippet.
Body: Grizzly hackle wound around hook and trimmed.
Wings: Grey mottled Partridge tied spent.
Hackle: Brown.

No. 17   BLUE DUN
Tail: Blue grey hackle fibres.
Body: Blue grey fur; ribbing, primrose silk.
Wings: Blue grey quill sections.
Hackle: Blue grey.

No. 18   BLUE QUILL
Tail: Blue grey hackle fibres.
Body: Peacock quill.
Wings: Blue grey quill sections.
Hackle: Blue grey.

No. 19   BLUE UPRIGHT
Tail: Blue dun hackle fibres.
Body: Peacock quill.
Hackle: Blue dun.

No. 20 BRADLEY SPECIAL
Tail: Dark red hackle fibres.
Body: Red squirrel fur; on red silk.
Wings: Grey Mallard.
Hackle: Dark reddish brown.

No. 21   BRADLEY
(Don Martinez)
Tail: None. Natural red hackle fibres are sometimes used.
Body: Red Macaw quill.
Wings: Brown hackle tips.
Hackle: One furnace and one grizzly dyed silver doctor blue.

No. 22   BRADY
Tail: Light brown hackle fibres.
Body: Peacock quill.
Wings: Light brown hackle tips.
Hackle: Grizzly and light brown tied on together.

No. 23   BROWN ANT
(W. F. Blades)
Body: Reddish brown tying silk, use cement on silk to form two humps for ants body.
Wings: Four blue dun hackle tips.
Hackle: Brown.

No. 24   BROWN BIVISIBLE
Tail: Brown hackle tips or fibres.
Body: Brown hackle tied palmer, and two to four turns of white at the head. Other good patterns are Black, Badger, Ginger, Blue, etc.

SELECTED DRY FLY PATTERNS
(See Plate XXVI)

No. 1   CAHILL (DARK)
Tail: Brown hackle fibres.
Body: Grey Muskrat fur.
Wings: Wood Duck.
Hackle: Brown.

No. 2   CAHILL
Tail: Brown hackle fibres.
Body: Grey Muskrat fur.
Wings: Wood Duck.
Hackle: Brown.

No. 3   CAHILL (LIGHT)
Tail: Ginger hackle fibres.
Body: Creamy white fur, Linx tail.
Wings: Wood Duck.
Hackle: Ginger.

No. 4   CAMPBELL'S FANCY
Tail: Golden Pheasant crest.
Body: Gold tinsel.
Wings: Mallard body feather.
Hackle: Furnace.

No. 5   CATSKILL
Tail: Wood Duck fibres.
Body: Orange floss; light brown hackle, tied palmer.
Wings: Wood Duck.
Hackle: Light brown.

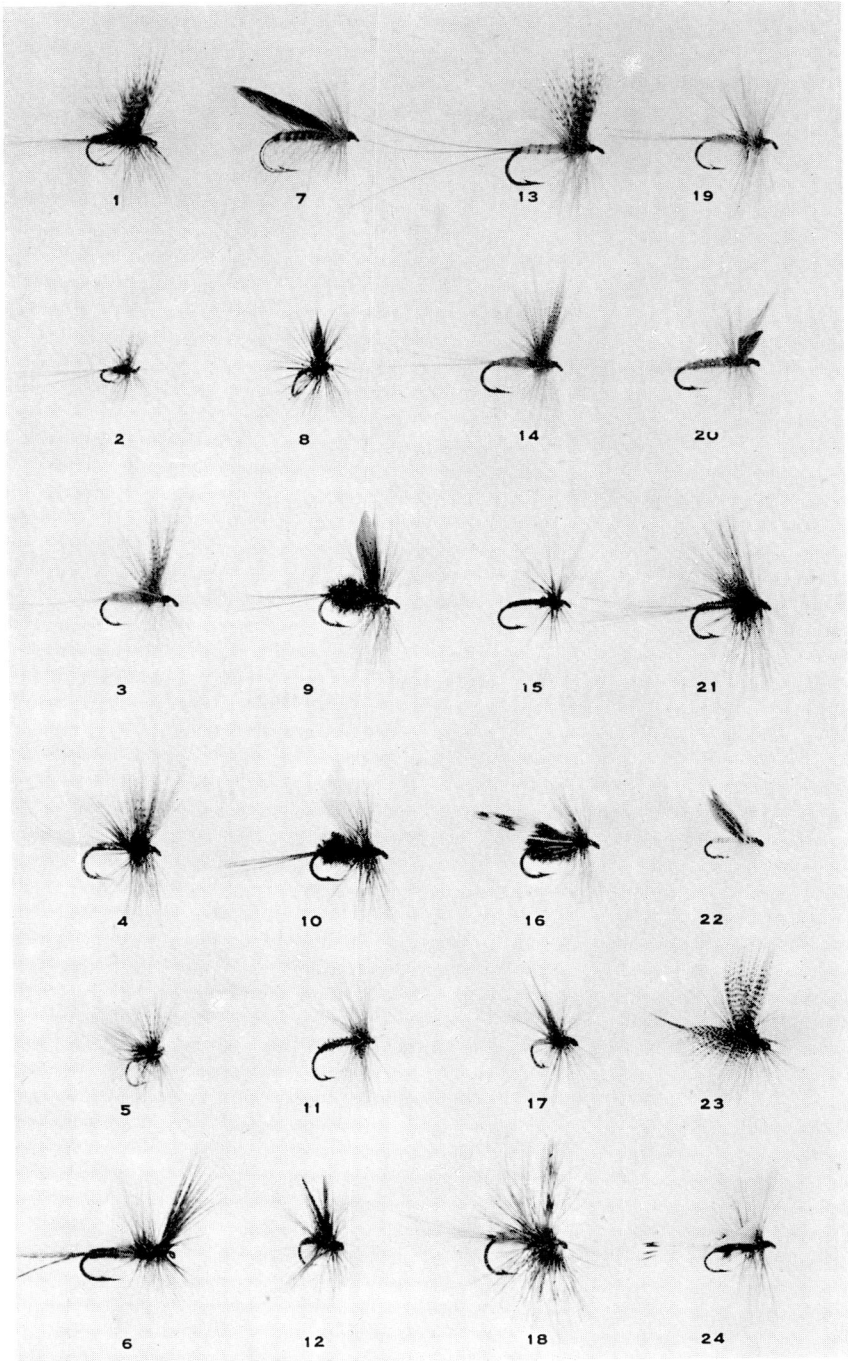

PLATE XXVI. DRY FLIES.

(See opposite page for descriptions)

No. 6   CHOCOLATE DUN
(Don Martinez)

Tail: Strands of brown Mallard.
Body: Chocolate brown fur dubbing; ribbing, gold wire.
Shoulder: Yellow chenille.
Hackles: One grizzly dyed silver doctor blue and one light brown.

No. 7   CINNAMON SEDGE

Body: Stripped Condor dyed dull yellow-green.
Ribbing hackle: Ginger.
Hackles: Two ginger cock hackles.
Wings: Mottled brown hen.

No. 8   CLARET SMUT

Body: Peacock quill dyed claret.
Wings: Pale Starling.
Hackle: Black cock.

No. 9
COACHMAN LEADWING

Tail: Brown hackle fibres.
Body: Peacock herl.
Wings: Dark grey Blackbird, Starling or Duck.
Hackle: Brown.

No. 10   COACHMAN

Tail: Brown hackle fibres.
Body: Peacock herl.
Wings: White goose quill section.
Hackle: Brown.

No. 11   CORKSCREW

Body: Central quill of a brown Partridge tail feather from which the fibres have been cut away.
Shoulder hackle: Brown ginger cock hackle.
Head hackle: Brown ginger hen hackle.

No. 12   COWDUNG

Body: Olive floss.
Wings: Dark grey quill sections.
Hackle: Brown.

No. 13   CROSS MAYFLY
(Reub Cross)

Tail: Three brown hackle stems with fibres stripped off.
Body: Natural raffia; ribbing, gold wire.
Wings: Wood Duck.
Hackle: Blue dun.

No. 14   CROSS SPECIAL

Tail: Grey hackle fibres.
Body: Pale cream fur.
Wings: Wood Duck.
Hackle: Grey.

No. 15
DARK OLIVE GNAT

Body: Peacock quill dyed dark olive.
Thorax: Dark olive herl.
Wings: Blue dun hackle tips.
Hackle: Furnace.

No. 16   DEER FLY

Body: Peacock herl.
Wings: Grizzly hackle tips.
Hackle: Brown.

No. 17   DEW FLY

Body: Primrose silk floss.
Hackle: Light red.
Wings: Starling.

No. 18
DONNELLY'S DARK VARIANT

Tail: Brown hackle fibres.
Body: Blue dun fur dubbing.
Wings: Furnace hackle tips.
Hackle: One brown and one grizzly.

No. 19
DONNELLY'S LIGHT VARIANT

Tail: Ginger hackle fibres.
Body: Cream fur dubbing.
Wings: White hackle tips.
Hackle: One ginger and one white.

No. 20   DRIFFIELD DUN

Tail: Pale ginger hackle fibres.
Body: Pale blue dun fur; ribbing, yellow silk.
Wings: Pale Starling.
Hackle: Pale ginger.

No. 21   DUNHAM
(Don Martinez)
Tail: Maroon fibres from Golden Pheasant breast feathers, or Amherst Pheasant crest fibres.
Body: Macaw quill red and blue.
Hackle: Furnace, and a few turns in front of Plymouth Rock dyed silver doctor blue.

No. 22   EMU
Tail: White hackle fibres.
Body: White Emu quill.
Wings: Pale Starling.
Hackle: White.

No. 23
FAN WING PROFESSOR
Tail: Scarlet duck quill section.
Body: Yellow floss; ribbing, gold.
Wings: Mallard mottled breast feather.
Hackle: Brown.

No. 24
FAN WING ROYAL COACHMAN
Tail: Dark brown hackle fibres.
Body: Scarlet floss; Peacock herl at each end.
Wings: White Wood Duck breast feathers.
Hackle: Brown.

SELECTED DRY FLY PATTERNS
(See Plate XXVII)

No. 1   FLYING CADDIS FLY
Tail: Grizzly hackle fibres (optional).
Body: Grey deer body, clipped; ribbing, yellow floss.
Wings: Double grizzly hackle tips, tied spent.
Hackle: Grizzly.

No. 2   GINGER BI-VISIBLE
Tail: Ginger hackle fibres.
Hackle: Ginger tied palmer, two or three turns of white at the head.

No. 3   GINGER QUILL
Tail: Ginger hackle fibres.
Body: Peacock quill.
Wings: Grey duck; grizzly hackle tips for spent wing.
Hackle: Ginger.

No. 4
GINGER QUILL SPENT-WING
(Parachute)
Tail: Ginger hackle fibres.
Body: Brown hackle stem.
Wings: Grizzly hackle tips, tied spent.
Hackle: Ginger.

No. 5   GORDON
Tail: Blue dun hackle fibres (or Wood Duck).
Body: Golden yellow floss.
Wings: Wood Duck tied upright.
Hackle: Blue dun.

No. 6   GOVERNOR
Body: Bronze Peacock herl; tag, orange floss.
Wings: Hen Pheasant or Woodcock secondary feathers.
Hackle: Ginger.

No. 7   GREEN DRAKE
(F. M. Halford) 1886
Tail: Brown Mallard, four strands.
Body: Raffia; ribbing, crimson tying silk. Ribbing, hackle ginger.
Wings: Wood Duck trimmed to shape.
Shoulder hackle: Grey hen dyed pale olive.

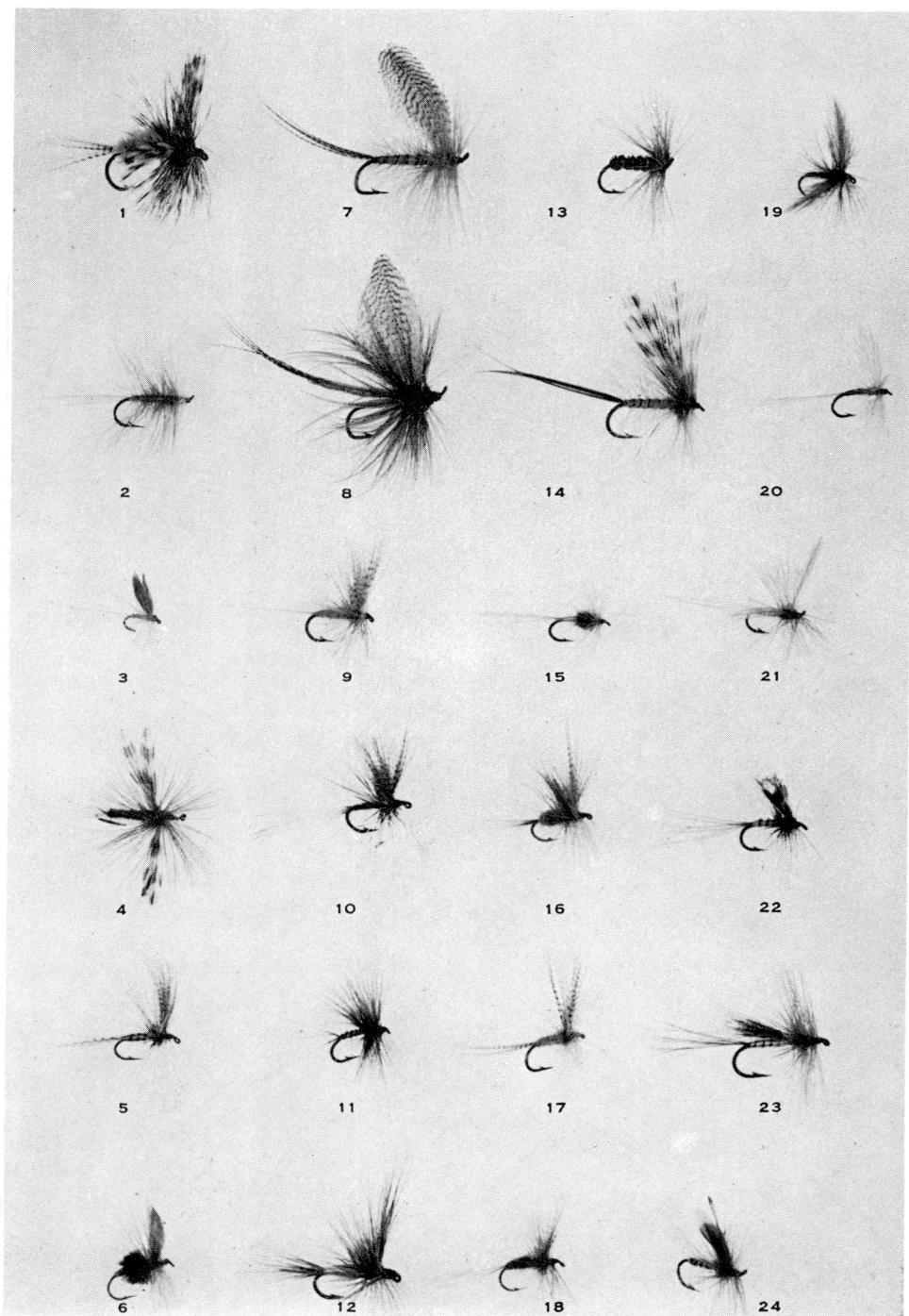

PLATE XXVII. DRY FLIES.
(*See page 121 for descriptions*)

No. 8   GREEN DRAKE
(F. M. Halford) 1886

Tail: Brown Mallard, four strands.

Body: Detached, of white horse hair over raffia, worked on two strands of nylon; ribbing, waxed yellow tying silk.

Wings: Wood Duck trimmed to shape.

Hackles: First Hen Pheasant dyed pale olive; front hackle, blue dun rooster.

Head: Bronze Peacock herl.

No. 9   GREY FOX

Tail: Ginger hackle fibres.

Body: Red Fox belly fur.

Wings: Grey mottled Mallard.

Hackle: One ginger, one grizzly front hackle.

No. 10   GREIG'S QUILL
(Elizabeth Greig)

Tail: Dark badger.

Body: Peacock quill.

Wings: Wood Duck.

Hackle: Dark badger.

No. 11
GREENWELL'S GLORY

Tail: Furnace hackle fibres.

Body: Yellow waxed tying silk; ribbing, gold wire.

Wings: Upright, made of blue dun hackle.

Hackle: Furnace.

No. 12   GRIZZLY WULFF
(Dan Bailey)

Tail: Brown bucktail.

Body: Pale yellow floss lacquered.

Wings: Brown bucktail.

Hackle: Mixed grizzly and brown.

No. 13   HACKLE SEDGE

Body: Central quill of Partridge tail feather, with fibres cut away; ribbing, gold twist.

Shoulder hackle: A ginger cock hackle.

Head hackle: Brown hens neck hackle.

No. 14
HACKLE WING MAYFLY

Tail: Three strands Cock Pheasant feather.

Body: Yellow raffia; ribbing, gold wire; body palmered with yellow hackle.

Shoulder hackle: Brown speckled grizzly.

Wings: Grizzly hackle tips dyed greenish yellow.

No. 15   HALF STONE

Tail: Blue dun hackle fibres (three).

Body: Rear half yellow; front, dark grey mole fur.

Hackle: Blue dun.

No. 16 HENDRICKSON (DARK)
(Roy Steenrod)

Tail: Wood Duck.

Body: Fawn colored fur from the Red Fox belly.

Wings: Wood Duck.

Hackle: One blue dun and one brown or rusty blue dun.

No. 17 HENDRICKSON (LIGHT)

Tail: Wood Duck.

Body: Cream fur.

Wings: Wood Duck.

Hackle: Light blue dun.

No. 18   HONEY DUN

Tail: Grey hackle fibres.

Body: Muskrat fur dubbing.

Wings: Lemon Wood Duck.

Legs: Grey or dun hackle.

No. 19 HOUGHTON RUBY

Tail: White hackle fibres.

Body: Stripped red hackle stem, dyed red and crimson.

Wings: Two light blue dun hen hackle tips, tied spent.

Hackle: Bright Rhode Island red.

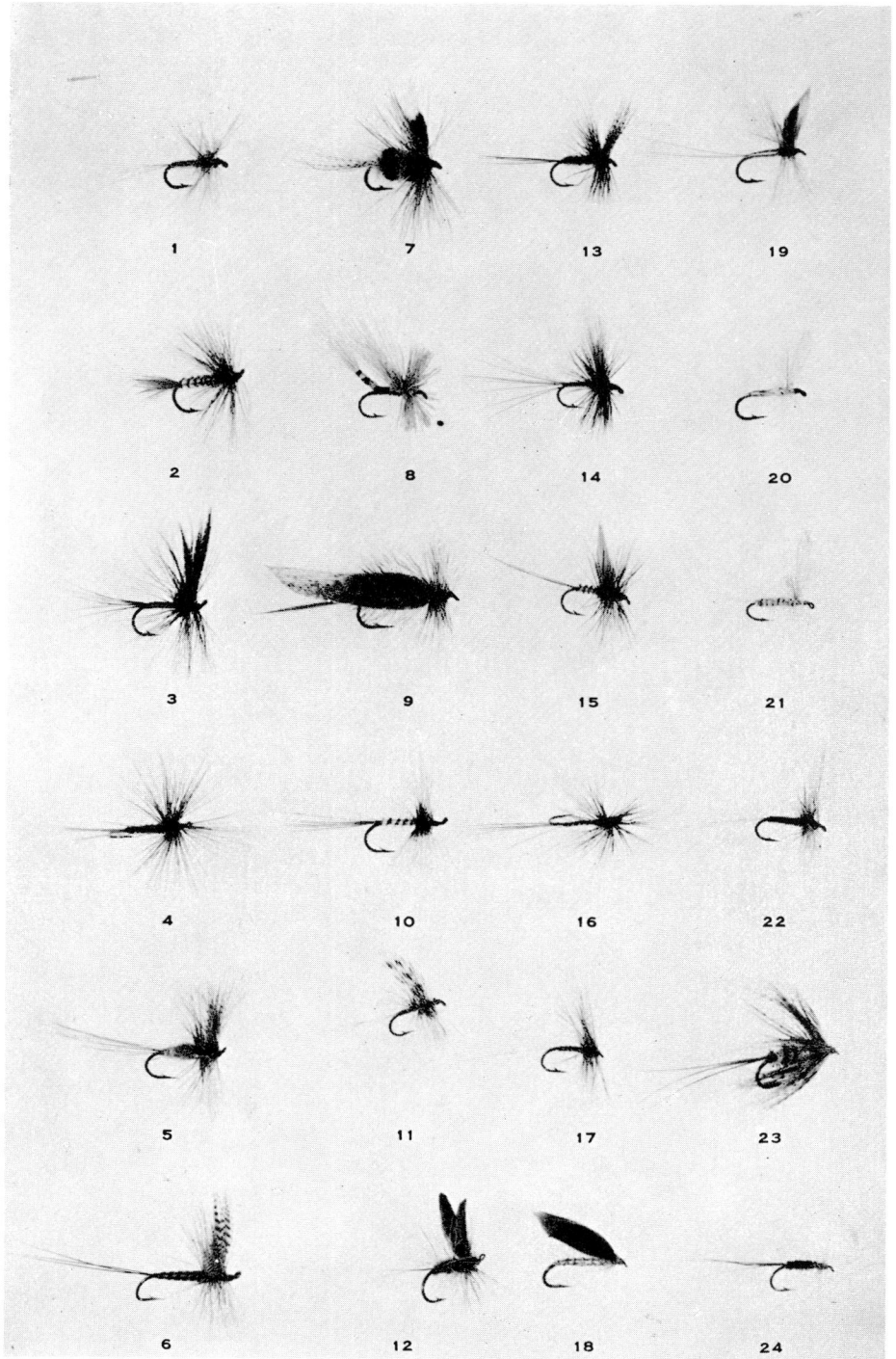

PLATE XXVIII. DRY FLIES.
(*See opposite page for descriptions*)

No. 20   JENNY SPINNER
(Spent Wing)
Tail: Light blue dun grey hackle fibres.
Body: White horse hair or polar bear;
orange tying silk at each end.
Wings: Light blue dun tips, tied spent
wing.
Hackle: Light blue dun.

No. 21
JULY DUN SPINNER
Tail: Ginger hackle fibres.
Body: Gold colored floss; ribbing, gold
wire.
Wings: Blue dun hackle tips, or pale
Starling, tips tied spent.
Hackle: Ginger.

No. 22   JUNGLE VARIANT
(Don Martinez)
Tail: Brown hackle fibres.
Body: Red and blue Macaw quill.
Wings: Small Jungle Cock.
Hackle: Furnace, dressed sparsely.

No. 23   KILLER DILLER
Tail: Red hackle fibres.
Body: Yellow floss; ribbing, gold tinsel.
Wings: Grey squirrel.
Hackle: Brown, tied upright and full.

No. 24   KIMBRIDGE
Body: White Condor, ribbing, silver wire,
palmered with pale ginger cock hackle.
Wings: Woodcock.
Hackles: Two pale ginger cock hackles
at shoulder.

SELECTED DRY FLY PATTERNS
(See Plate XXVIII)

No. 1
LUNN'S YELLOW BOY, WINGED
Tail: Pale buff hackle fibres.
Body: Yellow stripped hackle stem.
Wings: Buff hackle tips, tied spent.
Hackle: Light buff cock hackle.

No. 2   MACAW TAG
Tag: Ibis body feather fibres.
Body: Strand of yellow Macaw tail
feather.
Hackle: Two natural red hackles.

No. 3   MALLARD QUILL
Tail: Dark brown hackle fibres.
Body: Peacock quill.
Wings: Brown Mallard flank.
Hackle: Brown.

No. 4   MACAW TAG
(Parachute)
Tail: Ibis body feather fibres.
Body: Strand of yellow Macaw tail
feather.
Hackle: Natural red tied on horizontal.

No. 5   MARCH BROWN
(American)
Tail: Red hackle fibres.
Body: Red Fox belly and Hare's poll.
Wings: Grey Mallard or Wood Duck
flank feather.
Hackle: Red game cock; light grizzly in
front.

No. 6   MAY FLY
Tail: Three Porcupine hairs.
Body: Pale yellow floss; ribbing, dark
peacock quill.
Wings: Wood Duck.
Hackle: Brown.

No. 7   MC GINTY
Tail: Grey Mallard fibres and red hackle
fibres.
Body: Yellow and black chenille.
Wings: Mallard wing feathers, white
tipped.
Hackle: Brown.

No. 8   MC QUEEN PALE OLIVE
Entire fly constructed of pale olive deer body hair; ribbing, black silk.

No. 9   MICHIGAN HOPPER
Tail: Red hackle fibres.
Body: Yellow wool with yellow wool egg sack; palmered with grizzly and brown hackle.
Wings: Brown mottled Turkey.
Hackle: Brown and grizzly, tied on together.

No. 10   MICHIGAN SPIDER
(Don Martinez)
Tail: Dark brown hackle fibres.
Body: Blue and yellow Macaw quill.
Hackle: Badger saddle..

No. 11   MOSQUITO
Tail: Grizzly hackle fibres.
Body: Peacock quill.
Wings: Grizzly hackle tips.
Hackle: Grizzly.

No. 12   OAK
Tail: Brown hair or hackle fibres.
Body: Brown fur; ribbing, gold tinsel.
Wings: Brown mottled, Partridge, Pheasant, etc.
Hackle: Brown, tied palmer.

No. 13   OLIVE DUN
Tail: Olive hackle fibres.
Body: Olive fur.
Wings: Wood Duck or grey duck wing sections.
Hackle: Olive.

No. 14   OLIVE DUN HACKLED
Tail: Olive hackle fibres.
Body: Peacock quill, dyed olive.
Wings: Blue dun hackle fibres, tied upright.
Hackle: Olive.

No. 15   OLIVE QUILL
Tail: Olive hackle fibres.
Body: Peacock quill.
Wings: Grey duck wing sections.
Hackle: Olive.

No. 16   OLIVE QUILL
(Parachute)
Tail: Olive hackle fibres.
Body: Peacock quill.
Wings: Blue dun hackle tips.
Hackle: Olive.

No. 17   OLIVE SPIDER
Tail: Olive hackle fibres.
Body: Olive Peacock quill.
Hackle: Olive.

No. 18   ORANGE SEDGE
Body: Orange floss; ribbing, gold wire.
Wings: Landrail or substitute.
Hackle: Ginger tied palmer.

No. 19 PALE EVENING DUN
Tail: Blue grey hackle fibres.
Body: Greenish yellow.
Wings: Slate quill section.
Hackle: Blue grey.

No. 20
PALE WATERY SPINNER
(Female)
Tail: Pale golden yellow hackle fibres.
Body: Pale golden yellow seal fur; ribbing, gold tinsel.
Wings: Pale blue hackle tips, tied spent.
Hackle: Pale golden yellow.

No. 21
PALE WATERY SPINNER
(Male)
Tail: Pale cream hackle fibres.
Body: Celluloid over yellow tying silk; orange tip at tail and thorax.
Wings: Blue cock hackle tips, tied spent.
Hackle: Pale cream.

No. 22   PARTICULAR
Tail: Four natural red hackle fibres.
Body: Rhode Island cock hackle stem stripped.
Wings: Two medium blue dun hackle tips, tied spent.
Hackle: Medium Rhode Island red hackle.

No. 23   THE PARSON

Tail: Three strands cock Pheasant tail feather.

Body: Pale yellow wool dubbing with three ribs of Peacock herl at tail.

Hackles: Hen Pheasant neck and Wood Duck hackles.

No. 24
PHEASANT TAIL SPINNER

Tail: Three strands of purple Pheasant tail.

Body: Three strands of purple brown cock Pheasant tail wrapped around hook; ribbing, gold wire.

Hackle: Blue dun.

SELECTED DRY FLY PATTERNS

(See Plate XXIX)

No. 1
PHEASANT TAIL SPINNER
(Parachute)

Tail: Three strands of purple Pheasant tail.

Body: Three strands of purple brown cock Pheasant tail wrapped around hook; ribbing, gold wire.

Hackle: Blue dun tied on horizontal.

No. 2   PINK LADY
(Spent Wing)

Tail: Ginger hackle fibres.

Body: Pink floss; ribbing, gold.

Wings: Blue dun hackle tips (standard pattern Starling upright)

Hackle: Ginger.

No. 3   PINK LADY
(As Tied By Donnelly)

Tail: Ginger hackle fibres.

Tag: Primrose yellow floss.

Body: Pink wool or dubbing.

Hackle: First a ginger, then a blue dun next to the head.

No. 4   QUILL GORDON

Tail: Blue dun grey hackle fibres.

Body: Peacock quill; ribbing, gold wire counter clockwise.

Wings: Wood Duck.

Hackle: Blue dun grey.

No. 5   RAINBOW SPECIAL
(Reuben R. Cross)

Tail: Grey mottled Mallard fibres.

Body: Cream colored fur wound on pink crewel wool.

Wings: Grey mottled Mallard.

Hackle: Grey.

No. 6   RED QUILL
(Art Flick)

Tail: Blue dun hackle fibres.

Body: Rhode Island Red hackle stem; stripped, soaked, wrap tightly around the hook and lacquer when dry.

Wings: Wood Duck.

Hackle: Blue dun.

No. 7   RED QUILL
(English)

Tail: Natural red hackle fibres.

Body: Peacock quill.

Wings: Starling.

Hackle: Natural red.

No. 8   RED UPRIGHT

Tail: Reddish brown hackle fibres.

Body: Reddish brown stripped hackle stem.

Wings: Wood Duck

Hackle: Reddish brown.

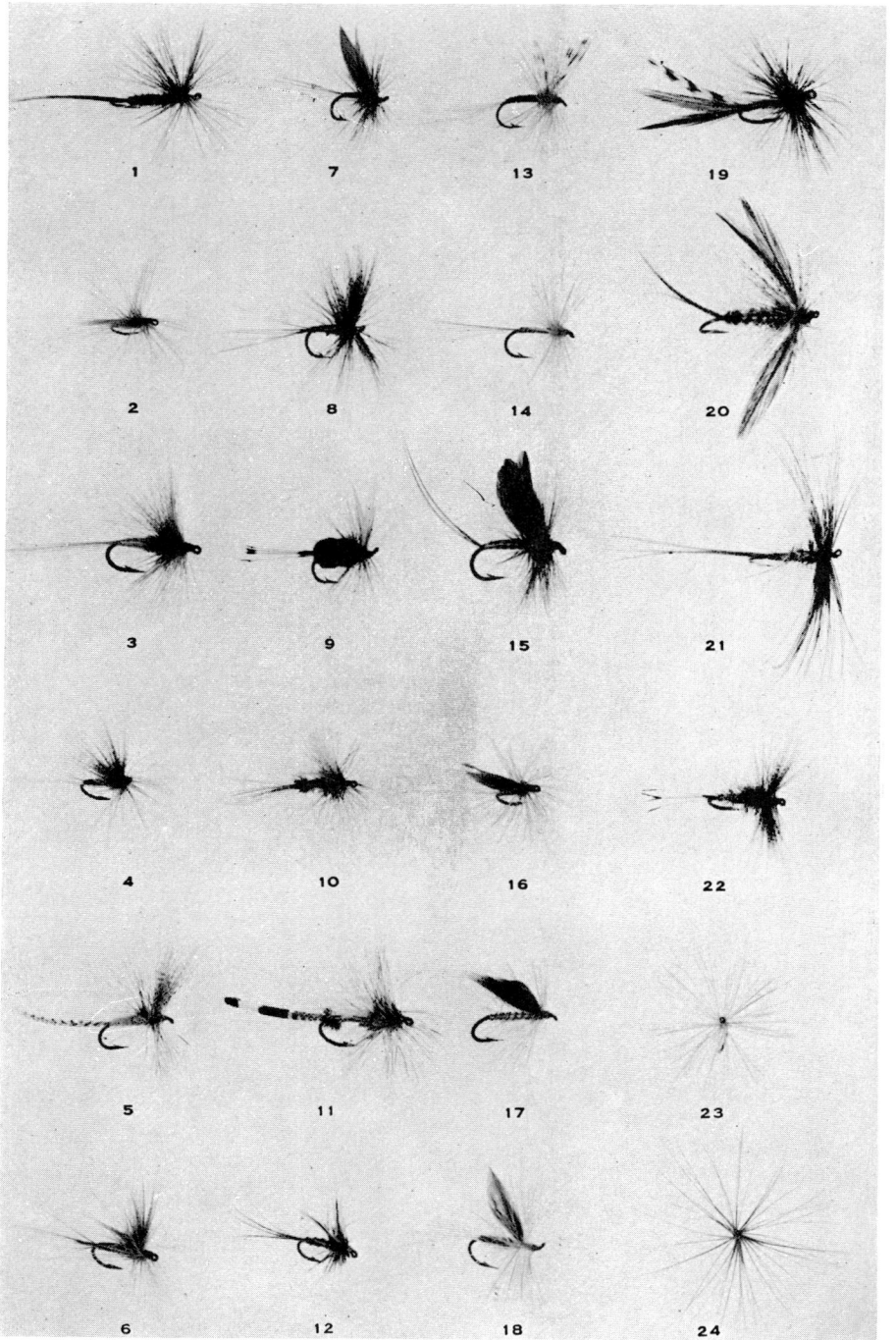

PLATE XXIX. DRY FLIES.

(See page 127 for descriptions)

No. 9   RIO GRAND KING
Tail: Golden Pheasant tippet fibres.
Body: Black chenille.
Wings: White.
Hackle: Brown.

No. 10 ROYAL COACHMAN
Tail: Golden Pheasant tippets, or brown hackle fibres.
Body: Peacock herl, red silk band centre.
Wings: White goose, quill sections.
Hackle: Reddish brown.

No. 11   A. K. ROYAL
Tail: Barred Wood Duck; red silk on top.
Body: Red floss; Peacock herl on each end.
Wings: White calf tail or soft bucktail.
Hackle: Grizzly.

No. 12
        RED SPINNER BADGER
Tail: Magenta hackle fibres.
Body: Red floss; ribbing, silver oval tinsel.
Wings: Badger hackle tips.
Hackle: Badger.

No. 13   RED QUILL
           (Spent Wing)
Tail: Pale blue grey hackle fibres.
Body: Reddish brown stripped hackle stems.
Wings: Grizzly hackle tips, tied spent.
Hackle: Pale blue grey.

No. 14   SAIL FLY
           (L. R. Hardy)
Tail: Blue dun.
Body: Peacock quill.
Wings: One white hackle tied upright, (for visibility).
Hackle: Blue dun.
(Many different color combinations are used.)

No. 15   SAND FLY
Tail: Two Turkey quill strands.
Body: Yellow floss; ribbing, gold tinsel.
Wings: Brown mottled Turkey, doubled.
Hackle: Brown.

No. 16   SALTOUN
Tail: Light brown hackle fibres.
Body: Black floss; ribbing, silver wire.
Wings: Pale Starling.
Hackle: Two pale ginger cock hackles.

No. 17   SILVER SEDGE
Body: White floss; ribbing, silver wire.
Wings: Landrail or substitute.
Hackle: Pale ginger tied palmer.

No. 18   SKY BLUE
Tail: Yellow hackle fibres.
Body: Blue rabbit's fur.
Hackle: Yellow.
Wings: Starling.

No. 19
       SNAKE RIVER VARIANT
Tail: Three hackle tips, grizzly, brown centre, black.
Body: Tip of black floss, remainder orange floss.
Hackles: Brown, black and grizzly, tied medium long.

No. 20   SPENT GNAT
           (F. M. Halford) 1886
Tail: Brown Mallard, four strands.
Body: White floss; ribbing, unstripped Peacock herl, cinnamon color at root and dark at point, start with dark portion at tail.
Ribbing hackle: Badger cock.
Shoulder hackle: Grey Partridge.
Wings: Four blue Andalusian hackle tips, tied spent, and having ginger points.
Head: Bronze Peacock herl.

No. 21
       SPENT WING MAY FLY
Tail: Three Pheasant tail fibres.
Body: Raffia; ribbing, gold wire, palmered with badger hackle.
Wings: Natural black hackle, tied spent.
Hackle: Natural black.

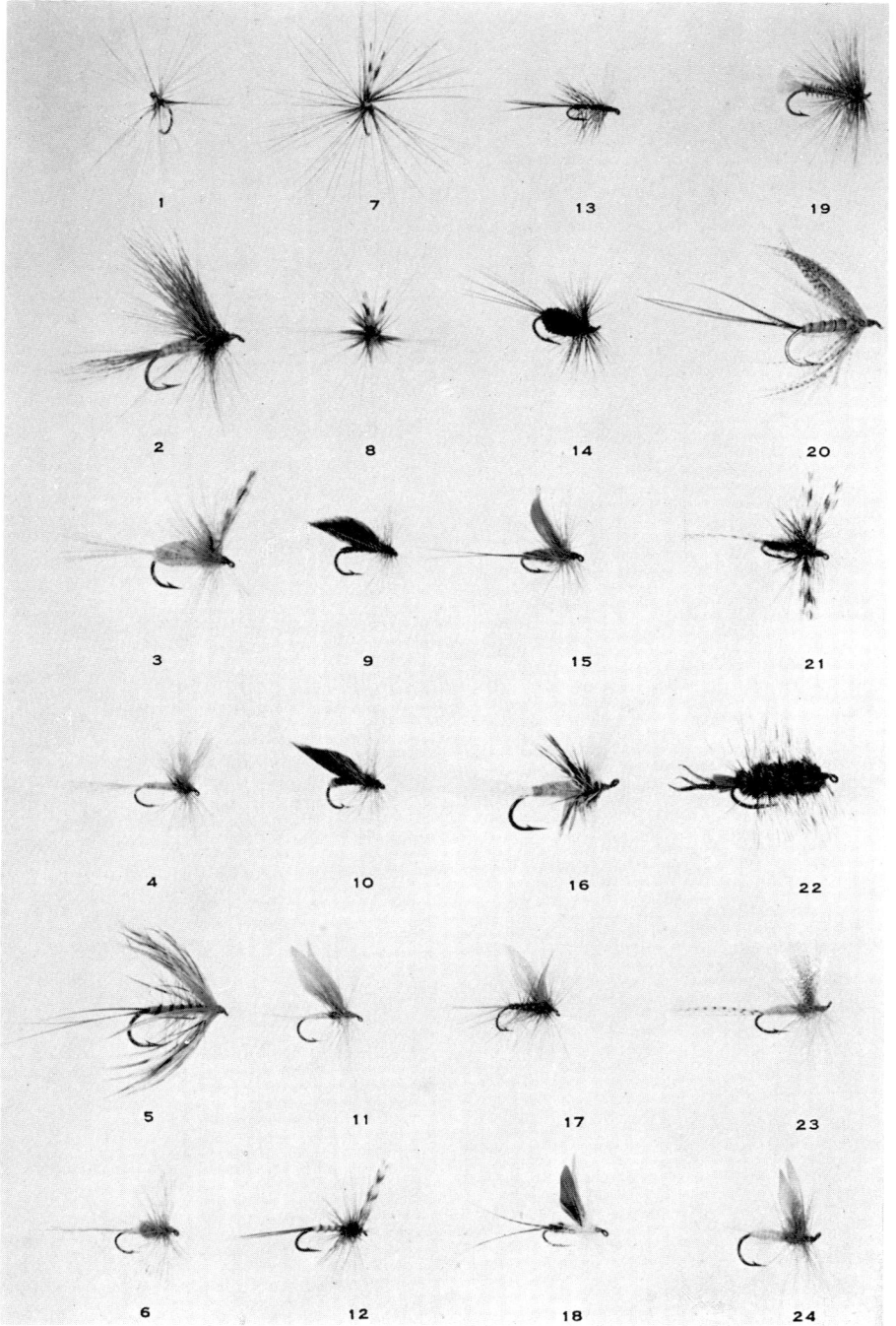

PLATE XXX.   DRY FLIES.

(See opposite page for descriptions)

No. 22
SPENTWING WOOD DUCK

Tail: Golden Pheasant tippets.

Body: Grizzly hackle wound around hook and clipped.

Wings: Wood Duck tied spent.
Hackle: Brown.

No. 23   SPIDER
(Blue Grey)
Body: Peacock quill.
Hackle: Blue grey.

No. 24   SPIDER
(Brown)
Body: Gold tinsel.
Hackle: Brown.

SELECTED DRY FLY PATTERNS
(See Plate XXX)

No. 1   SPIDER
(Furnace)
Body: Gold tinsel.
Hackle: Furnace.

No. 2   STONE FLY
Tail: Tan deer tail hair.
Body: Yellow wool; ribbing, tan silk.
Wings: Tan deer body hair, tied upright and divided.
Hackle: Brown.

No. 3   STRAW MAY
(E. B. & H. A. Darbee)
Tail: Ginger hackle fibres.
Body: Natural grey brownish reindeer or deer body hair.
Wings: Four red grizzly hackle tips.
Hackle: Straw colored or light ginger.

No. 4   TETON SPECIAL
(Don Martinez)
Tail: Ginger hackle fibres.
Body: Pale cream fur from Fox belly, or cream kapok.
Wings: Ginger hackle points.
Hackle: One ginger, and one Plymouth Rock dyed blue grey, tied on together.

No. 5   THE FRENCHMAN
Tail: Three strands cock Pheasant tail feather.
Body: Yellow raffia; ribbing; gold wire; body palmered with brassy dun cock.
Shoulder Hackle: French Partridge feather.

No. 6 TUPS INDISPENSABLE
Tail: Three fibres of honey dun hackle.
Body: Claret and yellow seal fur, mixed with Hare's poll.
Tag: Primrose floss or tying silk.
Hackle: Dark ginger and light blue dun.

No. 7   BROWN VARIANT
Body: Peacock quill.
Wings: Grizzly hackle points.
Hackle: Brown.

No. 8   NELSON'S VARIANT
(W. F. Blades)
Body: Peacock quill.
Wings: Jungle Cock.
Hackle: Ginger.

No. 9
WELSHMAN'S BUTTON
(Male)
Body: Peacock quill dyed brown; ribbing, maroon horse hair.
Wings: Dark brown hen quill feather.
Hackle: Furnace cock.

No. 10
WELSHMAN'S BUTTON
(Female)
Body: Three turns of cinnamon Turkey tail strands; remainder, Peacock quill dyed brown; ribbing, maroon horse hair.
Wings: Dark brown hen.
Hackle: Furnace.

No. 11 WHITCHURCH DUN
Tail: Pale ginger hackle fibres.
Body: Primrose floss.
Wings: Pale Starling.
Hackle: Pale ginger.

No. 12   WHITCRAFT
(Don Martinez)
Tail: Brown hackle fibres.
Body: Blue and yellow Macaw quill.
Wings: Plymouth rock hackle points.
Hackle: One brown, one Plymouth Rock, tied on together.

No. 13
WHITE WINGED BLACK MIDGE
(E. B. & H. A. Darbee)
Tail: Black hackle fibres.
Body: Black tying silk.
Wings: White hackle tips.
Hackle: Black palmered,. tied sparsely.

No. 14
WHITE WINGED BLACK GNAT
(Harry Darbee)
Tail: Stiff black hackle fibres.
Body: Clipped deer hair dyed black.
Wings: White hackle tips tied upright.
Hackle: Natural black cock.

No. 15   WHIRLING BLUE
Tail: Guinea fowl dyed brown red, or natural brown hackle fibres.
Body: Water rat fur dubbing.
Wings: Medium Starling; or grey Mallard.
Hackle: Two ginger cock hackles.

No. 16   WHITE WULFF
(Lee Wulff)
Tail: White deer tail.
Body: Cream wool or fur.
Wings: White deer tail.
Hackle: Light badger.

No. 17   WICKHAM'S FANCY
Tail: Natural red hackle fibres; ribbing, gold tinsel.
Body: Gold tinsel.
Wings: Starling or Duck.
Hackle: Natural red, tied palmer.

No. 18   WINSLOW MIDGE
Tail: Three brown Mallard strands.
Body: Rear half, dark grey dubbing; front, light grey; ribbing, light grey silk.
Wings: Brownish grey from Mallard wing.
Hackle: White or cream.

No. 19   WILLOW FLY
Tag: Primrose floss.
Body: Condor or Peacock quill dyed orange.
Shoulder hackle: Orange ginger cock hackle.
Head hackle: Dark honey dun hen hackle.

No. 20   THE WOOD DUCK
Tail: Three strands Cock Pheasant tail feather.
Body: Undyed raffia; ribbing, gold wire, palmered with ginger hackle.
Shoulder hackle: Wood Duck.

No. 21   WOODRUFF
(Chester Mills)
Tail: Barred grey Mallard.
Body: Bright green seal fur.
Wings: Grizzly, tied spent.
Hackle: Brown.

No. 22   WOOLLY WORM
(Black)
Tail: Red floss and Peacock sword.
Body: Black chenille; ribbing, gold tinsel.
Hackle: Plymouth rock, tied palmer; tied in by the butt to make it point forward.

No. 23   YELLOW DUN
Tail: Ginger hackle fibres.
Body: Light yellow wool.
Wings: Starling.
Hackle: Ginger.

No. 24   YELLOW MALLARD
Tail: Grey mottled Mallard.
Body: Yellow wool or fur.
Wings: Grey Mallard.
Hackle: Ginger.

Chapter XI

NATURAL MAY FLIES
AND IMITATIONS

HILE I am not an authority on the subject of entomology, I have collected on the streams and lakes many flies and nymphs that form a great part of the food for all game fish. I also thank my many friends for the specimens they have sent to me from different parts of the country.

The female fly deposits the eggs in the water and they sink to the bottom where they hatch into a grub or larvae. They live under stones and in mud until they are ready to transform from a nymph to the first winged stage, which is called a subimago, (most anglers call it a dun).

I have watched the nymphal skin split open on the surface of the water; the fly then works its way out and dries off its wings; many of them are taken by birds and fish at this time, but the lucky ones fly off into the trees, where they make another great change from the subimago to the imago; most anglers call this the spinner.

By all means take off a little time to watch this change from the subimago to the imago. The fly works its way out of the present skin (which may be a dull grey in color) and change into a pale yellow body with brown markings. The front legs are much longer and the tails more than double in length.

I have found a very easy way to collect May Flies; park your car near the stream or lake in the evening and put on the bright lights; at times you will get more flies than you want. The flies can be preserved in 70 percent rubbing alcohol, with 5 percent of glycerine added; this keeps the bodies soft and preserves the color. I also keep some flies out of the alcohol; and by all means, make a note of the colors when you first get them; the colors will change quickly. I have, several times, stored some duns in the evening (alive) and found them changed into spinners the next morning.

Put a couple of the flies you collect in alcohol, and if the live ones have turned into spinners you definitely know you have the subimago and imago of that hatch.

I have given the scientific names of the flies and also the name of the artificial that is made to imitate the natural; this will assist the angler to ascertain what flies are hatching on the stream.

When making these May Flies, if you find the detached bodies are hard to make at first, use a 2X hook and make the bodies on the hook.

The female spinners are larger than the male spinners and when they are full of eggs one can easily see why the trout prefer them to the males. After the eggs have been disposed of, the wings lay flat on the water and the fly floats down the stream; this is called a spent-wing fly; the body is just an empty shell and of very little value for food.

The above few lines have been written to assist the fisherman; for further information read the books on this subject written by James G. Needham, Ph. D. and Paul R. Needham, Ph. D.; also Ann Haven Morgan and J. H. Comstock.

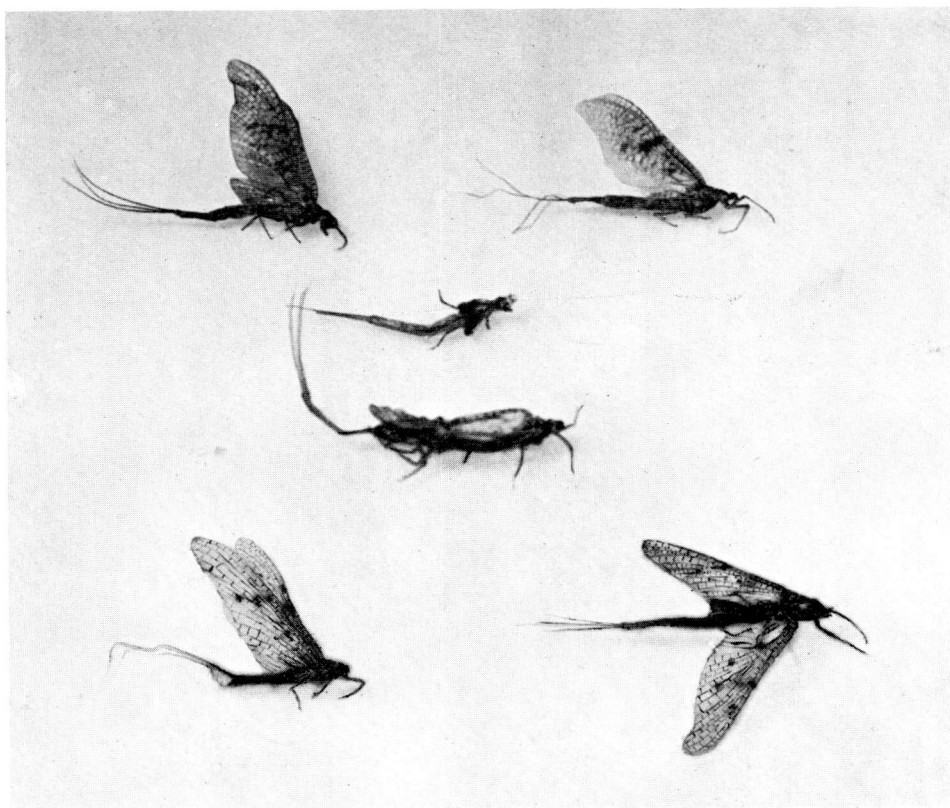

Alan Wallace

PLATE XXXI. METAMORPHOSIS OF THE SUBIMAGO.

EPHEMERIDAE, EPHEMERA SIMULANS WALKER
Lake Michigan, August, 1949.

This is a photograph of the actual May Flies making their change from a subimago to an imago.

Left to right, top to bottom:

No. 1: The subimago, called the dun.

No. 2: The imago, called the spinner.

No. 3: The skin or shuck that the spinner has emerged from.

No. 4: The actual change in progress.

No. 5: A female spinner, showing the egg sack.

No. 6: The female dun in the position tail downwards, ready to make the change from a subimago to an imago.

[135]

BLADES' EPHEMERA SIMULANS

(See Plate XXXII, No. 1)

CLASSIFICATION:

ORDER: *Ephemeroptera*
FAMILY: *Ephemeridae*

GENUS: *Ephemera*
SPECIES: *simulans* (Walker)
Subimago female

DESCRIPTION OF THE INSECT
Tails: Three, grey.
Body: Reddish brown with dark brown markings.
Wings: Grey, mottled with dark brown spots.
Legs: Front legs, dark brown; rear legs dark grey.

MATERIAL FOR THE ARTIFICIAL
Tails: Three Wood Duck fibres dyed grey. Length, 11/16".
Body: Reddish brown raffia; markings, brown enamel. Length, ¾".
Wings: Grey hackle tips, or veined wing material, with brown enamel spots. Length, ¾".
Legs: Trimmed hackle stems; front legs dark brown; rear, grey.
Hackle: Brown-and-grey variant.
Collected in Wilmette, Illinois. (Lake Michigan)

BLADES' EPHEMERA SIMULANS

(See Plate XXXII, No. 2)

CLASSIFICATION:

Order: *Ephemeroptera*
Family: *Ephemeridae*

Genus: *Ephemera*
Species: *simulans* (Walker)
Subimago male

DESCRIPTION OF THE INSECT
Tails: Three, dark grey.
Body: Dark brown.
Wings: Transparent, smoky grey in color, mottled with dark brown.
Legs: Front legs, dark brown; hind legs, dark grey.

MATERIAL FOR THE ARTIFICIAL
Tails: Three dark grey hackle fibres. Length, ⅝".
Body: Dark grey-brown raffia; markings, dark brown enamel. Length, 11/16".
Wings: Veined wing material, spotted with brown enamel, or dark grey hackle tips. Length, ¾".
Legs: Trimmed hackle stems; front legs, dark brown; rear legs, brown.
Hackle: Brown and grey variant.
Collected in Wilmette, Illinois. (Lake Michigan)

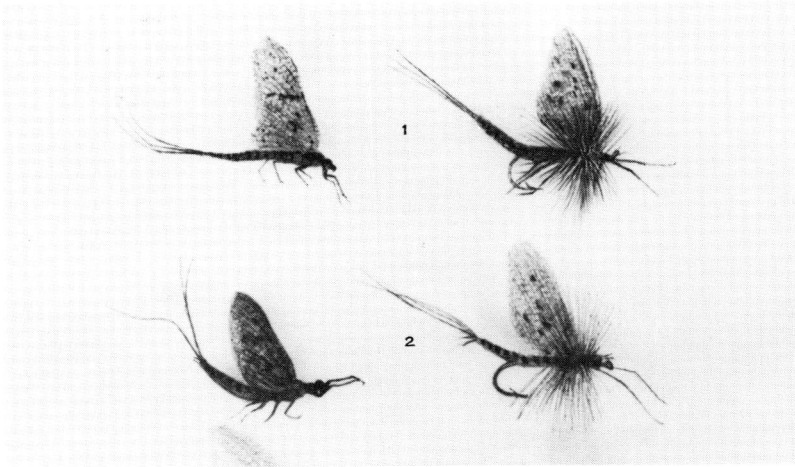

Natural   Artificial

Photograph of painting by William F. Blades

PLATE XXXII.   MALE AND FEMALE SIMULANS.

BLADES' HEXAGENIA MUNDA

(See Plate XXXIII, No. 1)

CLASSIFICATION:

Order: *Ephemeroptera*

Family: *Ephemeridae*

Genus: *Hexagenia*

Species: *munda* (Eaton)

Imago male

DESCRIPTION OF THE INSECT

Tails: Two, tan with brown markings.

Body: Color, tan with reddish brown markings on back and thorax.

Wings: Transparent, with brownish grey cast. Brown veins on outer edge.

Legs: Front legs, reddish brown; rear and middle legs, dirty tan.

MATERIAL FOR THE ARTIFICIAL

Tails: Two, tan Wood Duck fibres. Length, 1½".

Body: Tan raffia; markings, brown enamel. Length, ¾".

Wings: Tan-and-brown variant hackle tips. Length, ⅝".

Legs: Trimmed hackle stems; front pair, reddish brown; rear and middle legs, dirty tan.

Hackle: Tan and brown variant.

Collected in Florida.

| | | | |
| Natural | Artificial | Natural | Artifi|

Photograph of painting by William F. Blades

PLATE XXXIII.   MAY FLIES AND IMITATIONS.

BLADES' HEXAGENIA MUNDA

(See Plate XXXIII, No. 2)

CLASSIFICATION:

Order: *Ephemeroptera*
Family: *Ephemeridae*

Genus: *Hexagenia*
Species: *munda* (Eaton)
Subimago female

DESCRIPTION OF THE INSECT

Tails: Two, brown with dark brown segment markings.

Body: Tan with reddish brown markings on back and thorax.

Wings: Transparent, with a pale cast, veins not prominent.

Legs: Front pair, reddish brown; rear and middle legs, pale tan.

MATERIAL FOR THE ARTIFICIAL

Tails: Two dark Wood Duck fibres, or brown Mallard. Length, 13/16".

Body: Tan raffia; markings, reddish-brown enamel. Length, 1".

Wings: Pale blue-dun hackle tips. Length, 13/16".

Legs: Trimmed hackle stems; front pair, reddish brown; rear and middle, pale tan.

Hackles: Tan-and-fiery-brown variant, or two hackles tan and brown.

Collected in Florida.

BLADES' HEXAGENIA MUNDA

(See Plate XXXIII No. 3)

CLASSIFICATION:

Order: *Ephemeroptera*
Family: *Ephemeridae*

Genus: *Hexagenia*
Species: *munda* (Eaton)
Subimago male

DESCRIPTION OF THE INSECT

Tails: Two, brown with dark segment markings.

Body: Tan, with reddish brown markings on back and thorax.

Wings: Transparent, with a grey cast.

Legs: Front pair, reddish brown; rear and middle legs, dirty tan.

MATERIAL FOR THE ARTIFICIAL

Tails: Two brown Mallard or dark Wood Duck. Length, 1".

Body: Tan raffia; markings, reddish brown. Length, 15/16".

Wings: Pale blue dun hackle tips, or veined wing material. Length, 11/16".

Legs: Trimmed hackle stems, front pair, reddish brown; rear and middle legs, dirty tan.

Hackle: One tan-and-brown variant, or one tan and one brown.

Collected in Florida.

[139]

BLADES' PENTAGENIA VITTIGERA

(See Plate XXXIII, No. 4)

CLASSIFICATION:

Order: *Ephemeroptera*
Family: *Ephemeridae*

Genus: *Pentagenia*
Species: *vittigera* (Walsh)
Subimago female

DESCRIPTION OF THE INSECT

Tails: Two, grey banded.
Body: Underside, tan; the back has brown markings.
Wings: Transparent, with a grey cast, veins black and prominent.
Legs: Front legs, brown with dark markings; rear legs, tan.

MATERIAL FOR THE ARTIFICIAL

Tails: Two Wood Duck fibres, dyed grey. Length, ⅞".
Body: Cream raffia; markings, brown and grey enamel. Length, ⅞" to 1".
Wings: Veined wing material, or Wood Duck dyed grey; also grey hackle tips. Length, ⅞".
Legs: Trimmed hackle stems; front legs, tan-and-brown variant; rear legs, tan.
Hackle: One variant, grey-and-tan.
Collected in Michigan.

BLADES' HEPTAGENIA HEBE

(See Plate XXXIII, No. 5)

CLASSIFICATION:

Order: *Ephemeroptera*
Family: *Heptageniidae*

Genus: *Heptagenia*
Species: *hebe* (McD)
Imago male

DESCRIPTION OF THE INSECT

Tails: Two, grey.
Body: Yellowish tan, brown markings on back.
Wings: Transparent brownish tint; veins, light brown.
Legs: Grey.

MATERIAL FOR THE ARTIFICIAL

Tails: Two grey hackle fibres. Length, ½".
Body: Yellowish tan raffia; brown enamel markings on back. Length, ¼".
Wings: Blue dun hackle tips. Length, 5/16".
Legs: Greyish brown trimmed hackle stems.
Hackle: Blue dun.
Collected in New York.

[140]

BLADES' HEPTAGENIA HEBE

(See Plate XXXIII, No. 6)

CLASSIFICATION:

Order: *Ephemeroptera*
Family: *Heptageniidae*

Genus: *Heptagenia*
Species: *hebe* (McD)
Imago female

DESCRIPTION OF THE INSECT

Tails: Two, grey.
Wings: Transparent; veins, light brown.
Body: Yellowish tan.
Legs: Grey.

MATERIAL FOR THE ARTIFICIAL

Tails: Two grey hackle fibres. Length, ½".
Body: Yellowish tan. Length, 5/16".
Wings: Pale blue dun hackle tips with brown cast. Length, 5/16".
Legs: Grey trimmed hackle stems.
Hackle: Light blue dun.
Collected in New York.

BLADES' EPHEMERELLA SP

(See Plate XXXIII, No. 7)

CLASSIFICATION:

Order: *Ephemeroptera*
Family: *Ephemerellidae*

Genus: *Ephemerella*
Species: *sp*
Subimago female

DESCRIPTION OF THE INSECT

Tails: Three, light blue dun.
Body: Underside, yellowish olive green; some are olive, back markings, dark olive green.
Wings: Transparent; color, smoky blue dun.
Legs: Front legs, olive; rear legs, dirty pale yellow.

MATERIAL FOR THE ARTIFICIAL

Tails: Three blue dun hackle fibres. Length, ⅜".
Body: Raffia, dyed yellowish olive green. Markings, dark olive green enamel. Length, ⅜".
Wings: Smoky blue dun hackle tips. Length, ½".
Legs: Trimmed hackle stems. Front pair, olive green; rear legs, dirty pale yellow.
Hackle: Olive green.
Collected in New York.

[141]

BLADES' EPHEMERELLA SP

(See Plate XXXIII, No. 8)

CLASSIFICATION:

Order: *Ephemeroptera*
Family: *Ephemerellidae*

Genus: *Ephemerella*
Species: *sp* (McD)
Subimago male

DESCRIPTION OF THE INSECT
Tails: Three, color, grey.
Body: Blue dun, brownish shade.
Wings: Brownish tint; veins, light brown.
Legs: Greyish brown.

MATERIAL FOR THE ARTIFICIAL
Tails: Three light grey hackle fibres. Length, ¼".
Body: Brownish, blue dun, trimmed hackle stems. Length, ¼".
Wings: Brownish, blue dun hackle tips. Length, ¼".
Legs: Grey brown andalusian, trimmed hackle stems.
Hackle: Grey brown andalusian.
Collected in New York.

BLADES' HEXAGENIA LIMBATA MALE IMAGO

(See Plate XXXIV, No. 1)

CLASSIFICATION:

Order: *Ephemeroptera*
Family: *Ephemera*

Genus: *Hexagenia*
Species: *limbata* (Serville)

DESCRIPTION OF THE INSECT
Tails: Two, color, tan with brown markings at segments.
Body: Rich fiery brown; markings, dark brown.
Wings: Transparent; veins, brown; front outer edge, brown.
Legs: Front legs, dark brown; rear legs, tan.

MATERIAL FOR THE ARTIFICIAL
Tails: Two dark Wood Duck fibres dyed tan; length, 1⅛".
Body: Fiery brown raffia; markings, dark brown enamel; length, ⅞".
Wings: Transparent, hackle tips or veined wing material. Brown enamel markings on outer edge; length, ⅞".
Legs: Trimmed hackle stems; front legs, dark brown; rear legs, tan; length, ⅝".
Hackle: Tan-and-brown variant.
Collected in Michigan.

[142]

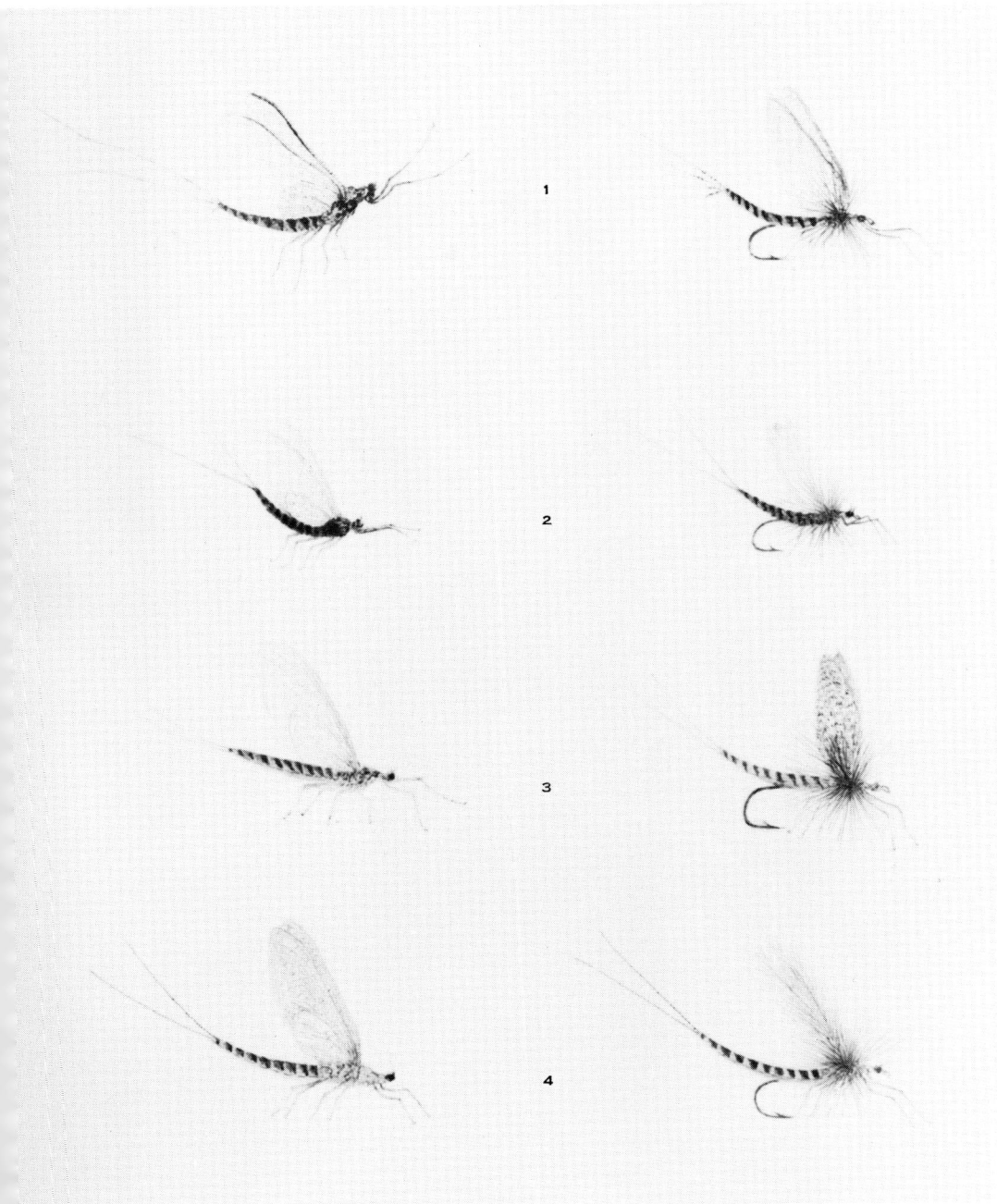

PLATE XXXIV. MAY FLIES AND IMITATIONS.

Photo by William F. Blades

BLADES' ISONYCHIA ALBOMANICATA

(See Plate XXXIV, No. 2)

CLASSIFICATION:

Order: *Ephemeroptera*
Family: *Baetidae*

Genus: *Isonychia*
Species: *albomanicata* (Needham)
Subimago female

DESCRIPTION OF THE INSECT

Tails: Two, color, pale tan.
Body: Reddish brown; segment markings, light tan.
Wings: Smoky grey; veins, prominent; color, dark grey.
Legs: Rear legs, cream; front legs, dark brown, except the tips, which are tan with brown markings.

MATERIAL FOR THE ARTIFICIAL

Tails: Two pale Wood Duck fibres. Length, ⅝".
Body: Raffia, dyed a pale reddish brown; markings, dark brown enamel. Length, ⅝".
Wings: Blue-dun hackle tips. Length, 11/16".
Legs: Trimmed hackle stems; rear legs, cream; front legs, fiery-brown variant, with light tips, or the fiery brown white tipped Narobi hackle.
Hackle: Tan, grey and brown variant.
Collected in New York.

BLADES' HEXAGENIA RIGIDA

(See Plate XXXIV, No. 3)

CLASSIFICATION:

Order: *Ephemeroptera*
Family: *Ephemeridae*

Genus: *Hexagenia*
Species: *rigida* (McDunnough)
Subimago female

DESCRIPTION OF THE INSECT

Tails: Two, color, tan.
Body: Cream; back, pale orange; markings, brown.
Wings: Transparent, veins, brown.
Legs: Cream.

MATERIAL FOR THE ARTIFICIAL

Tails: Two fine tan hackle stems. Length, ⅞".
Body: Natural raffia; pale orange enamel tint; markings, brown enamel. Length, ⅞".
Wings: Wood Duck or transparent hackle tips. Length, 1".
Legs: Cream trimmed hackle stems.
Hackle: Cream.
Collected in New York.

BLADES' PENTAGENIA VITTIGERA

(See Plate XXXIV, No. 4)

CLASSIFICATION:

Order: *Ephemeroptera*
Family: *Ephemeridae*

Genus: *Pentagenia*
Species: *vittigera* (Walsh)
Subimago male

DESCRIPTION OF THE INSECT
Tails: Two, color, grey, banded.
Body: Underside, tan; the back has brown markings.
Wings: Transparent, with a grey cast, veins black and prominent.
Legs: Front legs, brown with dark markings; rear legs, tan.

MATERIAL FOR THE ARTIFICIAL
Tails: Two Wood Duck fibres dyed grey. Length, 13/16".
Body: Tan raffia; markings, brown enamel. Length, 13/16".
Wings: Grey hackle tips. Length, ¾".
Legs: Trimmed hackle stems; front legs, tan-and-brown variant, rear legs, tan.
Hackle: One variant grey-and-tan.
Collected in Michigan.

BLADES' ISONYCHIA ALBOMANICATA

(See Plate XXXIV)

CLASSIFICATION:

Order: *Ephemeroptera*
Family: *Baetidae*

Genus: *Isonychia*
Species: *Albomanicata*
Imago female

DESCRIPTION OF THE INSECT
Tails: Two, color, pale cream.
Body: Reddish brown; markings, dark-brown enamel.
Wings: Transparent.
Legs: Front legs, brown with light tips; rear legs, creamy white.

MATERIAL FOR THE ARTIFICIAL
Tails: Two pale cream hackle fibres. Length, 1".
Body: Raffia, dyed reddish brown; markings, dark brown enamel. Length, ⅝".
Wings: Pale grey hackle tips. Length, ⅝".
Legs: Trimmed hackle stems; front legs, brown with light tips; rear legs, creamy white.
Hackle: Cream and brown variant.
This fly is known to fishermen as the White Gloved Howdy. The natural fly was taken on the Beaverkill River in early June 1951.

[145]

Natural   Artificial

Photograph of painting by William F. Blades

PLATE XXXV. MAY FLY AND IMITATION.

BLADES' HEXAGENIA LIMBATA

(See Plate XXXVI, No. 1)

<small>CLASSIFICATION:</small>

Order: *Ephemeroptera*   Genus: *Hexagenia*
Family: *Ephemeridae*   Species: *limbata* (Serville)
                             Imago female

<small>DESCRIPTION OF THE INSECT</small>
Tails: Two, color, cream with yellow cast faintly marked.
Body: Underside cream. The back has brown markings.
Wings: Transparent, with a greenish yellow cast on the outer edge.
Legs: Front legs, brown with dark brown markings; rear legs tan.

<small>MATERIAL FOR THE ARTIFICIAL</small>
Tails: Two pale Wood Duck fibres dyed greenish yellow. Length, 1⅜″.
Body: Cream raffia; markings, brown enamel. Length, ⅞″.
Wings: Transparent veined wing material. Length, ⅞″.
Legs: Trimmed hackle stems; front legs tan-and-brown variant; rear legs tan.
Hackle: One tan-and-brown variant and one tan.
Collected in Michigan.

[146]

PLATE XXXVI. IMITATION MAY FLY WITH SPECIAL WING MATERIAL.

BLADES' HEXAGENIA LIMBATA

(See Plate XXXVI, No. 2)

CLASSIFICATION:

Order: *Ephemeroptera*
Family: *Ephemeridae*

Genus: *Hexagenia*
Species: *limbata* (Serville)
Subimago male

DESCRIPTION OF THE INSECT

Tails: Two, color, tan banded darker shade.
Body: Fiery brown; markings, dark brown.
Wings: Transparent smoky grey cast.
Legs: Front legs, dark brown; rear legs, tan.

MATERIAL FOR THE ARTIFICIAL

Tails: Two Wood Duck fibres dyed grey. Length, ¾".
Body: Fiery brown raffia; markings, dark brown enamel. Length, ¾".
Wings: Grey hackle tips or veined wing material. Length, ⅞".
Legs: Trimmed hackle stems; front legs, dark brown-grey variant; rear legs tan.
Hackle: Ginger, brown-and-grey variant.
Collected in New York.

BLADES' HEXAGENIA RIGIDA

(See Plate XXXVI, No. 3)

CLASSIFICATION:

Order: *Ephemeroptera*
Family: *Ephemeridae*

Genus: *Hexagenia*
Species: *rigida* (McDunnough)
Imago male

DESCRIPTION OF THE INSECT

Tails: Two, tan with dark brown markings.
Body: Tan with purple fiery brown markings.
Wings: Transparent; veins, brown; front outer edge, tan brown.
Legs: Front legs, fiery brown; rear legs, tan.

MATERIAL FOR THE ARTIFICIAL

Tails: Two large Mallard breast-feather fibres dyed tan or Wood Duck. Length, 2¼".
Body: Tan raffia; markings, purple fiery brown enamel. Length, ⅞".
Wings: Veined wing material, front edge marked with tan-brown enamel. Wood Duck fibres and hackle tips can also be used. Length, ¾".
Legs: Trimmed hackle stems; front legs, fiery brown ⅝" long; rear legs, tan.
Hackle: Tan and brown variant.
Collected in New York.

BLADES' SIPHLONURUS QUEBECENSIS

(See Plate XXXVII, No. 1)

CLASSIFICATION:

Order: *Ephemeroptera*
Family: *Baetidae*

Genus: *Siphlonurus*
Species: *quebecensis*
Subimago female

DESCRIPTION OF THE INSECT

Tails: Two, dark grey brownish cast.
Body: General color reddish brown, with dark brown markings at each segment.
Wings: Smoky grey, with prominent blackish brown veins.
Legs: Two front legs, blackish brown; rear legs, tan.

MATERIAL FOR THE ARTIFICIAL

Tails: Two dark blue dun hackle fibres. Length, $9/16''$.
Body: Raffia, dyed fiery brown; markings, brown enamel. Length, $5/8''$.
Wings: Veined wing material, or iron blue dun hackle tips. Length, $5/8''$.
Legs: Trimmed hackle stems; front legs, brown and grey variant; middle and rear legs, tan.
Hackle: Variant, tan, brown and grey.
Collected in New York.

BLADES' EPHEMERELLA INVARIA

(See Plate XXXVII, No. 2)

CLASSIFICATION:

Order: *Ephemeroptera*
Family: *Ephemerellidae*

Genus: *Ephemerella*
Species: *invaria*
Subimago male

DESCRIPTION OF THE INSECT

Tails: Three, grey ringed.
Body: Yellowish tan; markings, reddish brown.
Wings: Medium grey.
Legs: Light grey.

MATERIAL FOR THE ARTIFICIAL

Tails: Three grey Mallard or Wood Duck fibres. Length, $1/4''$.
Body: Yellowish tan raffia; markings on back, reddish brown. Length, $3/8''$.
Wings: Medium grey hackle tips. Length, $3/8''$.
Legs: Grey trimmed hackle stems.
Hackle: Medium blue dun.
Collected in New York.

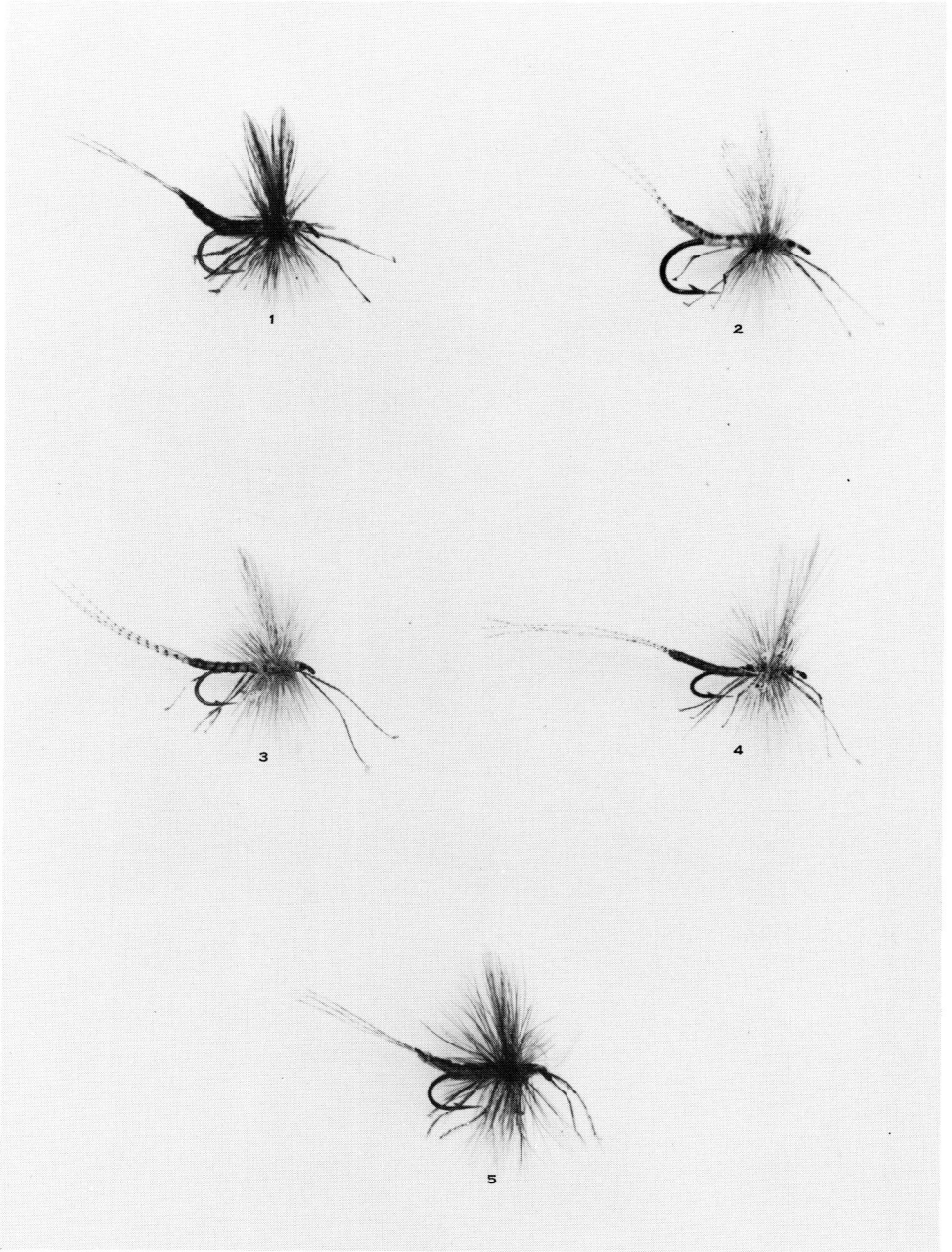

PLATE XXXVII. IMITATION MAY FLIES WITH HACKLE TIP WINGS.

BLADES' EPHEMERELLA SUBVARIA

(See Plate XXXVII, No. 3)

CLASSIFICATION:

Order: *Ephemeroptera*
Family: *Baetidae*

Genus: *Ephemerella*
Species: *subvaria*
Imago female

DESCRIPTION OF THE INSECT
Tails: Three, grey, segments, brown.
Body: Tan; with faint brown markings.
Wings: Clear; with a pale tan cast.
Legs: Grey.

MATERIAL FOR THE ARTIFICIAL
Tails: Three grey Wood Duck fibres.
  Length, ½″.
Body: Natural red hackle stem, or raffia
  dyed natural red. Length, ⅜″.
Wings: Hackle tips, clear with tan cast.
  Length, ½″.
Legs: Grey trimmed hackle stems.
Hackle: Grey and tan variant.
Collected in New York.

BLADES' EPHEMERELLA SUBVARIA

(See Plate XXXVII, No. 4)

CLASSIFICATION:

Order: *Ephemeroptera*
Family: *Baetidae*

Genus: *Ephemerella*
Species: *subvaria*
Imago male

DESCRIPTION OF THE INSECT
Tails: Three, tannish grey, segments,
  brown.
Body: Fiery brown; segments, brown.
Wings: Transparent, with grey cast.
Legs: Rear legs, grey; front legs, tan and
  light brown.

MATERIAL FOR THE ARTIFICIAL
Tails: Three pale Wood Duck fibres.
  Length, ⅜″.
Body: Pale fiery brown raffia; markings,
  brown enamel. Length, $5/16$″.
Wings: Pale-grey hackle tips. Length, ⅜″.
Legs: Trimmed hackle stems. Front
  two, tan and light brown variant;
  rear legs grey. Length, ½″.
Hackle: Tan and grey variant.
Collected in New York.

[151]

BLADES' EPHEMERELLA

(See Plate XXXVII, No. 5)

CLASSIFICATION:

Order: *Ephemeroptera*
Family: *Baetidae*

Genus: *Ephemerella*
Species: *sp*
Subimago female

DESCRIPTION OF THE INSECT
Tails: Three, tannish grey.
Body: Light grey; back markings, dark grey.
Wings: Light brownish grey.
Legs: Brownish grey.

MATERIAL FOR THE ARTIFICIAL
Tails: Three grey hackle fibres. Length, ⅜".
Body: Grey trimmed hackle stems. Length, ⅜".
Wings: Brownish grey hackle tips. Length, ⅜".
Legs: Grey, trimmed hackle stems.
Hackle: Tan and grey variant.
Collected in New York.

BLADES' ANTOCHA SP

(See Plate XXXVIII)

CLASSIFICATION:

Order: *Diptera*
Family: *Tipulidae*

Genus: *Antocha*
Species: *sp* (Det by Alan Stone)

DESCRIPTION OF THE INSECT
Body: Light tan with an amber tint.
Wings: Transparent.
Legs: Greyish ginger.

MATERIAL FOR THE ARTIFICIAL
Body: Light amber raffia, markings; brown horse hair. Length, ¼".
Wings: Transparent hackle tips. Length, ¼".
Legs: Greyish ginger hackle fibres. Length, ¹¹⁄₁₆".
Collected in New York.

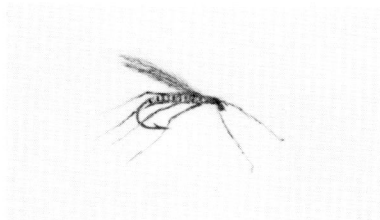

PLATE XXXVIII. DIPTERA, ENLARGED.

PLATE XXXIX. ARTIFICIAL MAY FLY WITH DETACHED BODY.

BLADES' ISONYCHIA RUFA

(See Plate XXXIX)

CLASSIFICATION:

Order: *Ephemeroptera*
Family: *Baetidae*

Genus: *Isonychia*
Species: *rufa*
Imago male

DESCRIPTION OF THE INSECT
Tails: Two, color, pale grey.
Body: Reddish brown; markings, dark brown.
Wings: Transparent, pale brown veins.
Legs: Front legs, brown with light tips; rear legs, creamy white.

MATERIAL, FOR THE ARTIFICIAL
Tails: Two pale-grey hackle fibres. Length, 1″.
Body: Reddish-brown raffia; markings, dark-brown enamel. Length, ½″.
Wings: Pale-grey hackle tips with brownish cast. Length, ⁷⁄₁₆″.
Legs: Trimmed hackle stems; front legs, reddish brown with light tips; rear legs, creamy white.
Hackle: Cream-and-white variant.
Collected in New York.

[153]

PLATE XL. ARTIFICIAL MAY FLY, RUFA SPINNER, FEMALE.

BLADES' ISONYCHIA RUFA

(See Plate XL)

Order: *Ephemeroptera*
Family: *Baetidae*

Genus: *Isonychia*
Species: *rufa* (McDunnough)
Imago female

DESCRIPTION OF THE INSECT
Tails: Two, pale grey.
Body: Pale amber; markings, fiery brown.
Wings: Transparent.
Legs: Front legs, brown with light tips; rear legs, creamy white.

MATERIAL FOR THE ARTIFICIAL
Tails: Two pale grey hackle fibres. Length, 1″.
Body: Pale amber raffia; markings, fiery brown horse hair. Length, ½″.
Wings: Pale grey hackle tips. Length, ½″.
Legs: Trimmed hackle stems; front legs, reddish brown with light tips, rear legs, creamy white.
Hackle: Cream and brown variant.
Collected in New York.

PLATE XLI. ARTIFICIAL MAY FLY, RUFA DUN, FEMALE.

BLADES' ISONYCHIA RUFA

(See Plate XLI)

CLASSIFICATION:

Order: *Ephemeroptera*
Family: *Baetidae*

Genus: *Isonychia*
Species: *rufa* (McDunnough)
Subimago female

DESCRIPTION OF THE INSECT
Tails: Two, grey.
Body: Amber; markings, reddish brown.
Wings: Dark grey.
Legs: Front pair, reddish brown; rear and middle legs, pale grey.

MATERIAL FOR THE ARTIFICIAL
Tails: Two grey hackle fibres. Length, ½".
Body: Amber raffia; markings, brown horse hair. Length, $\frac{9}{16}$".
Wings: Dark grey hackle tips. Length, ½".
Legs: Trimmed hackle stems; front legs, reddish brown; rear legs, pale grey.
Hackle: Grey-and-brown variant.
Collected in New York.

[155]

PLATE XLII. ARTIFICIAL MAY FLY, LEUKON SPINNER, MALE.

BLADES' EPHORON LEUKON

(See Plate XLII)

CLASSIFICATION:

Order: *Ephemeroptera*
Family: *Ephemeridae*

Genus: *Ephoron*
Species: *leukon* (Will)
Imago male

DESCRIPTION OF THE INSECT

Tails: Two, pale grey, brown at the base.
Body: White, tan at the tip; thorax, tan.
Wings: Transparent, with reddish brown veins.
Legs: Front legs, reddish brown; rear and middle legs, pale grey.

MATERIAL FOR THE ARTIFICIAL

Tails: Two pale grey hackle fibres. Length, $\frac{7}{8}''$.
Body: White quill, tip marked with pale tan enamel. Length, $\frac{7}{16}''$.
Wings: Pale grey hackle tips. Length, $\frac{7}{16}''$.
Legs: Trimmed hackle stems; front pair, reddish brown; rear legs, pale grey.
Hackle: Grey-and-brown variant.
Eyes: Black. Tie on a piece of black hackle stem or use black enamel.
Collected in New York.

[156]

PLATE XLIII. ARTIFICIAL MAY FLY, GREEN DRAKE SPINNER.

EPHEMERA GUTTULATA SPENT WING

(See Plate XLIII)

Tail and Body: Swan or Goose body
  feather pulled in reverse.
Wings: Teal, fibres pulled in reverse.
Hackle: White or light Badger.
Hook: Short shank.

This is a pattern of the wing of the Ephemera Guttulata female imago. The hackle tips are Badger. I bore a hole as shown, and place a hackle tip, stem down, in it and close the stiff paper pattern together. Now cut off the fibres to shape. Teal or Wood Duck feathers can also be used. This method can be used on any May Fly.

PLATE XLIV. WING—A COMBINATION OF PAPER AND HACKLE ILLUSTRATES THE BLADES' METHOD OF CUTTING WINGS WITH A PAPER PATTERN.

Plate XLV illustrates how near we can come to copying the natural fly, Hexagenia Limbata, Imago male.

The vein wings make the fly look more natural and they have taken many trout for me.

This fly can also be made with hackle tips, which I believe is more popular among fly fishermen.

PLATE XLV. MAY FLY AND THREE IMITATIONS OF IT.

PLATE XLVI. IMITATIONS WITH DIFFERENT TYPE WINGS.

BLADES' STENONEMA VICARIUM

(See Plate XLVI)

CLASSIFICATION:

Order: *Ephemeroptera*
Family: *Heptageniidae*

Genus: *Stenonema*
Species: *vicarium*
Imago male

DESCRIPTION OF THE INSECT

Tails: Two.
Body: Tan; markings, brown.
Wings: Transparent, brown markings.
Legs: Brown, mottled.

MATERIAL FOR THE ARTIFICIAL

Tails: Two dark Wood Duck fibres, length, ⅞″.
Body: Tan raffia; markings, brown enamel, length, ⅝″.
Wings: Pale grey hackle tips, or veined wing material, length, ⅝″.
Legs: Trimmed hackle stems, tan-and-brown variant.
Hackle: Brown-and-tan variant, or medium brown.
Known by fishermen as the Great Red Spinner.

Why should we expect an intelligent trout, a creature of keen close-range vision, to take an old attractor type Red Spinner if the above fly is what he is feeding on and looking for?

[160]

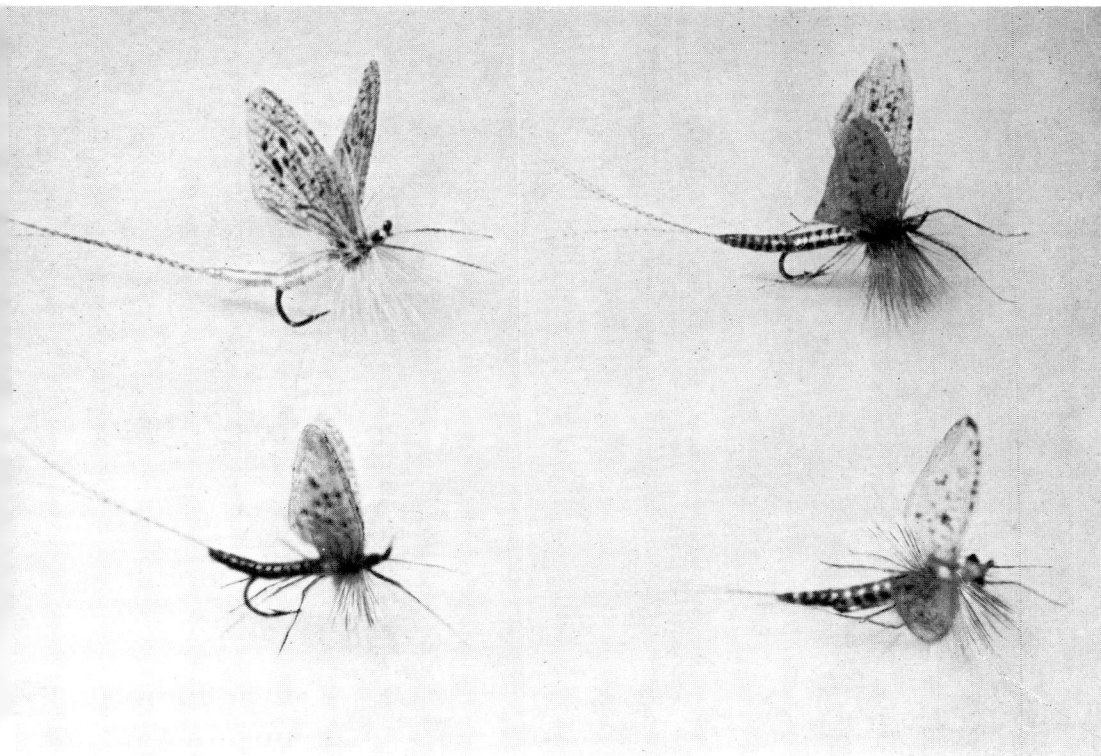

Left to right, top to bottom:

ARTIFICIAL MAY FLIES

Photograph No. 1: Blades' Ephemera guttulata—Spinner of the Green Drake (Coffin Fly).

Photograph No. 2: Blades' Ephemera guttulata Female Sub-Imago (Green Drake).

Photograph No. 3: Blades' Ephemera guttulata Male Imago, (Black Drake).

Photograph No. 4: Blades' Hexagenia recurvata Male Sub-Imago (Brown Drake).

STENONEMA VICARIUM—MAY FLY

Most fishermen are acquainted with the May Fly, which is known as the American March Brown. After learning to tie this fly in the detached body style, you will be able to tie any of your favorite drakes and spinners, if you have the list of materials used or the natural fly as a copy.

These flies appear on the Beaverkill and Delaware early in May, and the natural I am using was picked up on June 7th, 1949 on the Delaware.

The wings are a tannish grey, the veins are dark brown, and are also marked with dark brown mottles. The body is a yellowish tan, or cream on the underside, with reddish brown markings on the back. Legs are yellowish tan with dark brown markings in the first section near the body and at the first joint. Tails are light brown with dark markings.

To tie the fly, place a No. 10 or No. 12 light hook in the vise and coat it with liquid cement, then wrap it with 6-0 tying silk from the eye to where

Drawing No. 1

Drawing No. 2

the body becomes detached from the hook; now tie in a piece of eight-pound test nylon and take the tying silk to the head, as shown in Drawing No. 1.

I now tie in two fibres of brown Mallard for the antennae and form the head with the tying silk and a little cement; the eyes are black enamel. Take the tying silk to where the detached body leaves the hook and coat the nylon with cement; now take a few turns of silk around the nylon, then lift the nylon up and go back on the hook with a few turns; do this two or three times using cement each time and you will notice the detached body will be much stiffer.

The next step is to cut off the nylon the length of the body and tie in two strands of brown Mallard on the hook at the joint; coat the detached nylon with cement and carefully wind the tying silk to the end of the body and back to the hook, keeping the tail fibres on top of the nylon.

Drawing No. 2. Now tie in a fine strand of white or cream floss and form the underbody to the required size, using a little cement on the windings. Take the tying silk to where the body leaves the hook and tie on a fine piece of cream raffia; now take the tying silk to the position of the first pair of legs.

Put a little cement on the body and carefully wind the raffia up to the end of the body and back to the position of the first pair of legs.

To tie on the wings, take the tying silk to the wing position and place the tip of a Wood Duck flank feather on top of the hook with the best side down. I now raise the tying silk almost vertical and tilt the tip to about 45 degrees, and with one quick turn of the silk I roll it on top of the hook; take a few more turns of tying silk around the butt of the tip; trim off the surplus ends and take a few turns of silk in front of the wings to bring them back to about 60 degrees.

Drawing No. 3

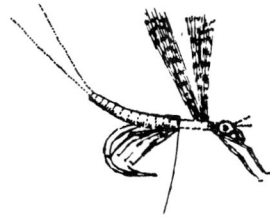

Drawing No. 4

Drawing No. 3. For the legs I trim four variant tan and dun hackles. This mottled effect looks very natural; if these are not available, a yellowish tan or light brown will be suitable. Tie in the first pair of legs in the following manner: Put a little cement on the hook and hold the hackle stem on the side of the hook and secure it with two or three turns of silk; now pass the hackle stem over the body, and take a few more turns of silk while holding the stem

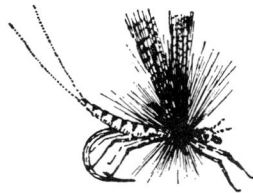

Drawing No. 5

with your left hand fingers; take a few turns of raffia, then tie in the second pair of legs. The next step is to tie in the front legs which are two separate hackle stems. This gives the fly a more natural look. Drawing No. 4. For the hackle I prefer two variants with colors of tan, grey and brown; you can also use one tan and one grizzly. I use the best portion of two hackles taking only a few turns—and if you have a long thin hackle of good quality, one is sufficient.

Tie off with the whip finish and apply a little cement. I bend the legs with my thumb nail and first finger, and cut them off to the proper length. Drawing No. 5 is the finished fly.

The body markings are a yellowish brown enamel applied with a fine camel's hair brush, on the back only.

This is not an easy fly to tie, and should not be attempted by the beginner, —but any good fly tyer can make it with a little practice.

My imitations of the natural flies have been experimented with by two expert fishermen during August, 1949 and they took twice as many fish as the general attractor type.

They were also very deadly on the wary brown trout. I have also used these may flies in Canada with success when no flies were hatching.

STENONEMA VICARIUM—MAY FLY—WET

Follow the same instructions as given for the dry fly, but omit the hackles. Fill in this space with tying silk and cover it with raffia, marking it with yellowish brown enamel which forms a fine thorax and makes one of the most natural looking flies I have had the pleasure of making.

This fly has also been proved to be successful in New York State and Wisconsin.

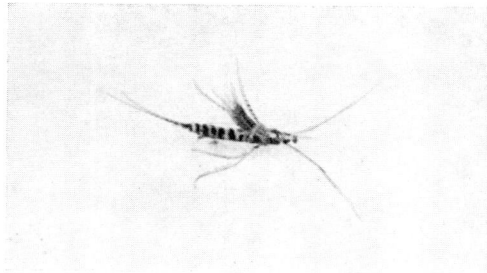

PLATE XLVIII.   MAY FLY.

When tying the following list of May Flies use the instructions for tying the Stenonema Vicarium May Fly, and follow each material list of the fly you are tying.

[164]

BLADES' BLASTURUS CUPIDUS SAY—FEMALE IMAGO

CLASSIFICATION:

Order: *Ephemeroptera*   Genus: *Blasturus*
Family: *Baetidae*   Species: *cupidus*

The artificial fly is known as the Brown Spinner. This fly resembles the March Brown very much, except that the body markings are more pronounced and the wings are not mottled as in the March Brown.

DESCRIPTION OF THE INSECT

Tails: Brown, banded. Two outer tails ⅝th inch long; center ⅜th inch.

Body: Underside, fiery brown; markings, dark fiery brown, especially on the back.

Legs: A dirty yellow.

Wings: Transparent, with a brownish cast, darker on the front edge and tips. Size ½ inch to 9/16ths long.

Actual Insect

Artificial

MATERIALS FOR THE FEMALE IMAGO ARTIFICIAL

Tails: Three strands of Mandarin duck, centre tail short.

Body: Fiery brown raffia, with dark fiery brown enamel markings.

Legs: Trimmed red-brown hackle stems or a variant with gold, grey and brown.

Wings: Transparent, grey-brown cast hackle tips.

Hackle: Brownish yellow; this shade can be found in a variant, or dye a yellow hackle brown.

Head: Brown. Eyes, black.

[165]

BLADES' BLASTURUS CUPIDUS SAY—MALE SUB-IMAGO

This artificial is known as the Black Quill Dun and Dark March Brown. This fly is darker than the Female Imago.

DESCRIPTION OF THE INSECT

Tails: Three, grey, banded with brown, about ⅜ths inch long.
Body: Blackish brown, with bands of a lighter shade.
Legs: Blackish brown.
Wings: Blue grey. Size ⅜th to ½ inch long.

MATERIALS FOR THE MALE SUB-IMAGO ARTIFICIAL

Tails: Three strands of brown Mallard nashua feather (dark).
Body: Fiery brown raffia, banded with blackish brown enamel.
Wings: Blue grey hackle tips.
Legs: Trimmed blackish brown hackle stems.
Hackle: Blackish brown.
Head: Brown tying silk or enamel; Eyes, black.

BLADES' EPHEMERA GUTTULATA—FEMALE SUB-IMAGO
(See Plate XLVII)

CLASSIFICATION:

Order: *Ephemeroptera*	Genus: *Ephemera*
Family: *Ephemeridae*	Species: *guttulata*

The artificial is known as the Green Drake.

This fly is one of our largest May Flies; the length of the wings varies from ⅞ths inch to 1 1/16th inch. The wings are a transparent pale green, mottled with dark brown patches.

The body is a tan yellow with brown markings on the back.

The front legs are brown in the first section near the body; remainder, yellow. Rear legs, yellow.

Tails, brown with a green tint.

Actual Insect

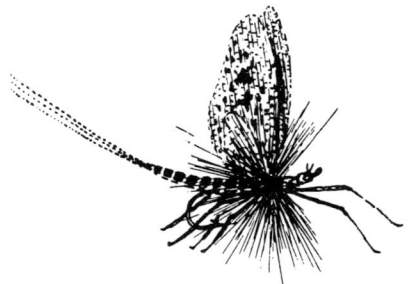

Artificial

To tie the Green Drake, use my instructions for tying the Stenonema Vicarium—May Fly, and use the following materials:

Tail: Mandarin fibres, natural, or dyed olive.

Body: Raffia, natural or dyed yellow. Markings, brown enamel.

Wings: Mandarin body feathers dyed green, or veined wing material painted with pale green enamel and blotched with brown.

Legs: Yellow; Trimmed hackle stems.

Hackle: Light ginger, dyed olive.

Head: Yellow tying silk. Eyes, brown enamel.

BLADES' IRON EPEORUS—MALE DUN

This fly is imitated by the Quill Gordon, (dark).

This is one of the first May flies to appear; the males are smaller and darker than the females.

I would suggest that you try the wet fly and fish it a little below the surface if the fish refuse the dry fly. To make the wet fly, copy the dry fly and omit the hackle.

Actual Insect

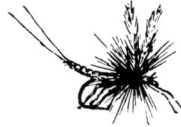

Artificial

The two tails are grey. Body, ruddy tan with prominent dark brown markings. *The legs* are tan grey. *The wings* are dark blue grey. *The hackle,* tan grey variant.

Material for the Male Dun Artificial

Tails: Two dark grey hackle fibres.

Body: Ruddy tan raffia, markings, brown enamel.

Legs: Trimmed tan grey variant or dye a grizzly hackle a fiery brown.

Wings: Dark blue dun hackle tips.

Hackle: Tan grey variant.

[167]

This is a small fly and should be made on a No. 14 hook. *Wing size* is about ⅜ths inch. *Body,* from the head to the tip, ⅜th inch. *Head,* Brown tying silk. *Eyes,* black enamel.

To make the female dun, use a No. 12 hook and make all the material a shade lighter than the male.

The wings and body increase a good 1/16th of an inch.

Artificial: Quill Gordon.

BLADES' EPHEMERA GUTTULATA—MALE IMAGO

CLASSIFICATION:

Order: *Ephemeroptera*   Genus: *Ephemera*
Family: *Ephemeridae*   Species: *guttulata*

The artificial is known as the Coffin Fly. The Coffin Fly, which is known by most trout fishermen, is the Green Drake after it has shed its skin and turned into a spinner. This is a great change, but it still is the same fly.

Tails: Three, which can be well imitated with strands of Mandarin duck or brown Mallard.

Body: Waxy white, with fiery brown on the top of the thorax.

Wings: Transparent and mottled, with brown and black spots. Size of wings, ½ to 11/16ths of an inch.

Legs: Front, black and brown mottled. Back legs are a yellowish white.

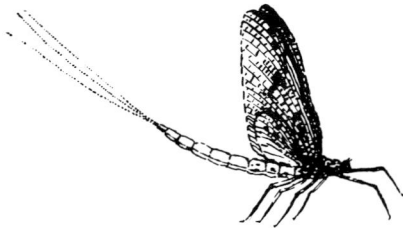

Actual Insect   Artificial

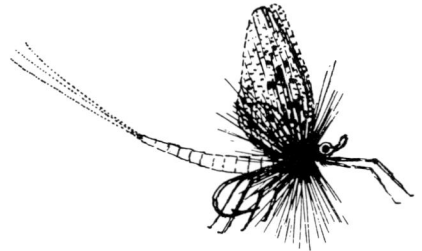

MATERIAL FOR THE ARTIFICIAL

Tails: Mandarin duck.

Body: White quill stripped from a Swan's small wing feather.

Wings: Transparent veined wing material, mottled with brown and black enamel, or Teal body feathers.

Legs: Trimmed hackle feathers; front variant hackles; rear legs, cream hackles.

Hackle: Badger.

Head: White tying silk. Eyes, black enamel.

Antennae: Two cream hackle fibres.

[168]

BLADES' EPHEMERA VARIA—FEMALE IMAGO

CLASSIFICATION:

Order: *Ephemeroptera*   Genus: *Ephemera*
Family: *Ephemeridae*   Species: *varia*
This fly is known as the Yellow Drake.

Actual Insect

Artificial

DESCRIPTION OF THE INSECT

Tails: Three. Pale yellow or cream, with brown bands.
Body and Thorax: Cream, with grey-brown markings on the back.
Legs: Front cream with tan-brown markings. Rear legs, cream.
Wings: Transparent with a cream cast. Mottled with tan-brown. Size 8/16ths to 11/16ths of an inch long.

MATERIALS FOR THE FEMALE IMAGO

Tails: Three strands of Wood Duck or ginger cock hackle.
Body: Cream raffia; markings, grey brown enamel on the back only.
Legs: Trimmed hackle stems. Front, cream variant; rear, cream.
Wings: Cream hackle tips, or a cream badger spotted, if available. Also veined wing material.
Hackle: Cream; for the wet fly, omit the hackle.
Head: Cream silk; Eyes, black enamel.

BLADES' LITTLE MARRYAT

CLASSIFICATION:

Order: *Ephemeroptera*   Family: *Baetidae*
Genus: *Ephemerella*   Species: *dorothea*
Named by Paul R. Needham
This fly has proved to be very successful in taking the wary Brown Trout on the Beaverkill and Delaware rivers by my friend Charles B. Woehrle. Charles says: "Bill, I hope the day will never come when I am without one."

Most of my noted angling friends agree that these flies will catch fish, but they put them in their favorite collections.

This fly is similar to the English fly that is imitated by the Pale Evening Dun and Little Marryat.

Wings: Transparent. Size 4/16ths to 6/16ths of an inch.

Body: Very pale yellow.

Tails: Three, white.

Legs: Cream.

Actual Insect

Artificial

MATERIAL FOR THE ARTIFICIAL

Tail: Cream hackle fibres.

Body: Cream raffia, tied over nylon. This can be plain or faintly marked with brown enamel.

Wings: Pale Wood Duck, or cream hackle tips.

Hackle: Cream.

Head: White tying silk. Eyes, black enamel.

BLADES' STENONEMA FUSCUM—MALE IMAGO

CLASSIFICATION:

Order: *Ephemeroptera*   Genus: *Stenonema*
Family: *Heptageniidae*   Species: *fuscum*
The artificial name for the fly is the Ginger Quill.

DESCRIPTION OF THE INSECT

Tails: Two; Ginger with brown bands.

Body: Tan cream, with light brown markings on the back.

Legs: Light amber, or ginger, with brown markings in the section near the body.

Wings: Transparent with reddish ginger markings near the tip. Size 1/4 to 7/16ths.

Tails: Two ginger cock hackle fibres or Mandarin.

Body: Tan cream raffia; markings, brown enamel on back only.

Legs: Trimmed ginger variant hackle stems.

Wings: Veined wing material marked on the front tips with a reddish ginger enamel, or cream hackle tips.

Hackle: Light multi-variant.

Head: White tying silk; Eyes, black.

Actual Insect   Artificial

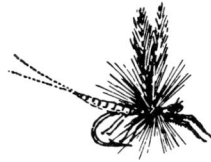

BLADES' STENONEMA FUSCUM—FEMALE DUN

CLASSIFICATION:

Order: *Ephemeroptera*   Genus: *Stenonema*
Family: *Heptageniidae*   Species: *fuscum*

The artificial for this fly is the Ginger Quill.

DESCRIPTION OF THE INSECT

Tails: Two; Ginger with brown bands.

Body: Cream raffia with a yellowish tint; markings, brown enamel on top only.

Legs: Cream to ginger.

Wings: Transparent with yellow-tan cast. Size 7/16ths to 9/16ths.

MATERIALS FOR THE FEMALE DUN ARTIFICIAL

Tails: Two ginger cock hackle fibres or Mandarin.

Body: Cream raffia; markings, brown enamel on top only.

Legs: Trimmed cream ginger hackle stems.

Wings: Pale Mandarin drake flank or pale cream ginger hackle tips.

Hackle: Cream, or cream badger.

Head: White tying silk. Eyes, black enamel.

CLASSIFICATION:

Order: *Ephemeroptera* Genus: *Stenonema*
Family: *Heptageniidae* Species: *ithica*

This May Fly is known as the Light Cahill. It is a very attractive fly, and a "killer" for trout.

The wings are a pale yellow, and are slightly spotted with tan. The wing sizes vary from 6/16ths to 9/16ths of an inch.

Tails, two light tan hackle fibres. *The body* is a pale yellowish cream with faint tan markings.

The legs are a cream tan, with a few brown markings.

Actual Insect

Artificial

MATERIAL FOR THE ARTIFICIAL

Tails: Two tan hackle fibres.
Body: Cream raffia. Tan enamel markings.
Legs: Trimmed ginger or cream hackles.
Hackle: Pale ginger.
Wings: Pale ginger hackle tips or pale Wood Duck.
Head: White silk. Eyes, black enamel.

BAETIDAE CALLIBEATIS SP. (WEST YELLOWSTONE)

(Caught around August 15, 1950) (Cold summer).

DESCRIPTION OF MALE SPINNER

Tails: Two; color, cream; length, ⅝ of an inch.

[172]

Body: Light grey, with sepia brown markings that are prominent on the back and faintly marked on the underside. The thorax is a dark sepia brown with a purple tint. Length of the body, 5/16 of an inch.

Wings: Transparent. Length 5/16 to ⅜ inches.

Legs: Color, dirty white or cream. The front legs are a little darker in the portion near the body and they have brown markings at the joints and feet. The four rear legs have faint brown markings at the joints. Length of front legs, approximately 5/16 of an inch, rear and middle legs, 3/16 of an inch.

Actual Insect

Artificial

MATERIALS FOR THE ARTIFICIAL

Tails: Two creamy white hackle fibres.

Body: Natural raffia; markings, sepia brown enamel.

Wings: Hackle tips, glossy creamish white. Try to imitate a transparent wing.

Legs: Trimmed hackle stems, cream-white speckled; these can be found in a freak badger neck.

Hackle: One tan and one cream, or a variant of the same color.

Head: Prominent; color, pinkish tan.

Eyes: Black enamel.

Suggested name: Sepia cream male spinner, BLADES.

CORK BODIED MAY FLIES

These flies are excellent for fishing in moving streams, and they allow you to give action to the fly without sinking it. Fishing these flies just under the surface is also very effective.

When making the elongated bodied fly, put the tails on a needle and thread them all the way down the cork body before placing it on the hook; put liquid cement on the wrapped hook and in the slot in the cork; allow

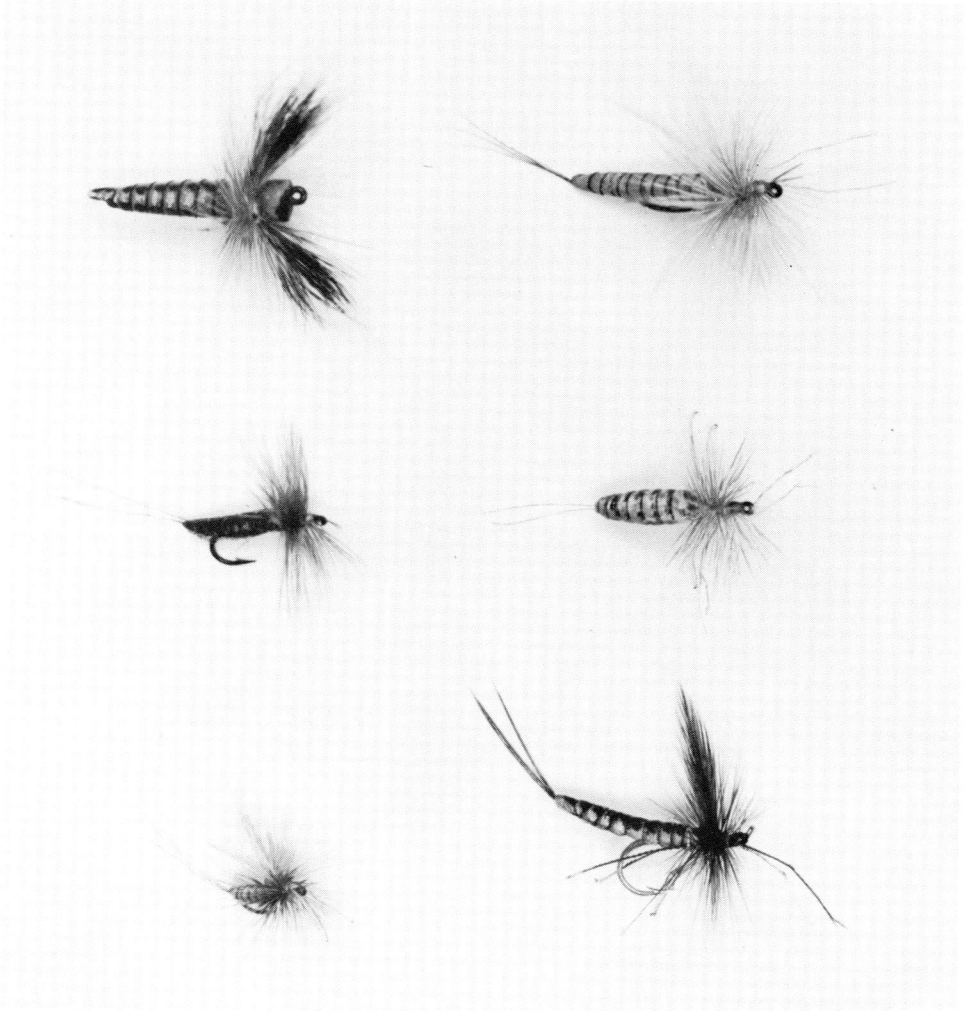

PLATE XLIX. MAY FLIES CONSTRUCTED WITH CORK BODIES.

the cement to set, then tie on the legs, wings and hackle, using my material lists for the May Fly you desire.

The elongated bodies are rather delicate, but the ones tied on the hook will give long service, with care. Fly number six has the body made of fine sheet cork.

I have caught trout very early in the season on the surface with one of these flies. Bass would take No. 1 when a May Fly hatch is in progress.

Chapter XII

OTHER TYPES OF TROUT STREAM INSECTS

NCE I was fishing a little lake in Ontario, Canada for small-mouth bass, using small popping bugs.

The bass were hitting all day—until about four P.M.—when a large mating flight of brown ants appeared and which were falling on the lake. From this time on, I could not interest the fish with bass flies—or any fly— proving to me that the fish are very selective when a flight of ants is available.

MAKING THE "BLADES" BLACK ANT

CLASSIFICATION:

Order: *Hymenoptera*   Family: *Formicidae*

When tying the Brown Ant, use the tying instructions for the Black Ant, with the following materials:

Body—reddish brown tying silk.

Wings—four light grey hackle tips.

Legs—reddish brown Moose mane, or trimmed hackle stems. Hackle— reddish brown.

When making the body, use fine tying silk and, as you wind the silk, apply several coats of cement sparsely as you wind the body. This prevents the silk from sliding.

To raise the body above the hook (which I feel is only for looks) tie on a piece of Peacock quill on the top of the hook and make your windings over it. Now reverse the quill and wind over it again, keeping the quill on

Drawing No. 1

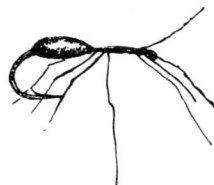

Drawing No. 2

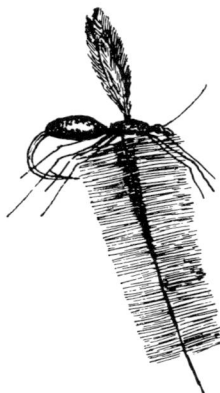

Drawing No. 3

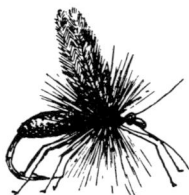

Drawing No. 4

Drawing No. 5

top of the hook. Do this several times and, when you reverse the quill, stop before you get to the end of the body or the ends of the body will be straight.

To tie the Black Ant, place a No. 10 hook in the vise, coat it with cement, and wrap it with No. 5-0 black tying silk to the end of the body. I selected a No. 10 hook to make the tying more simple when tying your first fly. Now wind the first portion of the body with black tying silk and cement. Take the tying silk and tie in two pieces of black Moose mane for the antennae and form the head with the tying silk. Your fly will be the same as Drawing No. 1.

Now tie in the legs, as shown in Drawing No. 2. These three pieces of brown Moose mane, or trimmed hackle stems, form six legs—three on each side. Let these be long until the fly is finished, then cut them to the proper size. Your fly will be the same as Drawing No. 2.

The next step is to tie in the wings which are pale grey hackle tips and consist of two large and two small, as shown in Drawings No. 3 and No. 4. Now make the front body with the black tying silk and tie in the hackle, also finish off the bodies with black enamel or clear before winding the hackle. Your fly will be the same as Drawing No. 3.

Now wind the cocky bondu hackle and tie off; also, cut the legs to size and kink them with the thumb nail. You will now have the finished fly, as shown in Drawing No. 4.

Drawing No. 5 is a drawing made from the natural Ant.

CRANE FLY

CLASSIFICATION:

Order: *Diptera*   Genus: *Tipula*
Family: *Tipulidae*   Species: *bella*

Body: Tan; or natural raffia with brown enamel markings.

Legs: Cock Pheasant tail fibres, knotted twice to form joints.

Wings: Tan variant hackle tips, tied on horizontally.

Hackle: Tan variant, or light brown.

This fly provides a major portion of food for trout and many game fish, and I sincerely feel that the artificial fly will bring many fish to the creel if it is given the opportunity.

The many different spiders and variants are made to imitate some of these different Crane Flies.

If you collect the natural fly and find it has different colors from the one I have listed, simply change the colors to suit the one you are imitating, and also copy the size.

Some tyers use grizzly hackle for the wings, and these can be dyed green, yellow and orange. Light blue dun is also used for this purpose.

To tie the Crane Fly—place a No. 10 3X hook in the vise and coat it with cement and tie in the antennae with No. 5-0 or No. 6-0 white tying silk; the antennae are tan hackle fibres or Pheasant tail fibres. Now continue the tying silk to the end of the body, as shown in Drawing No. 1.

Shape the underbody with a piece of fine white floss, as shown, and tie in a piece of natural raffia at the front of the body; this should be wet and long enough to wrap the body all the way down and back to the starting point again, and also long enough to wrap the thorax. Keep the raffia narrow as it makes a neater fly—your fly will now be the same as Drawing No. 2.

Drawing No. 1

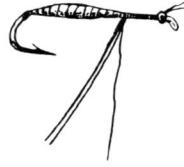

Drawing No. 2.

Drawing No. 3

Drawing No. 4

Drawing No. 5

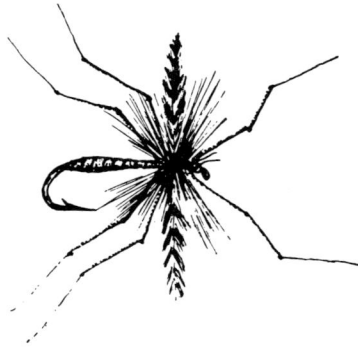

Drawing No. 6

TYING THE CRANE FLY.

Now take six strands of cock Pheasant tail fibres and knot them, as shown in Drawing No. 3. Tie in the first pair of legs which point to the rear of the fly; then take a couple of turns of raffia and tie in the second pair of legs which point out and back.

Tie in the wings, as shown, which are tan variant hackle tips—they are marked like the grizzly.

To tie in the wings, cut them to the proper size, leaving the centre quill long. Put the glossy sides together and straddle the hook with the butts; secure with three or four turns of thread, then criss-cross your thread in between the wings, bringing them to a horizontal position. Your fly will be the same as Drawing No. 4.

Now tie in a tan variant hackle, or tan if the variant is not available, between the wings and second pair of legs; next tie in the front pair of legs which point forward.

Wind the raffia over the thorax and tie off. Now wind on the hackle, and tie off; then put on the whip finish and head cement, and your fly will represent Drawing No. 6.

I tie this fly with a fairly large streamer hackle tied on horizontally, which is called "parachute." This is an excellent fly.

TYING THE CADDIS FLY

CLASSIFICATION:
      Order: *Trichoptera*   Genus: *Stenophylax*

DESCRIPTION OF THE INSECT

Body: Tan, segment markings, brown; length of body, ⅝ of an inch.
Wings: Cinnamon—a tannish brown; length, from the head to the wing
        tips, ⅞ths of an inch.
Legs: Tannish brown (could also be called dark ginger).
Antennae: The same color as the legs.

MATERIALS FOR THE ARTIFICIAL

Body: Tan raffia.
Ribbing: Brown Peacock quill, or raffia.
Legs: Trimmed, dark ginger hackle stems.
Wings: Four cinnamon hackle tips.
Head: Tan tying silk.
Eyes: Black enamel.

To tie the Caddis Fly, place a No. 6, 7, or 8 hook in the vise; coat it with cement and wrap it with tying silk to the end of the body. Now tie in a strand of tan raffia and a finer strand of brown raffia. Form the under body with fine floss and cover it with cement. Wind the tan raffia to the end of the body and form the ribbing with the fine brown raffia or Peacock quill to the location shown in Drawing No. 1.

Take the tying silk to the head and tie in two finely trimmed ginger hackle stems and form the head with tying silk. Take the tying silk to the end of the body, and tie in the first pair of legs; take a few turns of tying

Drawing No. 1

Drawing No. 2

Drawing No. 3

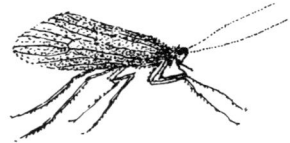

Drawing No. 4

silk and the tan raffia, and tie in the second pair of legs. Fill in the thorax as before, and tie in the front legs.

See that you have left enough space between the head and thorax to tie in the wings.

Now select four cinnamon-colored hackles and cut off the butts until you have the proper length for the wings. A prepared hackle is shown in Drawing No. 5. To tie on the wings, first see that you have prepared the base and put a little cement on it; now put a little cement on the butts of the two pairs of wings. Take the far side pair and place them on the side of the hook, leaning then *towards* you and low enough to cover the body; take a couple of turns of tying silk carefully over the butts; now tie in the near side wing, leaning it *away* from you. This will form a roof over the body, which is typical of all the Caddis flies. Take a few turns of your fine silk; trim off the butts and finish with the whip knot; your fly will now be the same as Drawing No. 3.

Drawing No. 4 is a drawing of the natural Caddis Fly.

If you make the padding of the body out of kapok dubbing and cover it with raffia, your fly will float much better.

I will explain how I make this ribbed body with the ribbing at right angles to the hook, not spiraling up the body. I am presuming you have prepared the body and have tied in two pieces of raffia a little less than 1/16th of an inch wide. Take two turns of the tan raffia over the brown to the under-

Drawing No. 5

side of the hook. Keep a strain on the tan raffia, and with the left hand make two turns with the brown raffia; keep a strain on the brown raffia and make two turns with the tan leaving a small amount of the brown showing which will make a fine rib.

Continue this operation for the entire length of the body. If you stain the top of the body, and give it a coat of cement after it has dried, you will have a very fine, natural looking body.

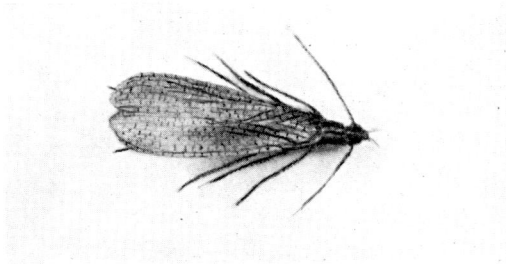

PLATE L. STONE FLY, WINGS CLOSED.

STONE FLY

CLASSIFICATION:

Order: *Plecoptera*

DESCRIPTION OF THE INSECT

Body: Fiery brown on the back; underside, orange tan.
Thorax: Dark brown.
Legs, Tails and Antennae: Dark brown.
Wings: Transparent, with a brownish cast; veins, brown.

MATERIALS FOR THE ARTIFICIAL

Body: Light fiery brown raffia; this can be dyed an orange shade, or orange enamel can be applied on the underside, and brown enamel markings on the back.
Legs, Tails and Antennae: Dark brown trimmed hackle stems.
Wings: Veined wing material; veins can be painted on with brown enamel.

PLATE LI. NATURAL STONE FLY, WINGS SPREAD.

TYING THE STONE FLY WITH FOLDED WINGS

Place a No. 8, 4X hook in the vise; coat it with liquid cement and wrap it with No. 4-0 tying silk. Now tie in the dark brown trimmed hackle stems for the tails and antennae. Form the under-body with floss or fur dubbing and wind the first portion of the body with light fiery brown raffia to the first pair of legs; wind the body up to the second pair of legs and tie them in.

Now form the portion of the body to the front legs and tie in the veined wings; these can be bought from Herter's, Waseca, Minnesota, cut ready to tie in. The material can also be had in sheets so that you can cut your own wings.

Form the front section to the antennae and tie off with the whip finish. Give the body a coat of clear enamel and put on the markings with brown enamel or any color to imitate the fly you are copying. Most of them have a decided orange tint.

To make this fly in flight, use the same wing tied spent for the top wing and cut out the lower wings from a sheet of veined-winged material, or the wings can be made from hackle tips.

The natural Stone Fly was collected near West Yellowstone, Montana, and many large trout were feeding on the surface when this hatch was in progress. I made the padding for the spentwing fly body of kapok and yellow floss before winding on the raffia; this improves the floating qualities of the flies.

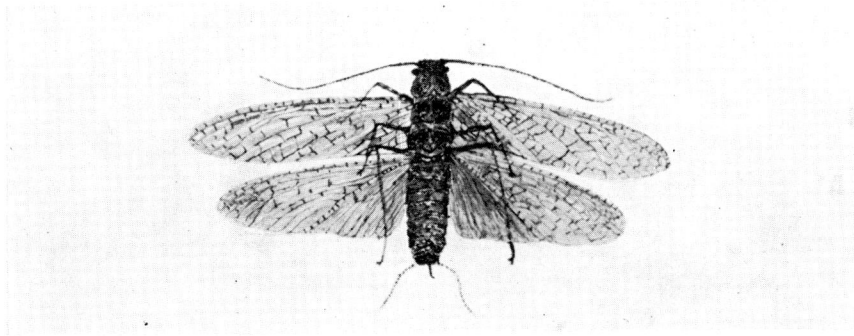

DRAWING OF NATURAL STONE FLY IN FLIGHT.

THE AUTHOR GIVING FLY TYING INSTRUCTIONS.

TYING THE DAMSEL FLY

CLASSIFICATION:

Order: *Odonata* Family: *Agrionidae*
Sub-Order: *Zygoptera* Genus: *Calopteryx*
Species: *maculata*

I picked up this fly on a trout stream near Redgranite, Wisconsin. There are many different species of Damsel Flies so, by all means, collect a specimen from your own location and change the size and color to suit the insect you are making.

The wings are heavily veined, and are a glossy, transparent brown in color. The body is dark brown, tinted with a blue dark green.

Drawing No. 1

Drawing No. 2

The thorax and head are the same color as the sword feather of the Peacock, which is blue green.

The legs are a dark greenish brown, grey blue.

To tie the Damsel Fly, place a No. 8 3X hook in the vise, coat it with liquid cement, and wrap it with No. 4 or 5-0 tying silk. Now take a piece of 6-pound test nylon and double it; then tie it on the hook with the loop end projecting over the bend, the desired length of the body, which in this case is 1⅝ths inches from the front of the head to the end of the body. Coat the nylon with cement and wrap it with tying silk; this forms an excellent foundation for the floss and raffia body. Your fly is now the same as Drawing No. 1.

The next step is to tie in a fine piece of brown floss and form the body, which is a little over 1/16th of an inch thick in this fly. Tie off the floss and take the tying silk to the bend of the hook. Now tie in a long, fine length of raffia, dyed a dark blue, green, brown color. This raffia must have been soaked in warm water, or it will be difficult to handle, as raffia is rather brittle when dry. I tie the raffia in at the bend of the hook and wrap the elongated portion of the body down to the tail and back to the hook, continuing down the body to the thorax.

Your fly will now be the same as Drawing No. 2.

[185]

To make the head and eyes, I lay a small piece of black hackle stem on the hook and criss-cross the tying silk over it, then cut off the ends to the desired length and apply the head cement; after this has set, apply a little dab of black enamel on each end.

The transparent veined wings can be bought already cut to shape from Herter's, Waseca, Minnesota, and you can also buy the material in sheets so that you can cut any size you desire. This material is only available in the

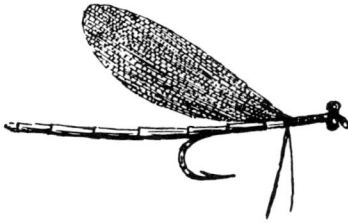

Drawing No. 3

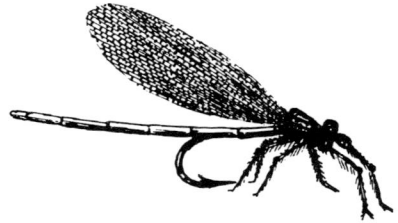

Drawing No. 4

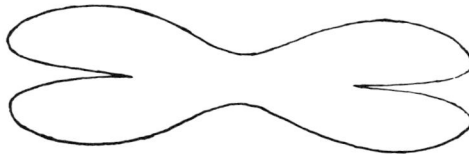

Drawing No. 5

natural color at the present time, but you can color it with a very thin coat of celluloid enamel, any color you desire.

These wings are easy to tie on; simply fold them and tie them on, holding them in the proper position all of the time. Your fly will now be same as Drawing No. 3.

Trim two long hackles for the first two pairs of legs and two smaller ones for the front legs. Tie in the two small front legs and cut off the surplus ends; then bring the tying silk to the base of the wings. To make the raised thorax, tie in four strands of dark Peacock sword quill and bind them on top of the hook with the tying silk up to the first pair of legs. Now reverse the quills and wind over them, taking them back to the wing base—do not cut them off, as they will form the top of the thorax. Take the tying silk forward and tie in the two pairs of legs in location, as shown in the drawing.

Wind the raffia over the thorax and lay the strands of Peacock herl over the top of the thorax, and tie off.

[186]

Cut the legs to the proper length and kink them with your thumb nail. Mark the body segments with black-green enamel, and also touch up the head.

Your fly will be as shown in Drawing No. 4.

Use kapok dubbing for padding on the body and thorax if you desire it to float better.

Drawing No. 5 is a copy of the wings. Trace this drawing on a piece of strong, flexible paper, and cut out a pattern. Lay it on the veined wing material and cut out the wings.

You can also take the fly wing and make a pattern of any fly you are making.

Chapter XIII

NYMPHS AND NYMPH
FISHING

Y ALL means do not overlook the fact that nymphs form a
great part of the food for all game fish; also it is an established fact that fish
are very selective when feeding on nymphs of all kinds; which means you
will have a much better opportunity to hook a fish if you have a close imitation of the nymphs, in place of using an attractor-type wet fly.

The plastic under-body assists in taking the nymphs down. I also wrap
the hook with soft copper wire for extra weight on some nymphs. The Dragon
and Stone Fly nymphs are very good for brown trout fished at almost any
depth. The Damsel Fly nymph proved to be very successful for Frank R.
Steel in the colored movie short "Fighting Rainbows."

At the present time I sincerely believe America is outstanding for its
patterns of nymphs. The following pages will give you a good selection of
nymphs and by all means collect some in your location and use my tying
instructions.

Fishing with nymphs requires skill and you must be able to discern the
slightest strike. Fish with a floating line and a nine foot to twelve foot tapered

leader; if your eyes are good watch the knot at the end of your line; if it moves quickly or in the opposite direction in which it is coming, raise the rod tip carefully and set the hook. For better visibility on long casts, take a very small cork and paint it white, then bore a hole down the centre with a bodkin and thread it up your leader until you reach the line connection, then watch the cork for your strikes.

You can get some good practice on this type of fishing on your local lakes, fishing for bluegills and crappies in the early season.

When nymph fishing on a stream for trout, my first method would be to fish upstream and across; my reason for this is that the trout are generally swimming with their heads upstream, which means the angler is not so visible to the trout. Another reason is that you are not fishing in murky water caused by your wading. Cast the nymph lightly on the water and allow it to sink two or three feet, then raise the rod tip and bring the nymph naturally up near the surface and at the same time take in the slack line caused by the current; now let it sink again and once more bring it up near the surface. At the end of the cast let the nymph sink to the bottom and make it crawl towards you as naturally as you can, with a slow retrieve.

If the fish are down deep, stand still at the head of a pool, then cast a long slack line downstream and allow the nymph to sink near to the bottom, then retrieve it with a jerking movement; also try this at several different depths, for if the fish are feeding on nymphs that are about to change to a subimago, they are feeding at any depth. For early fishing when the water is cold, let the nymph sink to or near the bottom and again move it along with a natural movement. The current will often take your nymph under a stone if you don't keep it working and, of course, if this does happen you are not fishing. You do not need special tackle for nymph fishing; your dry fly action rod, tapered line and a long fine leader are sufficient.

If the nymphs are not weighted, put a little tin foil on the leader. Most anglers prefer dry fly fishing or just under-the-surface, but at times it is nearly impossible to take fish on a dry fly, therefore I hope the following pages will assist my angling friends to enjoy the art of nymph fishing.

To be a successful trout fisherman you have to learn how to read a stream; if you watch the current it will tell you which is the deep side. Look for dark looking water; these are deep spots which should be fished before you disturb them. Cast your fly under overhanging trees or bushes, using the curve cast. My advice is, try to figure out where you would be if you were a trout and carefully present your fly or nymph in that spot.

Edward R. Hewitt says: "These nymphs should take salmon when they are schooled up in low water, especially if you will use the one on which they are feeding and use an imitation near to the size of the natural."

TYING THE OLIVE NYMPH

This type of nymph is tied in many colors and sizes; after learning to tie this nymph, it will be very simple to tie many that closely resemble the Olive nymph.

Place a No. 12 2X hook in the vise, coat it with cement and wrap it with tying silk. Now tie in the tail, which is blue dun hackle fibres; also tie in the olive seal fur dubbing and gold tinsel ribbing. Your nymph will be the same as Drawing No. 1.

Wind the dubbing and gold tinsel to the thorax and tie in the orange crown which is orange floss, and saturate with clear enamel or cement; take the tying silk forward and your nymph will be the same as Drawing No. 2.

Drawing No. 1

Drawing No. 2

Drawing No. 3

Drawing No. 4

Now wind the thorax with the olive seal fur, which is saturated with cement. Allow this to set a little, then flatten it with pliers. Take the crown and tie it over the thorax, and tie it down. I then tie in a soft hackle by the tip and wind on about three turns, as shown in Drawing No. 3 and No. 4 is the finished nymph. To weight this nymph, wind soft copper wire under the body.

TYING THE WEIGHTED ORANGE NYMPH

Place the hook in the vise, cover it with cement, and wrap it to the bend. Now tie in a few black hackle fibres and also the orange dubbing.

Wrap the hook with soft copper wire and allow the end to hang down at the tail, as this will form the ribbing. Coat the wire with cement and wrap it with tying silk. (Drawing No. 1.)

Form the body with the orange seal fur, and saturate it with cement and flatten it; also rib it with the copper wire and your nymph now will be the same as Drawing No. 2.

Wind on about three turns of soft black hackle and finish off with the whip finish. Cover the back with black enamel, and your nymph will be the same as Drawing No. 3.

I sometimes make a flat plastic body over the copper wire, then cover it with the dubbing.

Drawing No. 1

Drawing No. 2

Drawing No. 3

THE WEIGHTED ORANGE NYMPH.

TYING THE DRAGON FLY NYMPH
Order: *Odonata*

Collected on the Delaware River, New York

The length of the nymph I am tying is one and one-half inches long; the hook is a No. 2 Allcock's extra-long shank.

DESCRIPTION OF THE INSECT

The entire nymph is a reddish brown. The back is darker than the underside.

Legs: Dark brown, mottled.
Eyes: Black.

MATERIAL LIST FOR THE ARTIFICIAL

Tails, antennae, and embryo wings are made of fibres from the Turkey wing (outer feathers) dyed dark brown.
Legs: Trimmed dark brown hackle stems (or variant).

[191]

Body: Moulded plastic filed to shape and covered with brown raffia.
Markings: Dark brown enamel.
Head: Brown.
Eyes: Black.

To tie the Dragon Fly Nymph, which is one and one-half inches in length, I have used a No. 2 Allcock's long shank hook. Coat the hook with cement and wrap it with tying silk.

The next step is to take a piece of plastic that is not too soft or too stiff, and press it around the hook. While the plastic is still soft, I roughly trim it to shape with scissors, as shown in Drawing No. 1.

Drawing No. 1

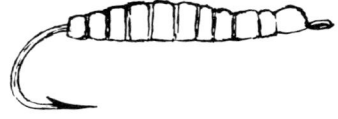

Drawing No. 2

After the plastic has set hard, file it to the proper size and shape; the back is shaped to a point, like a roof, as in Drawing No. 2.

Now tie in three Turkey wing quill fibres (dyed brown) for the tail, and a strand of brown raffia the color of the underside of the nymph; I stain the back darker and make the ribbing with brown enamel. Coat the plastic body with cement, and wind the raffia to the first leg position. Trim the six legs, using brown or brown variant hackles, and tie in the first pair of legs on the underside of the body. Wind the raffia to the second pair of legs and tie them in, then take your tying silk to the wing position. I use four of the largest Turkey wing quill fibres I can find, dyed dark brown.

Tie them in as shown, then tie in the front legs. Continue the raffia over the head, and tie off.

Drawing No. 3

The head can be marked with brown enamel, and I use black enamel for the two bulges at the eyes.

[192]

Carefully coat the nymph with cement; your nymph will be the same as Drawing No. 4.

Drawing No. 5 is the underside of the natural nymph. Drawing No. 6 is my drawing of the back of the natural nymph. I again suggest the tyer to obtain a specimen of the natural nymph in your location.

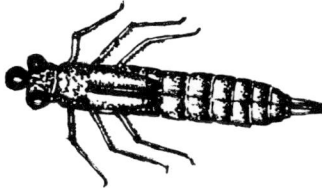

Drawing No. 4

Drawing No. 5

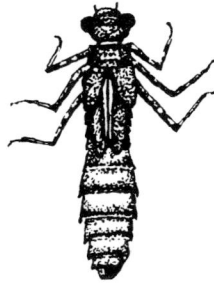

Drawing No. 6

THE DRAGON FLY NYMPH.

LARGE STONE FLY NYMPH

CLASSIFICATION:

    Order: *Plecoptera*   Family: *Pteronarcidae*

    Collected at West Yellowstone by Don and Dick Olson.

DESCRIPTION OF THE INSECT

The entire nymph is a blackish brown. The back is a little darker than the underside.

MATERIAL LIST FOR THE ARTIFICIAL

Tail, legs and antennae, blackish brown trimmed hackle stems. Embryo wings are made of fibres from the Turkey wing (outer feathers) dyed dark brown.

Body: Moulded plastic filed to shape and covered with blackish brown raffia.

Markings: Dark brown enamel.

Head: Dark brown.

Eyes: Black.

[193]

Read the instructions for tying the Dragon Fly Nymph before tying the Large Stone Fly Nymph as they are very much the same.

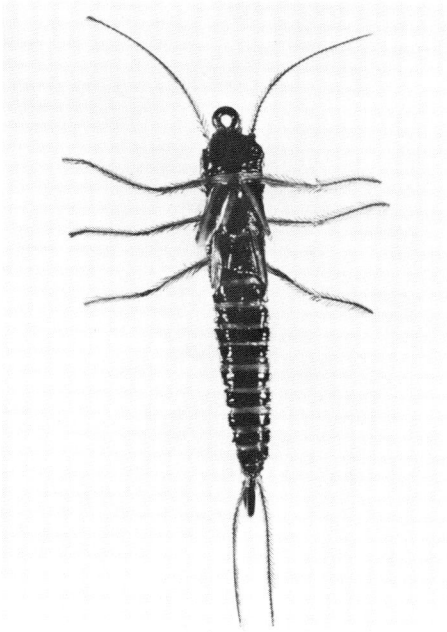 

Artificial   *Natural*

PLATE LII. LARGE STONE FLY NYMPHS.

TYING THE STONE FLY NYMPH

(Collected on the Delaware River)

The length of the nymph I am tying is one and one-sixteenth inches long; the hook is a No. 4, 3X long model perfect.

The tails, horns and antennae are made of trimmed ginger cock hackles.

First coat the hook with liquid cement, then tie in the antennae and horns and wind the hook with the tying silk to the bend; now tie in the tails and cut off the tying silk. (Your nymph should be the same as Drawing No. 1.)

The next step is to take a piece of plastic and mould the shape of the nymph on the hook with your fingers. Allow the plastic to harden a little, then cut it to shape with the scissors. After the plastic has set hard, file it to the shape of the nymph.

[194]

You will have to allow the liquid plastic to set until you can handle it like putty (Drawing No. 2).

Drawing No. 1

Drawing No. 2

Tie in at the tail a piece of natural raffia about three thirty-seconds of an inch wide and a brown Peacock quill; take the tying silk to the first pair of legs, then wind the raffia and quill to this location, tie off, and it will be the same as Drawing No. 3.

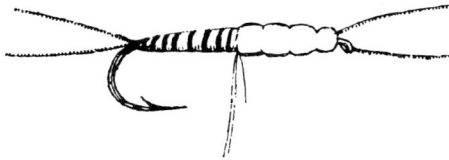

Drawing No. 3

Now trim three ginger hackles to make the six legs, tie in the first pair of legs, then wind the tying silk to the second pair of legs; now wet the natural raffia and wind it to this location, then tie off and tie in the second pair of legs.

The wing cases are made of a piece of natural raffia about three thirty-seconds of an inch in width and two grey Turkey wing quill fibres dyed tannish brown. These are taken from the flight quill, the largest feather on the wing. Put a little cement on the thorax then round off the corner of the raffia and two quills, tie on the raffia first, then tie on a quill on each side. Trim off the ends of the raffia and quills, then take the tying silk to the third pair of legs; wet the raffia and wind the second section of the thorax, then tie in the third pair of legs.

Tie on another piece of raffia and two quills as before described which will complete the wing cases. Wet the natural raffia and wind it on the last section of thorax and head, then tie off with the whip finish.

The top of the nymph is darkened a little with thin tan enamel, and the markings and eyes are painted with brown enamel. The underside is the natural raffia.

Drawings No. 4 and No. 5 are the finished nymph.

I suggest that you wind the hook with copper wire before putting on the plastic for early fishing. You can omit the markings and still have a good nymph.

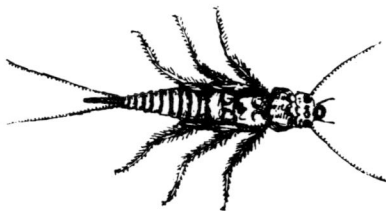

Drawing No. 4   *Drawing No. 5*

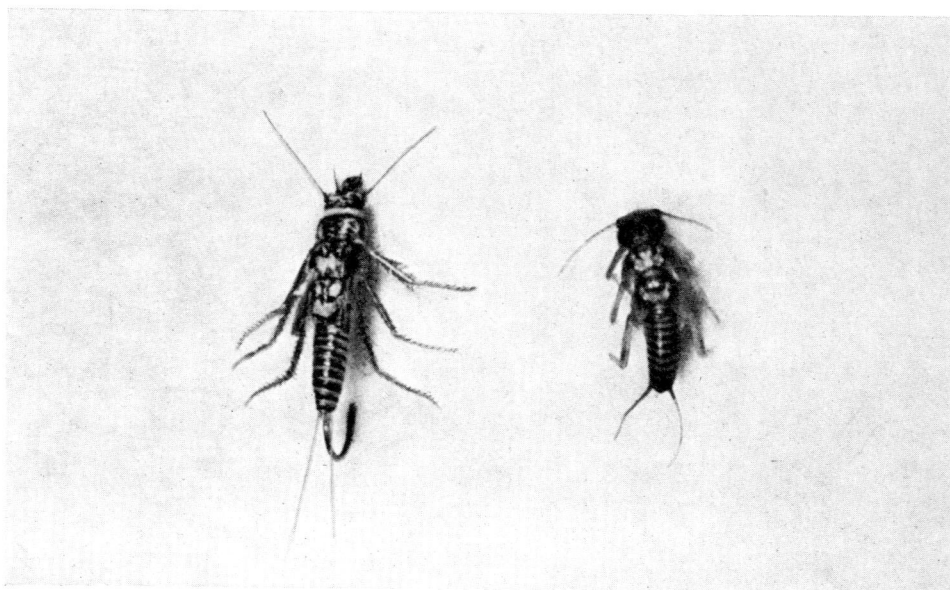

Artificial   *Natural*   Alan Wallace

PLATE LIII. STONE FLY NYMPHS.

TYING THE DAMSEL FLY NYMPH

CLASSIFICATION:

Order: *Odonata*

There are many different Damsel Fly Nymphs which vary in color and size, so again I advise you to collect some samples and copy them in the event the size and color of this nymph vary from the ones you obtain.

DESCRIPTION OF THE INSECT

The three tails, which by the way are gills, are transparent with tan markings; length, 5/16th of an inch.

Drawing No. 1

Drawing No. 2

The body is tan, darker on the back than on the underside; markings, brown. Length of the body from and including the head to the tails is ¾ of an inch.

Legs: Tan. Wing cases and thorax, brown.

Head: Tan. Eyes, grey, projecting rather prominently.

MATERIAL LIST FOR THE ARTIFICIAL

Tails: Three tan variant neck hackle tips.

Body and Thorax: Tan raffia; markings, brown enamel or a dark fine quill.

Legs: Trimmed ginger hackle stems.

Wing cases: Quills from the Turkey wing (outer feather) dyed brown tan.

Head: Tan tying silk. *Eyes:* Grey enamel.

To tie the Damsel Fly Nymph I use a No. 3X No. 10 hook. Secure it in the vise, then coat it with liquid cement. Now tie in two tan fibres for the antennae and wind the silk to the tail location. Tie in three tan variant hackle tips; these should be tied in on their edge. You will now be same as Drawing No. 1.

The next step is to form the under body with floss, as shown in Drawing No. 2. Also tie in, at the tail, a dark, fine, Peacock quill and a long piece of light tan raffia. Your nymph will now be same as Drawing No. 2.

Wind the raffia body to the position shown and wind the quill ribbing and cut it off. Take a trimmed ginger hackle stem, long enough to make the two rear legs; put a little cement on the leg position and tie in the leg on the near side, then pass it over the body and make a few turns over it on the far side, bringing them back in position shown. To make the bulging eyes, lay a piece of grey hackle stem across the front and form the head by criss-crossing the tying silk. Cut the hackle stem off to the proper length; give the head a coat of head cement, and put a little grey enamel on the ends of the hackle stem.

Now tie in two fine hackles for the front legs, and your nymph will be the same as Drawing No. 3. Take a couple of turns of raffia and tie in the second pair of legs.

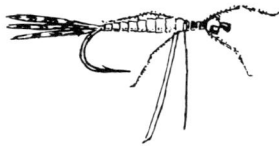

Drawing No. 3

Drawing No. 4

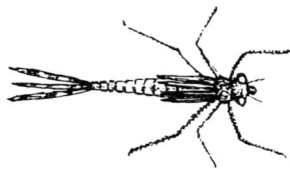

Drawing No. 5

Now tie in four tan colored Turkey wing quill fibres as in position shown in Drawings No. 4 and No. 5; cut off the ends at the head and wind the raffia over them to form the thorax.

Tie off with the whip finish, and your nymph will be the same as Drawings No. 4 and No. 5.

Give the nymph a thin coat of liquid cement on the body and thorax.

To make this nymph sink, wrap the hook with fine, soft copper wire and make the under body of plastic.

TYING THE MAY FLY NYMPH

Order: *Hexagenia*

Tying this nymph is not an easy task and the fly tyer should be an accomplished tyer before attempting this class of work.

Acquiring a real nymph will simplify the tying and greatly assist in getting the proper colors, which you will find vary in different locations.

The markings are very beautiful and can only be imitated briefly with enamel and a fine camel hair brush, all that is necessary for fishing purposes.

The under-body that is made of plastic can be made to the exact shape of the nymph if you wish to spend the time, and is an almost indestructible body. The weight of the plastic assists in taking the nymph down to where the fish are feeding. If additional weight is desired for early fishing, wrap

Drawing No. 1

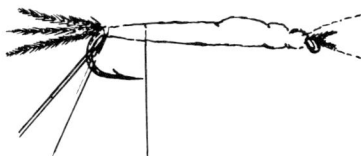

Drawing No. 2

the hook with fine soft copper wire before forming the plastic body. For the legs, I try to select natural colored hackles to imitate the color and strong enough to stand the wear, but flexible so as to give some action.

The length of the nymph I am tying is about one inch long, so I use a No. 8 hook 4X long. The tails, horns, and antennae are made of trimmed ginger cock hackles.

First, coat the hook with liquid cement, then tie in the antennae and horns and wind the hook with the tying silk to the bend; now tie in the tails and cut off the tying silk. (Your nymph should be the same as Drawing No. 1.)

The next step is to take a piece of plastic and mould the shape of the nymph on the hook with your fingers. Allow the plastic to harden a little, then cut to shape with scissors. After the plastic has set hard, file it to the shape of the nymph. Duco Household cement made by DuPont can be used as plastic. I take it out of the tube and allow it to set a little before using.

Tie in, at the tail, a piece of natural raffia about three thirty-seconds of an inch wide, and also a piece of brown raffia about one-sixteenth of an inch wide; this is used to mark the segments of the body which I will explain.

Now take your 5-0 tying silk to the location of the first pair of gills which number six pairs and are made of blue dun ostrich herl. (Your nymph should be the same as in Drawing No. 2.)

Soak the raffia in warm water and keep it wet all the while you are tying it on by wetting your fingers; also put a little cement on the plastic body. This prevents slipping.

Commence to wind the natural raffia over the brown raffia which is coming along on the underside of the nymph until you have completed the first body section.

I mark all the sections and gills on the plastic with black ink. This simplifies the tying very much. Now make a complete turn around the nymph with the brown raffia, and you have one section complete. Continue this method on nine sections up to the thorax, making the brown line very thin. Tie

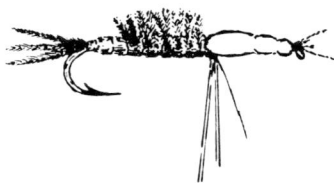

Drawing No. 3

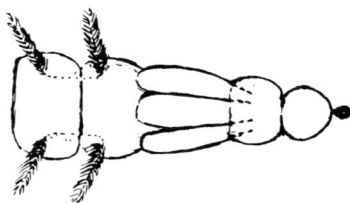

Drawing No. 4

in a pair of gills in sections 3, 4, 5, 6, 7 and 8 as you proceed in the following manner. Lay two pieces of blue dun ostrich herl lengthwise on top of the nymph (as shown in enlarged Drawing No. 4) and in the middle of the third section, then tie them down with the tying silk. Now wrap the remaining half of section No. 3 with the body raffia, also the brown segment and the first half of section No. 4; turn up each end of the herl and cut off to the desired length and you will have completed two pairs of gills. The tying silk comes along with all these operations while tying in the brown and natural raffia at each section and also tying on the gills. (Your nymph should be the same as Drawing No. 3.)

The next step is to securely tie in the first pair of legs that are made of trimmed ginger hackles. This can be made of one long stem or two short ones. Wind the raffia to the next pair of legs and tie them in, then wind the body raffia to the end of this section and take a turn of the brown raffia. The wing cases on top of the thorax are made of three fibres of grey Turkey dyed a tannish brown. These are taken from the flight quill, the largest feather on the wing. Trim the ends to shape and tie them in at the end of the thorax.

Now tie in the last pair of legs, wrap the last segment and head with raffia, then tie off with the whip finish.

I shade the top of this nymph with a brown and yellow enamel mixture, using the brown for the eyes and markings on the thorax; the tan I use on the top of the body. Leave the underside light natural raffia.

[200]

Drawing No. 5

Drawing No. 6

Drawing No. 5 is the finished nymph.

Drawing No. 6 is the natural nymph enlarged one and one-half times its natural size.

Drawing No. 7 is the natural nymph enlarged three times its natural size.

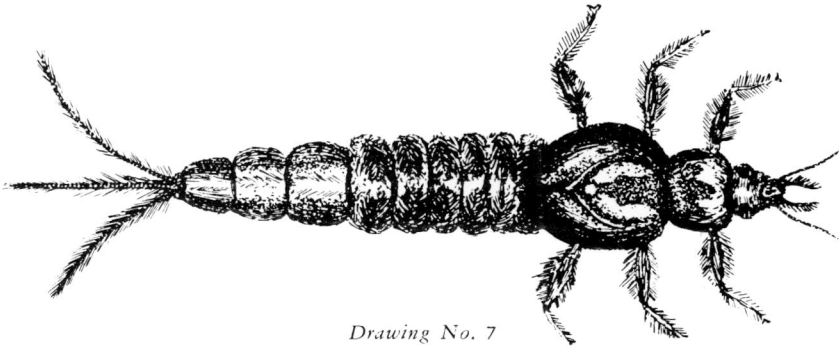

Drawing No. 7

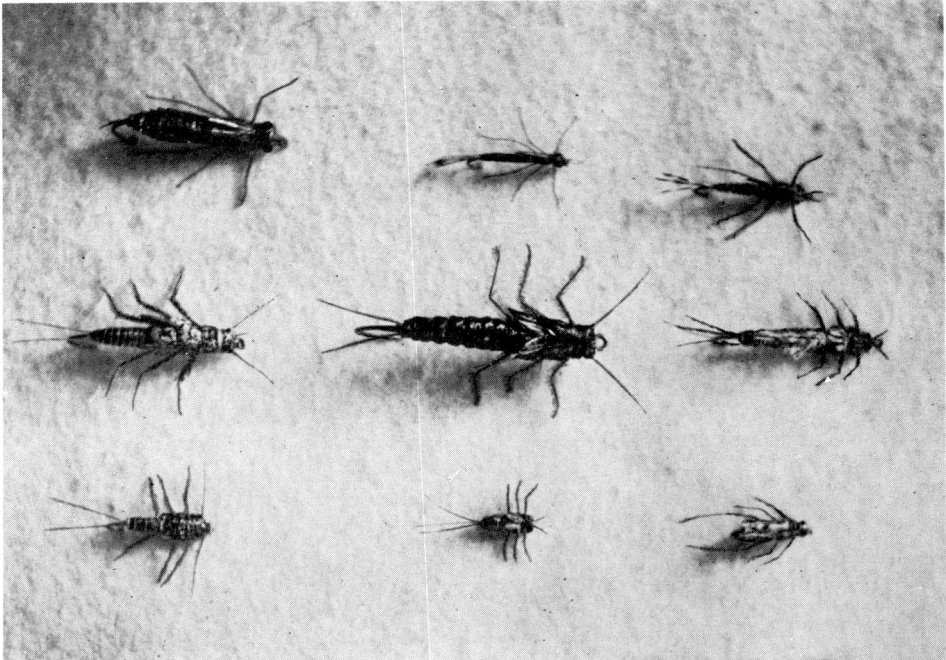

TYPICAL PLATE OF ARTIFICIAL NYMPHS.

BACK-SWIMMERS

Order: *Hemiptera*   Family: *NotonEctidae*

Drawing No. 1

Drawing No. 2

Drawing No. 3

Drawing No. 4

Drawing No. 5

Drawing No. 6

I was fishing in Ontario, Canada and my guide told me about a little lake he had stocked with brook trout about three years ago. He also said, "I would like you to try it out, Bill." The next morning we were on the lake shores and I was very much surprised to see and hear so many fish rising.

I couldn't get my tackle ready and into the canoe quick enough, but after I had cast many times, I knew the fish were very selective and were feeding on the surface; also below. I finally took three 15½ inch fish on a small badger popper and one on a white moth.

Around noon we pulled in for a little lunch, and while the guide was lighting the fire I opened the trout and found they were feeding on the nymph of the Back-Swimmer, which is Drawing No. 1. At this stage the legs are coiled closely to the body and look like easy prey for the hungry trout.

About two P. M. I noticed a nymph come to the surface as if he was rowing a boat. He took a look around, and down he went again. The next one I caught, and I got the most painful sting I have ever had, but I held on for I wanted him very much. They swim on their backs and are very strong and fast. At this stage, they are like Drawing No. 2.

When they get to the stage as shown in Drawing No. 3, they come to the surface and start to work, dry their wings, and take off (if they are lucky), for it is at this moment you hear the surface rises. This was a day I will never forget; I gained a little more knowledge about the things I adore.

Body: Orange and black.

Legs: Black or dark brown.

Thorax and Head: Black.

Wings: Can be well imitated with the English Woodcock stiffened with feather glazer.

MATERIALS FOR DRAWING No. 4 (ARTIFICAL)

Tail: Moose mane (short).

Body: Orange seal fur dubbing saturated with cement and made black at thorax and on the underside with black enamel.

Legs: Black trimmed hackle folded close to the body.

   On Drawings No. 5 and No. 6 make the legs of tan-brown trimmed hackle; all the other material is the same as No. 4.

Wings: Woodcock, stiffened with feather glazer or cement.

EPHEMERA GUTTULATA MAY FLY NYMPH

CLASSIFICATION:

Order: *Ephemeroptera*   Genus: *Ephemera*
Family: *Ephemeridae*   Species: *guttulata*

KNOWN AS THE GREEN DRAKE NYMPH

Description: Length of nymph including tails, one inch long.

Tails: Cream.

Body and Thorax: Light cream.

Legs: Cream.

Gills: White.

MATERIALS FOR THE ARTIFICIAL

Hook: 3X No. 12.

Tails: Three cream Emu plumes.

Antennae: Cream hackle fibres.

Body: Creamy-white raffia, with six pairs of white Emu plume gills.

Legs: Trimmed cream hackle stems.

Wing Cases: Swan wing quill fibres from the outer feather, tinted cream.

[203]

TYING THE CADDIS WORM (*TRICHOPTERA*)

The Caddis worm I am about to tie came from Michigan in 1949. Being a builder and mason myself, I can most certainly appreciate the wonderful work these little insects perform to construct, with small stones, wood and many assorted materials, the Caddis case. It is also lined with silk, which is a protection for the tender body of the worm. I have had these cases in alcohol for over a year and the stones and wood are just as secure as they were when I first got them.

The size of the worm is ⅞ of an inch in length and 5/32 of an inch in diameter. The body is light tan and has thirteen sections. The head is dark grey. The body has a few hairs at each section, which are about the same color as the body. The legs are dark brown; are short and resemble claws.

To tie the Caddis worm, place a No. 10 3x hook in the vise and coat it with liquid cement; wind the tying silk to the bend and back to a small distance from the eye; do not go to the eye or you will not be able to attach the leader when the worm is finished. Now double a piece of 6 lb. test nylon and tie it in so that it projects ¼ of an inch; wind the tying silk over the double nylon to the bend of the hook and keep the nylon on top of the hook; cut off the surplus ends of the nylon and tying silk and the worm will be the same as Drawing No. 1.

The next step is to wrap the body with fine soft copper wire and form the body to the proper thickness with fine yellow floss. Now tie in a fine piece of tan raffia that has been soaked, and tie in a small soft light ginger hackle that has been cut or stripped on one side of its fibres (Drawing No. 2). Wind the raffia and palmer the hackle to the first pair of legs (Drawing No. 3). Tie in three pairs of dark brown trimmed hackle legs, winding the tan raffia in between each pair; tie off and cut off the surplus raffia. Form the head with tying silk and paint it with dark grey enamel. The body segment markings are made with brown enamel. Drawing No. 4 is the finished worm.

You can make this worm on a 4x hook, but I think the elongated front portion makes it look more like the natural worm. There are many small sizes in the Caddis worms; some are only ¼ of an inch long.

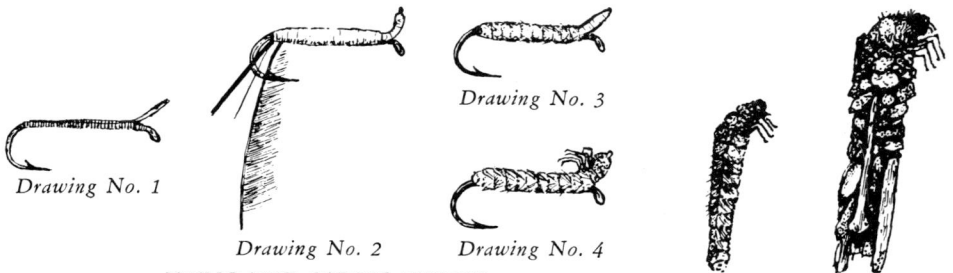

Drawing No. 3

Drawing No. 1

Drawing No. 2   Drawing No. 4
TYING THE CADDIS NYMPH.

THE CADDIS NYMPH
AND CASE.

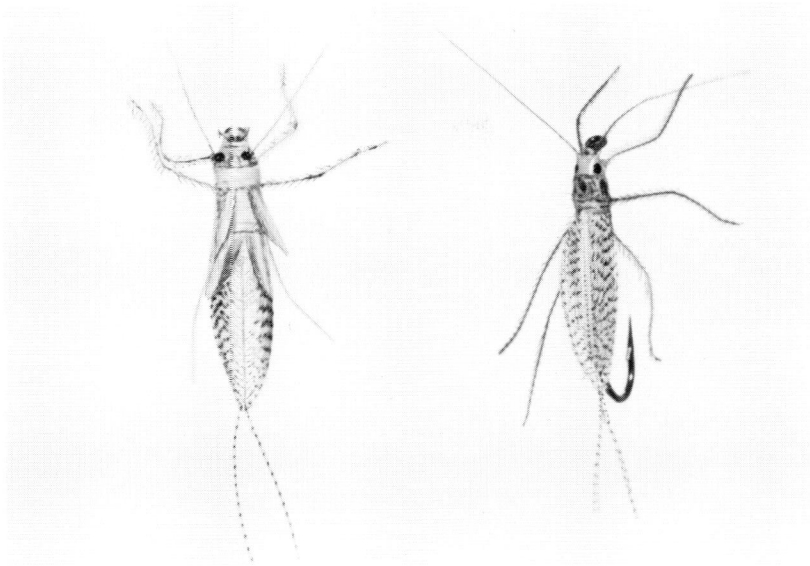

PLATE LIV. STONE FLY NYMPH WITH REVERSE HACKLE.

REVERSE WING STONE FLY NYMPH AND ADULT

Stone Fly nymph made to flutter on the surface to represent the nymph changing to an adult.

The body is a Wood Duck body feather with the fibres pulled forward; leave four fibres on the body for the tail and cement them in pairs. The front portion is described in the Stone Fly nymph instructions. Use a short shank hook; this will assist it to float.

STONE FLY ADULT

Wing and tail made of Wood Duck breast feather with fibres pulled in reverse. (See Stone Fly instructions.) This wing is strong and is a good representation of double wings at rest.

HELLGRAMMITE (CORYDALUS)

(*See Plate LV*)

The length of the Blade's Hellgrammite is two inches, but I have found out trout and bass will take them almost any size.

Place the hook in the vise; coat it with liquid cement and wrap it with tying thread. The tails, horns and gills are Turkey quill fibres dyed dark brown. Squeeze Household Duco Cement out of the tube on to the hook and wind the nylon thread through it as it drips; apply a good amount of cement, then allow it to set before applying more coats; mould the body to the shape and size; allow it to set, then file it smooth.

The body is raffia dyed a reddish brown; I make this a little over one sixteenth of an inch wide and keep it damp while tying. Before putting on the raffia, I file an indentation at the tail to start the tying thread, then file indentations at the three pairs of leg positions; then mark the gill positions in ink. Now tie in the raffia and wind the first segment; put a little cement on the body and tie in the first two gills with the tying thread; then make the second segment with the raffia; continue this until you reach the first pair of legs which are reddish-brown trimmed hackle stems.

My latest method for tying on the legs is to make one trimmed hackle stem form two legs on one side of the body, as shown in drawing. To do this, place the stem on an angle and take three turns over it; now bend the stem horizontal, taking a few turns over it until you reach the position of the next leg; bend the stem down to a vertical position and take a few turns of thread over and in front of it. Repeat this on the opposite side of the Hellgrammite and you will have completed the four legs. I tie on the four legs at the same time. My previous method was to go over the body, tying on the near-side and off-side legs at the same time. The two front legs can be tied on with two separate pieces of trimmed hackle or one going under or over the body.

PLATE LV. TOP: BACK AND UNDERSIDE OF HELLGRAMMITE, CORYDALUS. AT THE RIGHT IS THE BLADES IMITATION. BOTTOM: THE DOBSON FLY.

PLATE LVI. DRAGON FLY NYMPHS.

The Dragon Fly Nymphs marked Nos. 1, 2, 3 and 5 came from Yellowstone Park location;
No. 4 and No. 6 came from New York State. This plate clearly shows there are many different
sizes and shapes of this nymph.

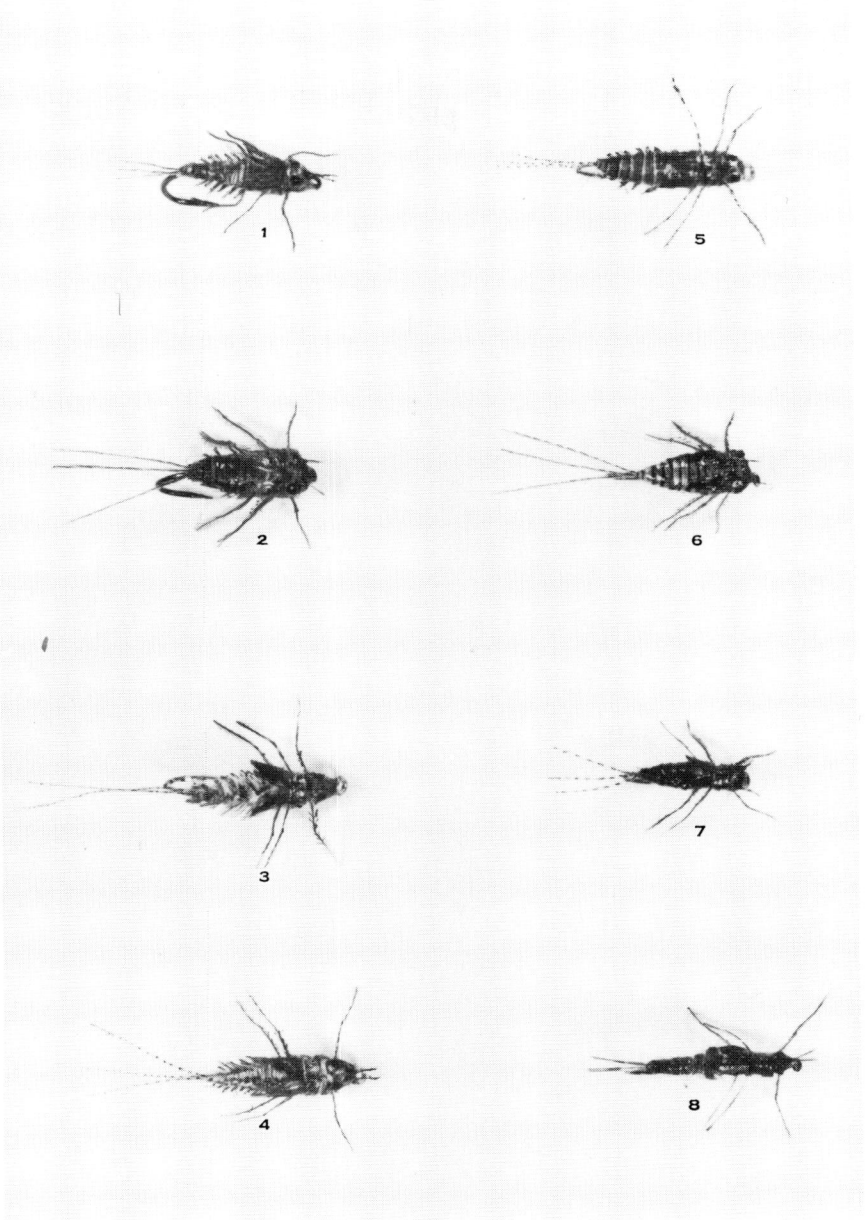

PLATE LVII. IMITATION MAY FLY OR DRAKE NYMPHS.

[209]

BLADES' EPHEMERELLA CORNUTA
(See Plate LVII, No. 1)

CLASSIFICATION:

Order: *Ephemeroptera*
Family: *Ephemerellidae*

Genus: *Ephemerella*
Species: *cornuta* (Morgan)

DESCRIPTION OF THE LIVE NYMPH

Tails: Three, pale tan.
Body: Tan.
Wing cases: Tan.
Gills: Pale grey.
Legs: Pale tan.

MATERIAL FOR THE ARTIFICIAL

Tails: Three pale Wood Duck fibres or hackle stems. Length, 1/4″.
Body: Under-body plastic, covered with pale tan raffia. Length, 5/16″.
Wing cases: Quills from turkey wing outer feather, dyed tan.
Gills: Pale grey Emu fibres.
Legs: Pale tan hackle stems.
Collected in New York.

BLADES' STENONEMA FUSCUM
(See Plate LVII, No. 2)

CLASSIFICATION:

Order: *Ephemeroptera*
Family: *Heptageniidae*

Genus: *Stenonema*
Species: *fuscum* (Clemons)

DESCRIPTION OF THE LIVE NYMPH

Tails: Three, dark ginger.
Body: Light tan; markings, reddish brown.
Gills: Light grey.
Wing Cases: Dark brown, almost black.
Legs: Tan, brown mottled.
Eyes: Blue-grey.

MATERIAL FOR THE ARTIFICIAL

Tails: Three dark-ginger, trimmed hackle stems. Length, 1/2″.
Body: Natural raffia; ribbings reddish brown raffia. Markings, tan enamel; under-body moulded plastic. Length, 1/2 to 5/8″.
Gills: Light grey Emu quill.
Legs: Trimmed ginger hackle stems; markings, brown enamel.
Collected in New York.

BLADES' EPEORUS VITREA
(See Plate LVII, No. 3)

CLASSIFICATION:
>   Order: *Ephemeroptera*
>   Family: *Heptageniidae*

>   Genus: *Epeorus*
>   Species: *vitrea* (Walker)

DESCRIPTION OF THE LIVE NYMPH
Tails: Two, greyish tan.
Body: Tan with brown markings.
Wing cases: Tan.
Gills: Pale tan.
Legs: Tan, prominent brown markings.

MATERIAL FOR THE ARTIFICIAL
Tails: Two fibres of Wood Duck. Length, ½".
Body: Under-body, plastic covered with raffia; markings, brown enamel. Length, ½".
Wing cases: Quills from turkey wing outer feather, dyed smoky tan.
Gills: Pale tan quill.
Legs: Wood Duck fibres or hackle stems.
Collected in New York.

BLADES' STENONEMA FRONTALE
(See Plate LVII, No. 4)

CLASSIFICATION:
>   Order: *Ephemeroptera*
>   Family: *Heptageniidae*

>   Genus: *Stenonema*
>   Species: *frontale* (Burks)

DESCRIPTION OF THE LIVE NYMPH
Tails: Three, yellowish pale green.
Body: Pale greyish tan; markings, pale sepia.
Wing cases: Greyish tan.
Gills: Grey.
Legs: Greyish tan cast.

MATERIAL FOR THE ARTIFICIAL
Tails: Three pale Wood Duck fibres dyed pale green. Length, ½".
Body: Under-body, plastic, covered with greyish-tan raffia; markings, pale sepia enamel. Length, 7/16".
Wing cases: Quills from turkey wing outer feather, dyed greyish tan.
Gills: Greyish tan hackle stems.
Collected in New York.

BLADES' HEPTAGENIA DIABASIA
(See Plate LVII, No. 5)

CLASSIFICATION:

Order: *Ephemeroptera*
Family: *Heptageniidae*

Genus: *Heptagenia*
Species: *diabasia* (Burks)

DESCRIPTION OF THE LIVE NYMPH
Tails: Three, tan; markings, dark brown.
Body: Light brown; segments cream.
Wing cases: Brown.
Gills: Grey.
Legs: Cream with grey-brown markings.

MATERIAL FOR THE ARTIFICIAL
Tails: Three Wood Duck fibres. Length, $\frac{3}{8}''$.
Body: Under-body, plastic, covered with light brown raffia; segment markings, cream silk or Emu quills. Length, $\frac{9}{16}''$.
Wing cases: Quills from turkey wing outer feather dyed brown.
Gills: Grey Emu quills.
Legs: Dirty cream; markings, grey, brown, cream-and-grey variant hackle stems.
Collected in New York.

BLADES' STENONEMA VICARIUM
(See Plate LVII, No. 6)

CLASSIFICATION:

Order: *Ephemeroptera*
Family: *Heptageniidae*

Genus: *Stenonema*
Species: *vicarium* (Walker)

DESCRIPTION OF THE LIVE NYMPH
Tails: Three, brown.
Body: Tan; markings, reddish brown.
Wing cases: Dark brown almost black.
Legs: Tan, brown markings.

MATERIAL FOR THE ARTIFICIAL
Tails: Three brown trimmed hackle stems. Length, $\frac{5}{8}''$.
Body: Under-body plastic, covered with tan raffia; markings, reddish-brown enamel. Length, $\frac{3}{8}$ to $\frac{1}{2}''$.
Wing cases: Quills from turkey wing outer feather dyed dark brown almost black.
Legs: Trimmed brown hackle stems, banded with darker brown enamel.
Collected in New York.

BLADES' EPHEMERELLA ROTUNDA
(See Plate LVII, No. 7)

CLASSIFICATION:

Order: *Ephemeroptera*
Family: *Ephemerellidae*

Genus: *Ephemerella*
Species: *rotunda* (Morgon)

DESCRIPTION OF THE LIVE NYMPH

Tails: Three, brown; markings, black.
Body: Dirty tan, brown markings.
Wing cases: Dark brown.
Legs: Tan, brown markings.

MATERIAL FOR THE ARTIFICIAL

Tails: Three dark Wood Duck fibres. Length, ³⁄₁₆″.
Body: Dirty tan raffia, brown enamel markings. Length, ⅜″.
Wing cases: Quills from the turkey wing outer feather dyed brown.
Legs: Tan-and-brown variant trimmed hackle stems.

Collected in New York.

BLADES' AMELETUS SP
(See Plate LVII, No. 8)

CLASSIFICATION:

Order: *Ephemeroptera*
Family: *Baetidae*

Genus: *Ameletus*
Species: *sp*

DESCRIPTION OF THE LIVE NYMPH

Tails: Three, grey and darker grey on tips.
Body: Light tan; markings, light brown, segment markings, grey, almost white.
Wing cases: Black.
Gills: Dirty white.
Legs: Grey mottled with tan.

MATERIAL FOR THE ARTIFICIAL

Tails: Three, trimmed badger hackle stems. Length, ¼″.
Body: Light tan raffia; markings, light tan enamel; segment markings, white tying silk. Length, ½″.
Gills: Trimmed Emu quills, six on each side.
Wing cases: Quills from turkey wing outer feather dyed black.
Legs: Trimmed dirty white hackle stems, mottled with tan enamel.

Collected in New York.

PLATE LVIII. ARTIFICIAL MAY FLY NYMPHS AND WATER BOATMAN (No. 6).

BLADES' STENONEMA ITHICA
(See Plate LVIII, No. 1)

CLASSIFICATION:

Order: *Ephemeroptera*
Family: *Heptageniidae*

Genus: *Stenonema*
Species: *ithica*

DESCRIPTION OF THE LIVE NYMPH

Tails: Tan, mottled with brown.
Body: Reddish tan, with brown segment markings.
Wing cases: Dark brown.
Legs: Tan.

MATERIAL FOR THE ARTIFICIAL

Tails: Three Wood Duck fibres or tan hackle fibres. Length, ½".
Body: Under-body, plastic, covered with reddish tan raffia; markings, brown enamel. Length, ⅜".
Wing cases: Quills from turkey wing outer feather, dyed dark brown.
Legs: Tan hackle stems, trimmed.
Collected in New York.

BLADES' SIPHLONURUS QUEBECENSIS
(See Plate LVIII, No. 2)

CLASSIFICATION:

Order: *Ephemeroptera*
Family: *Baetidae*

Genus: *Siphlonurus*
Species: *quebecensis*

DESCRIPTION OF THE LIVE NYMPH

Tails: Three, grey and tan cast.
Body: Brownish grey.
Wing cases: Brown.
Legs: Greyish brown.
Gills: Brown.

MATERIAL FOR THE ARTIFICIAL

Tails: Three tan-and-grey variant hackles with dark grey markings. Cut fibres off the outside edges of the two outside hackles. Length, ⅜".
Body: Under-body, plastic, covered with brownish grey raffia; brown enamel segment markings. Length, ⁷⁄₁₆".
Wing cases: Brown quill or feather.
Gills: Brown quill.
Legs: Trimmed grey-and-brown variant hackles.
Collected in New York.

BLADES' EPHORON LEUKON
(See Plate LVIII, No. 3)

CLASSIFICATION:

Order: *Ephemeroptera*
Family: *Ephemeridae*

Genus: *Ephoron*
Species: *leukon* (Will)

DESCRIPTION OF THE LIVE NYMPH

Tails: Grey.
Body: Cream.
Gills: Grey.
Wing cases: Dark brown.
Legs: Light grey, hairy.

MATERIAL FOR THE ARTIFICIAL

Tails: Three trimmed light grey hackle stems. Length, ⅜".
Body: Natural raffia, light color. Length, ½".
Gills: Light grey marabou tips, two on each gill, which are six pairs. (These can be omitted).
Wing cases: Dark brown quills.
Legs: Grey hackle stems, trimmed.
Eyes: Black enamel.
Collected in New York.

BLADES' STENONEMA NEPOTELLUM
(See Plate LVIII, No. 4)

CLASSIFICATION:

Order: *Ephemeroptera*
Family: *Heptageniidae*

Genus: *Stenonema*
Species: *nepotellum* (McD)

DESCRIPTION OF THE LIVE NYMPH

Tails: Three, pale tan.
Body: Pale tan; markings, sepia brown.
Wing cases: Light brown.
Legs: Pale tan.

MATERIAL FOR THE ARTIFICIAL

Tails: Three pale tan hackle stems. Length, ¼".
Body: Pale tan or natural raffia; under body, plastic. Length, ⁷⁄₁₆".
Wing cases: Light brown quills from turkey wing outer feather.
Legs: Pale tan trimmed hackle stems.
Collected in New York.

BLADES' EPHEMERELLA SP
(See Plate LVIII, No. 5)

CLASSIFICATION:

Order: *Ephemeroptera*
Family: *Ephemerellidae*

Genus: *Ephemerella*
Species: *sp*

DESCRIPTION OF THE LIVE NYMPH

Tails: Three, tan.
Body: Amber; segment markings, brown.
Wing cases: Amber.
Gills: Tannish grey.
Legs: Tan; markings, brown.

MATERIAL FOR THE ARTIFICIAL

Tails: Three pale Wood Duck fibres. Length, ⅜".
Body: Raffia dyed amber; ribbing, brown raffia or horse hair. Length, ⁷⁄₁₆".
Gills: Tan-grey quill.
Wing cases: Quills from turkey wing outer feather dyed black.
Legs: Trimmed tan hackle stems, mottled with tan enamel.
Collected in New York.

BLADES' WATER BOATMAN
(See Plate LVIII, No. 6)

CLASSIFICATION:

Order: *Hemiptera*
Family: *Corixidae*

Genus: *Hesperocorixa*
Species: *interupta* (Say)
Female

DESCRIPTION OF THE INSECT

Body: Golden-brownish tan; flat on the underside. Segment markings not prominent.
Wings: One pair is transparent with a pale tan cast. The top pair is mottled with dark brown grey markings.
Thorax and head: Brown, almost black.

MATERIAL FOR THE ARTIFICIAL

Body: Under-body; plastic, covered with golden-brownish tan raffia; ribbing, brown raffia or horse hair.
Wings: English Woodcock small wing feathers, saturated with liquid cement.
Legs: Brownish tan hackle stems; rear legs, long and hairy.
Collected in New York.

BLADES' PARALEPTOPHLEBIA
(See Plate LVIII, No. 7)

CLASSIFICATION:

Order: *Ephemeroptera*
Family: *Leptophlebiidae*

Genus: *Paraleptophlebia*
Species: *sp*

DESCRIPTION OF THE LIVE NYMPH
Tails: Three; pale tan.
Body: Reddish tan.
Wing cases: Black.
Legs: Pale tan.

MATERIAL FOR THE ARTIFICIAL
Tails: Three pale tan hackle stems. Length, ³⁄₁₆″.
Body: Reddish tan raffia. Ribbing; pale grey peacock quill.
Wing cases: Black feather or quill from turkey wing outer feather.
Legs: Pale tan hackle stems.
Collected in New York.

BLADES' ISONYCHIA RUFA
(See Plate LVIII, No. 8)

CLASSIFICATION:

Order: *Ephemeroptera*
Family: *Baetidae*

Genus: *Isonychia*
Species: *rufa* (McDunnough)

DESCRIPTION OF THE LIVE NYMPH
Tails: Three; grey.
Body: Amber; markings, reddish brown.
Wing cases: Black.
Legs: Mottled grey and black.
Eyes: Black.

MATERIAL FOR THE ARTIFICIAL
Tails: Three, trimmed grey hackle stems. Length, ½″
Body: Under-body moulded plastic. Covered with amber colored raffia. Markings, brown horse hair. Length, ⁹⁄₁₆″.
Wing cases: Black quill, or feather.
Legs: Trimmed hackle stems, grey-black-and-brown variant, mottled.
Eyes: Black.
Collected in New York.

RUBBER LEGGED NYMPHS

The nymphs shown in Plate LIX have been made with material to create action in the water, which I claim is very essential.

Nos. 1, 2 and 3 are Stone Fly Nymphs tied with rubber legs. No. 3 has brown tying silk knotted to form the joints, which can be omitted. No. 2 has a few turns of tan hen hackle for the front legs; this also increases the action.

Nos. 4, 5, and 6 are Hellgrammites; (Prob. Nigronia, sp). The front

PLATE LIX. RUBBER LEGGED NYMPHS.

legs on Nos. 4 and 5 are rubber; on No. 6 the legs are trimmed hackle stems. The gills are Turkey wing strands dyed brown; all this material gives very good action.

No. 7 is the Damsel Fly Nymph, also made with rubber legs. Nos. 8 and 9 are small Dragon Fly Nymphs made with rubber legs and hen hackle to increase the action. These are my favorites and will take their share of fish anywhere.

BLADES' EPHEMERA SIMULANS
(See Plate LX)

CLASSIFICATION:

Order: *Ephemeroptera*   Genus: *Ephemera*
Family: *Ephemeridae*   Species: *simulans* (Walker)

DESCRIPTION OF THE LIVE NYMPH
Tails: Three, dark brown.
Body: Tan.
Wing cases: Dark brown, nearly black.
Gills: Grey, dyed purple, (pale).
Legs: Brownish ginger.

MATERIAL FOR THE ARTIFICIAL
Tails: Three dark brown trimmed hackle stems. Length, ⅜".
Body: Tan raffia over plastic under-body; brown enamel on top of body. Length, ⅝".
Wing cases: Quills from Turkey wing outer feather dyed dark brown, almost black.
Gills: Grey Emu fibres dyed purple, (pale).
Legs· Brownish ginger trimmed hackle stems.
Read instructions for making the Hexagenia nymph as they are made very much alike.

PLATE LX. LEFT, LARGE ARTIFICIAL SIMULANS; CENTER, NATURAL SIMULANS NYMPH; AND RIGHT, TWO ARTIFICIAL NYMPHS.

PLATE LXI. A GROUP OF NYMPHS OF VARIOUS STYLE TIES.

TYING THE BLADES' FRESH WATER SHRIMP

CLASSIFICATION:

Order: *Amphipod*   Genus: *Gammarus*

Family: *Gammaridae*   Species: *sp*

Coat the hook with cement and wrap it with white nylon thread; then wrap it with fine copper wire of the weight you desire. Now tie in three or four strands of white Swan or Goose quill fibres. Drawing No. 1.

Now wrap the fibres round the hook to form the body; continue tying in the legs and wrapping the ends of fibres round the hook. See Drawing No. 2.

Take the tying thread to the front and form the head; continue tying in legs until you reach the centre, then tie off the thread. Give the Shrimp several coats of liquid cement. See Drawing No. 3.

This is one of the most reliable artificial Shrimps I have used for Rainbow Trout.

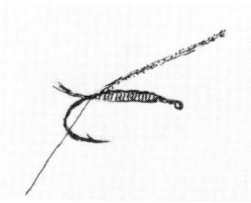  

Drawing No. 1   *Drawing No. 2*   *Drawing No. 3*

PLATE LXII. THE FRESH WATER SHRIMP. TWO NATURALS AND AN ARTIFICIAL.

[222]

CRAYFISH

Probably is *Orconestes Virilis* (Hagen)

This is an immature female that makes naming the species questionable. I removed three of these from the stomach of a fourteen-inch Brook Trout.

To make the crayfish, coat the hook with cement and wrap it with white nylon thread; now tie on the antennae, which are pale ginger hackle stems; also tie on the tail, which is pale ginger deer tail hair. If you desire the artificial to be weighted, wrap the hook with copper wire. I prefer to use a hump shank hook on my plastic bodies.

Now pour the Duco household cement on the hook out of the tube and wrap the nylon thread through it; this stops the cement from falling off the hook and speeds up the setting. Make the body to the location of the two claws and allow it to set; make the claws of pale ginger deer tail hairs and pour the cement over them and finish the body.

To put on the legs, put a little cement on the body and lay the rubber strands or soft hackle stems on the cement; allow it to set; then give it another coat. An easy way to finish this is to coat it with cream enamel

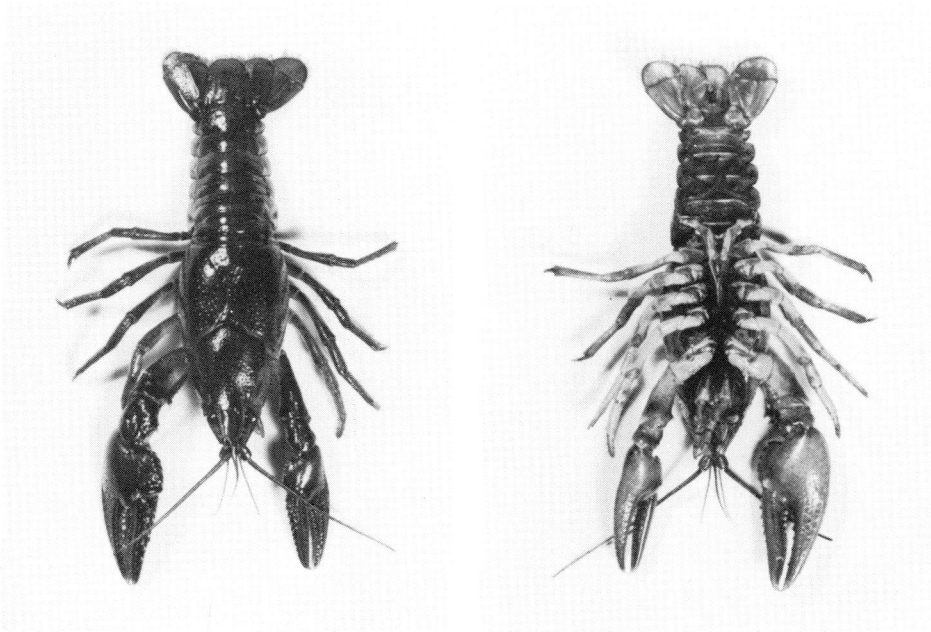

Photo by Wilfred Blades

PLATE LXIII. BACK AND UNDERPART OF CRAYFISH.

[223]

and make the markings with brown enamel. I also wrap the body up to and in between the legs with cream raffia and rib the tail portion with a pale brown ribbing of quill, horse hair or thread. Coat the body with two coats of liquid cement. Having a real crayfish to copy from will be a great help in construction.

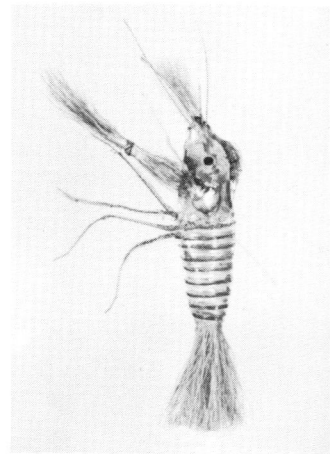

PLATE LXIV.   A NATURAL CRAYFISH AND THREE IMITATIONS.

ARTIFICIAL MINNOWS

(See Plate LXV)

Minnow No. 1: The Ghost Shiner. Also No. 5.

Minnow No. 2: The Black-Nosed Dace. Also No. 4.

Minnow No. 3: The Cayuga Minnow.

To make the minnows, coat the hook with liquid cement and wrap it with white nylon thread. If you desire them to be weighted, wrap the hook with copper or lead wire; weighting them too much will make them hard to cast.

Take two white duck breast feathers; place them back to back and insert them in liquid cement; take them out and allow the cement to set a little, then stroke them toward the tip, taking out the surplus cement, cut them to shape as shown, and tie them on the hook. Pour the Duco cement from the tube on the hook and wind the nylon thread through it as it is setting; this prevents the cement from falling off the hook and speeds up the setting.

After the body is filed to shape, give it two coats of white enamel. Paint the scales and head with a fine artist's camel-hair brush to represent the minnow you are making. A scale finish transfer can also be used. Professional tyers use a scale net and spray gun.

Cut the fins from a white hackle feather; pick one with a flexible centre stem; cut the fibres off on the underside and cut them off on the top side, leaving the shaped fins and also a piece of centre stem on each end about three-sixteenths of an inch; now put a little liquid cement on the underside of the fins and on the minnow pressing them on firmly. Allow the enamel to set before giving the minnow the final coats of liquid cement. This is the way I finished the Cayuga Minnow and the Ghost Shiner. No. 1 and No. 3.

No. 3, the Black-Nosed Dace body is wrapped with 2x limp nylon. I cut or file a slot all around the hook at the tail and at the back of the eye; this prevents the nylon from slipping; put a little cement in the slot at the tail and hold the end of the nylon at the underside of the body and take about four turns over it. Take the fins that you have prepared and wrap the nylon over the end until you have reached the first fin; now hang the hackle pliers on the hackle stem so that you can wrap the body nylon on to the length of the fin; lift the hackle up and wrap over the stem and the fin will be in place. The fins on top and bottom are put on together. After the fins are in place continue wrapping the body to the front slot and tie off. Do not put a heavy coat of liquid cement on the first coat; it may affect the enamel body. If this method is troublesome, put the fins on with cement and make them long; also tie in two narrow badger hackles to form the black stripe on the body of the Black-Nosed Dace and Cayuga Minnow. This will create action which I think is needed on these minnows.

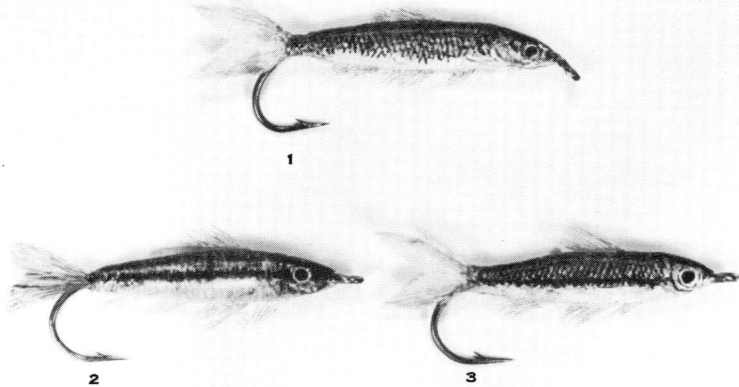

PLATE LXV. ARTIFICIAL MINNOWS.

PLATE LXVI. STREAMER FLIES UTILIZING MAY FLY PATTERNS.

ISONYCHIA MAY FLIES TIED AS WET STREAMERS

Use any of my material lists of my May Flies to make these streamers. These wings are Wood Duck; use small streamer or neck hackles where I call for hackle tips.

SELECTED NYMPH PATTERNS

(See Plate LXVII. Read top to bottom, left to right.)

No. 1
BLADES' MAY FLY NYMPH
STENONEMA FUSCUM

Tails: Three trimmed brown hackle stems.

Body and Thorax: Tan raffia; ribbing brown raffia. Under body moulded plastic.

Wing cases: Two Turkey wing quill fibres dyed tan.

Legs and antennae: Trimmed brown hackle stems, legs marked with dark brown enamel.

No. 2 May Fly Nymph Hexagenia
(See text for details)

No. 3 Back Swimmer Nymph No. 1
(See text for details)

No. 4
BLADES HACKLE NYMPH

Tail: Brown hackle fibres.

Body: Yellow and brown hackle clipped to shape; thorax, orange hackle clipped to shape; crown, grey goose quill fibres.

Hackle: Blue dun on throat only.

No. 5   CADDIS NYMPH

Body: Light grey wool; silver tinsel.

Legs: Six white fibres from goose wing outer feather, sharpened on both ends.

No. 6   CARROT NYMPH

Tail: Wood Duck or Mallard.

Body and thorax: Orange seal fur or wool saturated and flattened.

Ribbing: Gold tinsel.

Crown: Red floss (stiffen with cement).

Hackle: Badger hen, two or three turns.

No. 7   CADDIS GRUB NYMPH

Tail and horns: Peacock sword strands.

Body: Black and white chenille.

No. 8   DARK OLIVE NYMPH

Tail: Blue dun hackle fibres.

Body: Olive seal fur mixed with brown bear, heavy at the thorax.

Ribbing: Fine gold tinsel.

Hackle: Pale blue dun.

Crown: Purple floss.

No. 9   DARK MOSSBACK
(Dan Bailey)

Tail: Feelers, and antennae are from the Turkey wing feather, dyed brown.

Body: Pale yellow floss under body, over this is a woven horsehair body with brown and green on top and brown and yellow on the underside.

No. 10   Large Stone Fly Nymph
(See text for details)

No. 11   May Fly Nymph
Ephemera guttalata
(See text for details)

No. 12   Back Swimmer Nymph No. 2
(See text for details)

No. 13
DRIFTING MAY FLY NYMPH

Tail: Pheasant tail fibres.

Body: Pale yellow floss; ribbing, silver tinsel.

Hackle: Olive hen.

No. 14   GREEN DRAKE
(C. M. Wetzel)

Tail: Honey dun, very small tips.

Body: White fur, picked out for legs.

Wing cases: Jungle Cock.

Hackle: Pale honey dun.

No. 15   HALF STONE NYMPH

Body: Primrose silk; ribbing, gold tinsel.

Thorax: Mole fur, grey.

Hackle: Blue dun hen, two or three turns.

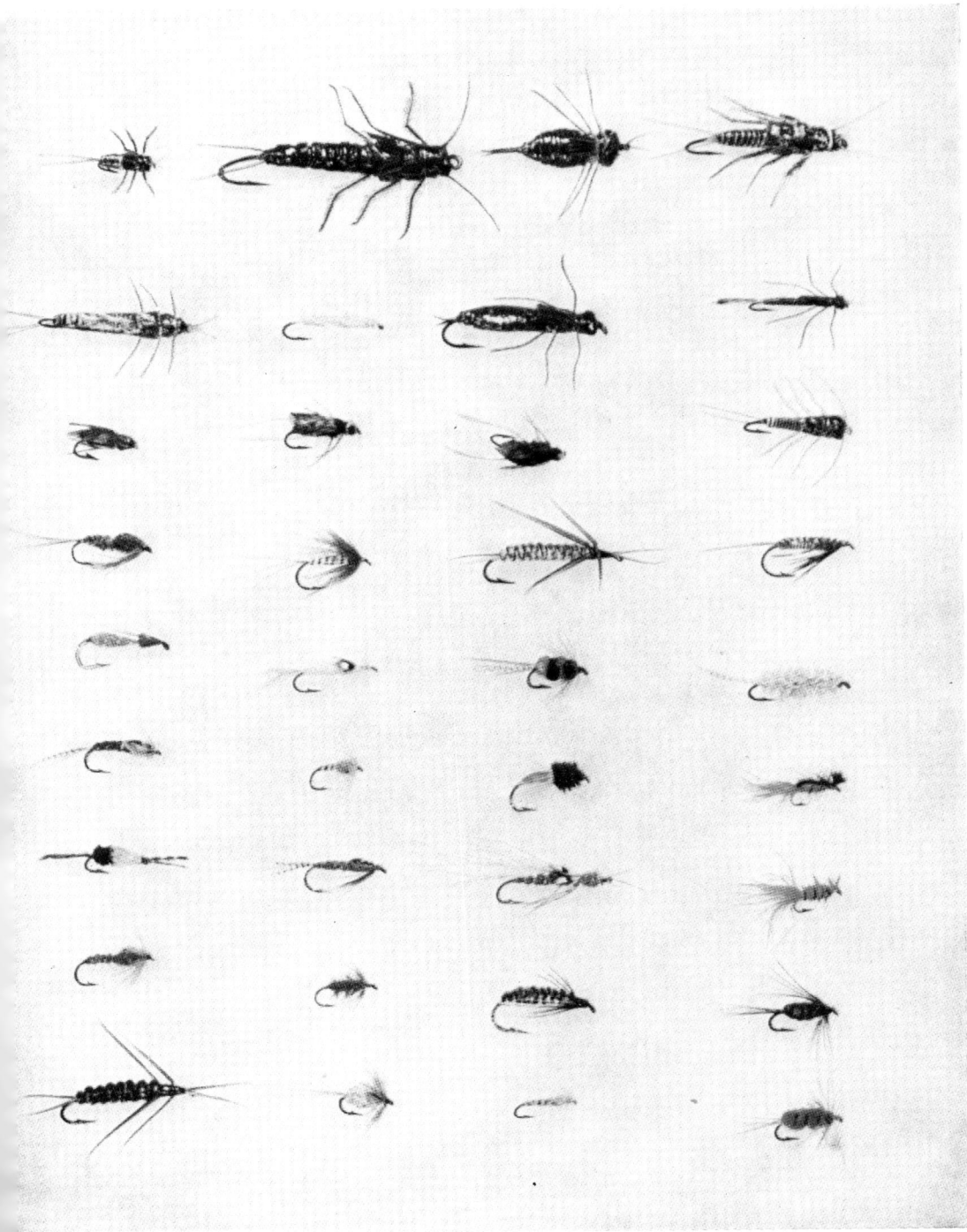

PLATE LXVII. NYMPHS.
(See pages 228, 230 and 231 for descriptions)

No. 16
HENDRICKSON NYMPH
(Art Flick)
Tail: Mandarin flank feather.
Body: Fur dubbing a greyish brown shade, made from grey fox belly fur, beaver, and claret seal.
Ribbing: Fine gold wire.
Wing case: Blue heron wing section.
Legs: Partridge hackle.

No. 17   IRON BLUE NYMPH
Tail: Soft white hackle fibres tied short.
Body: Mole fur spun on crimson silk, expose a few turns of silk at the tail.
Hackle: Two or three turns of blue dun hen, or Jackdaw throat hackle, short.

No. 18   IRRESISTIBLE
Tail: Brown deer tail.
Body: Grey deer body hair.
Hackle: Soft grizzly.

No. 19 DRAGON FLY NYMPH
(See text for details)

No. 20 DRAGON FLY NYMPH
      Nasiaesehna
(See text for details)

No. 21 BACK SWIMMER No. 3
      Ready for flight
(See text for details)

No. 22   LIGHT MOSSBACK
        (Dan Bailey)
Tail: Feelers and antennae are from the turkey wing feather, dyed brown.
Body: Cream floss under body, over this is a woven horsehair body with brown and pale green on top and white on the underside.

No. 23 MCGINTY NYMPH
Tail: Mallard and red hackle fibres.
Body: Yellow and black chenille.
Hackle: Brown.

No. 24   MIKE
Body: Yellow floss.
Legs: White polar bear.
Thorax: Peacock herl.

No. 25
MIDGET BUCKTAIL NYMPH
Tail: Antennae and throat hackle; fibres from the Partridge body feather, grey mottled, brown tipped.
Body: Brown mink fur dubbing; ribbing, Peacock quill.
Wings: Brown bucktail (about 15 hairs). Small Jungle Cock at thorax.

No. 26   MOSSY CREEPER
        (Dan Bailey)
Body: Cream floss under body, over this is a woven horsehair body with dark green on top and white on the underside.
Hackle: Badger hair.

No. 27   OLIVE NYMPH
Tail: Blue dun hackle fibres.
Body: Olive seal fur; ribbing, flat gold tinsel.
Thorax: Olive seal fur; crown, orange floss.
Hackle: Honey Badger.

No. 28 STONE FLY NYMPH
(See text for details)

No. 29   DAMSEL FLY NYMPH
(See text for details)

No. 30 SMALL STONE FLY NYMPH
(See text for details)

No. 31
STONE FLY CREEPER
(Art Flick)
Tail: Two strands from cock pheasant tail, half inch long.
Body: Large ginger cocks hackle stem.
Thorax: Seal fur dyed amber.
Wing case: Wide barred flank feather from Mandarin drake, tied flat extending full length of body.
Legs: Grouse hackle.

No. 32   STRAWMAN NYMPH
(Paul H. Young)

Tail: Barred grey Mallard.
Body: Grey deer body hair, clipped.
Ribbing: Yellow floss.

No. 33

YELLOW AND BLACK MARABOU
NYMPH

Tail: Yellow marabou.
Body: Yellow marabou over soft copper
wire, black marabou on back.
Ribbing: Soft maroon colored enameled
copper wire.

No. 34

YELLOW MARABOU NYMPH

Tail: Yellow marabou.
Ribbing: Soft maroon colored enameled
copper wire.
Body: Yellow marabou over copper wire.

No. 35

WEIGHTED ORANGE NYMPH

Tail and hackle: Black.
Body: Orange seal fur, saturated with
liquid cement and flattened.
Back: Black enamel.
Ribbing: Soft copper wire.

No. 36

WEIGHTED YELLOW NYMPH

Tail and hackle: Orange.
Body: Yellow chenille.
Ribbing: Dark enameled soft copper
wire.

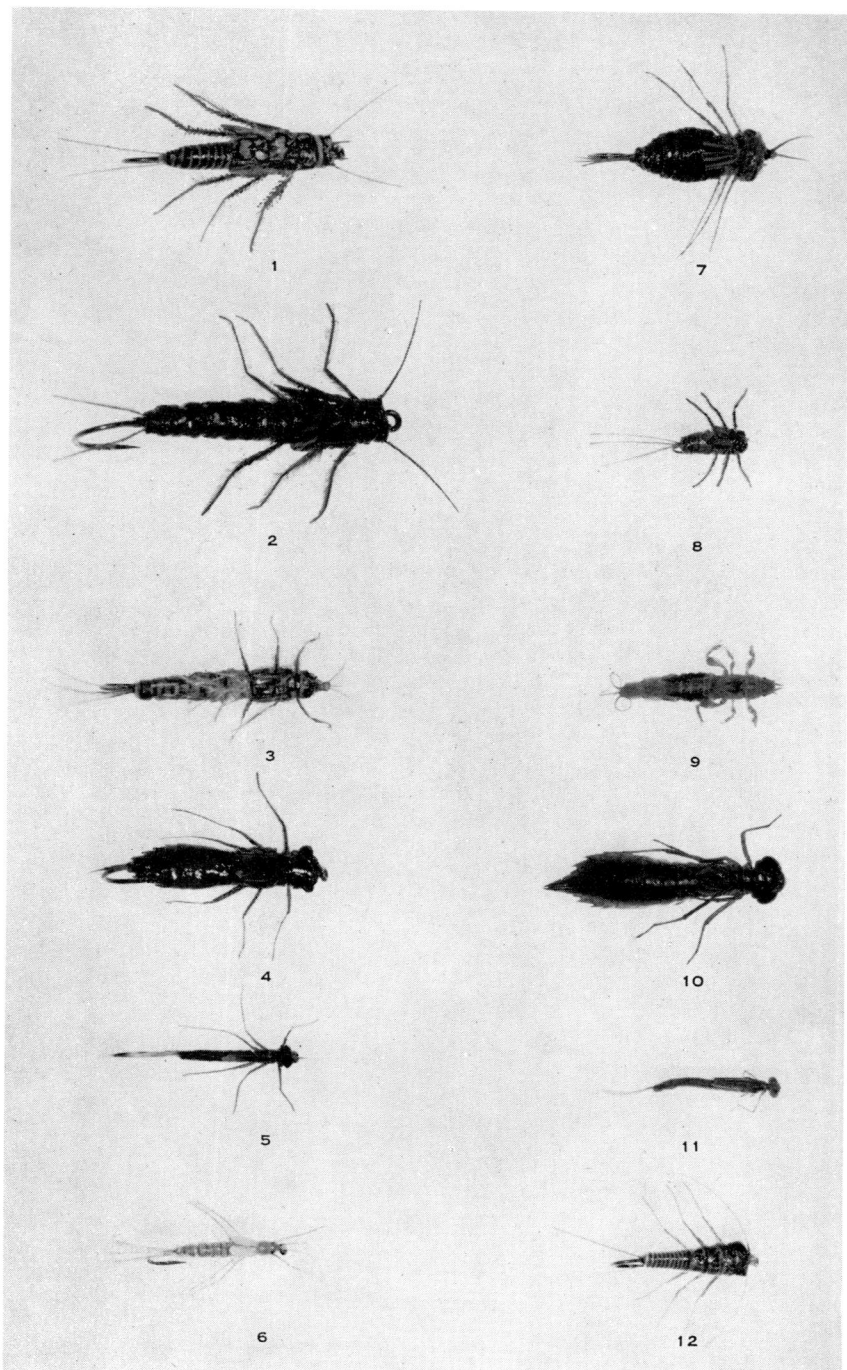

1

7

2

8

3

9

4

10

5

11

6

12

PLATE LXVIII. NATURAL AND ARTIFICIAL NYMPHS.

Left to right, top to bottom:

No. 1: Stone Fly Nymph.
No. 2: Large Stone Fly Nymph. Order: Plecoptera. Family: Pteronarcidae.
No. 3: May Fly Nymph, Hexagenia.
No. 4: Dragon Fly Nymph, Nasiaeschna.
No. 5: Damsel Fly Nymph.
No. 6: May Fly Nymph, Ephemera Guttulata.
No. 7: Dragon Fly Nymph.
No. 8: May Fly Nymph, Stenonema Fuscum.
No. 9: The Natural May Fly Nymph, Hexagenia.
No. 10: The Natural Dragon Fly Nymph.
No. 11: The Natural Damsel Fly Nymph.
No. 12: Small Stone Fly Nymph.

Chapter XIV

JIGS

HE jig is a single-purpose lure, designed to be fished near the bottom. It not only sinks rapidly, but can be retrieved and manipulated so that depth is maintained. With the single hook pointing upwards, the possibility of fouling is diminished. The hair has a tendency to open and close—"to breathe"—when the course through the water is broken by rod-tip action.

There are times when deep fishing is highly desirable, in fact, possibly the only hope of inducing the quarry to "take" and there are certain species, walleyes in particular, which have a decided preference for a lure which travels at what can be termed fish depth.

The jig is unwieldy to cast and the fishing of it is regarded by some as a desperation measure, but the fact remains, it has its place in the fish-taking scheme of things.

PLATE LXIX. JIGS FOR DEEP FISHING.

No. 1
Tail: Red marabou.
Body: Silver.
Wings: Red and white fine bucktail.
Hackle: White.

No. 2
Wings: Two red hackles with one white in the centre, on each wing.
Hackles: Red and white, tied on together.

No. 3
Wings: White marabou.
Hackle: Red hen hackle.

Nos. 4, 5 and 6
See instructions for the Stone Fly adult and nymph on page 205.

If your idea is catching fish for the frying pan, why not give them a good-looking last supper instead of enticing them to eat a nylon shaving brush.

Chapter XV

DRAGON FLIES

was fishing for rainbow trout in July of 1960 when I noticed a hatch of Dragon Flies that were mating and occasionally they would light on mossy weed patches. It was the first time I had seen trout rising to them. I did not have an artificial at this time but I have since made up two, one 2¼″ and one 1½″ body length. I prefer the smaller one; it is easier to cast and manipulate.

Even though dragon flies are seen far from water, they hatch from an aquatic nymph and deposit their eggs in quiet water; thus they are a common sight in, on and around lakes and bays and therefore are a part of the extensive menu of game fish, thus a factor in catching fish.

Photograph No. 3 is my imitation of the Dragon Fly.

The body is cork filed to shape with an emery board. Cut a slot in the cork and put it on a hump-shank hook with liquid cement. Paint the body with brown enamel; the segments are dark brown thread. Tie on six dark brown trimmed hackle stems for legs and use eight cream Badger hackles for the wings on the large fly and four on the smaller one. The large fly has yellow spots in each section; these can be omitted. These flies should take bass when they are surface feeding.

Photograph No. 1 is the natural Dragon Fly.

Photograph No. 2 is my imitation.

Body: Under-body; brown tying thread wrapped over double nylon to form the elongated body; cover with brown raffia.

Wings: Stiff Badger hackle fibres.

Legs: Trimmed brown hackle stems; markings and head, brown enamel.
The wings can also be made with four Chinchilla hackles.

PLATE LXX. DRAGON FLIES.

Chapter XVI

CORK BODIED BUGS

HE Badger Popper is one of my favorite poppers (not only for bass) which I prefer made on a No. 1 hook standard length, and also 3X long which has better hooking qualities inasmuch as the hook point is clear of the cork body. Making the cork too large and the hook too short is often the cause of not hooking the fish when they strike.

The cork bodies can be purchased in many different sizes and shapes at Herter's, Waseca, Minnesota. If you make your own, all you need is a razor blade, a box of emery boards and a small file. Be sure the body is sanded to a smooth finish, or you will never get a good enamel finish.

TYING THE BADGER POPPER

The bug on the accompanying drawings is made on a No. 6 model perfect hook. I have had success with this bug on brook trout.

Place the hump shank hook in the vise and coat it with liquid cement and wrap the portion that is inserted in the cork with tying silk (Drawing No. 1). Now cut a slot in the cork body with a razor blade or saw it with a very fine saw. This must fit tightly or the body will soon come loose.

Fill the slot and coat the hook with a good cement and press the hook in position.

Fill in the slot with cement or plastic wood and give the body two coats of liquid cement, or clear enamel, or wood sealer; allow it to dry. (Drawing No. 2.)

Now give the body two coats of enamel and one of clear enamel, if you want a good job.

  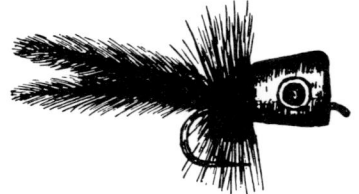

| *Drawing No. 1* | *Drawing No. 2* | *Drawing No. 3* |

When applying the enamel, use a quick light stroke (I have a bottle of thinner which I dip my brush into if the enamel is setting too quickly).

To paint the eyes, make two round sticks, one the size of the large white circle and one the size of the black centre. Insert the stick into the enamel so that only the end is covered, then put it straight down on the bug and off; allow the white to set a little, then put in the black centre in the same manner.

Select four or six badger neck hackles and tie them in so that they flare out; this gives them a life-like action.

Now wind on two or three soft hackles to form the collar; tie off and cement the winding.

I make the indentation in the cork which causes the popping, with the Burgess Vibro-tool which was presented to me for my first appearance with Patricia Stevens, tying a fly on television. I believe this was the first time this was performed in the Middle West.

Many color combinations can be made and many body styles and sizes can be used in making up these bugs.

If you will practice the method of putting on the enamel on a few bugs, you will very soon be making attractive bugs.

BLADES' GRASSHOPPER
Order: *Orthoptera*

I brought the real grasshopper, which I have tried to copy, from Ontario, Canada.

It is very easy to take trout and bass on this fly.

The hook is a No. 6 model perfect hump shank hook; place it in the vise and coat it with cement, then wrap it with tying silk (Drawing No. 1).

I then take a cork cylinder and shape it as shown in the drawings, cut a slot in the body, then fill the slot with liquid cement and coat the hook which is pressed into the slot.

Drawing No. 1

Drawing No. 2

Drawing No. 3

Drawing No. 4

Fill in the slot with cement or plastic wood and give the body two coats of liquid cement, then allow it to dry (Drawing No. 2).

Paint the body with two coats of yellow-green enamel and make the markings and eyes with brown enamel. I now tie in the two pairs of front legs which are two trimmed dark ginger hackle stems (Drawing No. 3).

The next step is to tie in the wings which are brown mottled Turkey sections that have been given a coat of cement on the inside of the feather to stiffen them. The two rear legs are trimmed ginger neck hackles bent to shape, as shown in the drawings.

Use fine tying silk to tie in the legs and wings (it cuts down the bulk), and cover the windings with brown enamel.

Drawing No. 4 is the finished "hopper."

CORK BODIED MOTH

Order: *Lepidoptera*

Hook: Humped shank, long.

Body: Cork, filed to shape and coated with liquid cement. Tie in near the tip, two strands of ostrich herl, one grey and one brown and wind them on together while the cement is tacky; this makes a life-like looking body and is an excellent floater.

Legs and Antennae: Trimmed, brown hackle stems.

Wings: Deer body hair, natural brown dyed yellow.

Head: Base of the hair wings, trimmed and marked with brown enamel.

Tie these moths in any color to imitate the natural moths. Grey and white moths are very good.

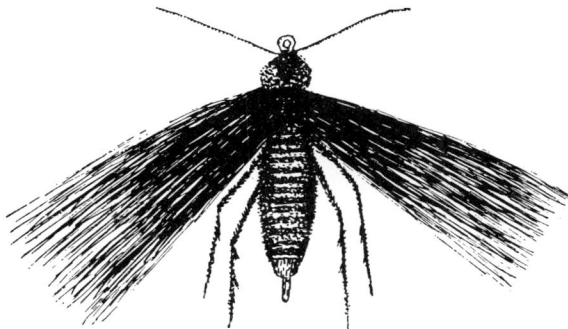

THE CORK BODIED MOTH.

[241]

PLATE LXXI.   CORK BODIED BUGS.
(See opposite page for descriptions)

CORK BODIED BUGS
(See Plate LXXI)

No. 1   BADGER POPPER
Body: Cork, painted black; eyes, white, black centre.
Tail: Four badger neck hackles.
Hackle: Badger.
Markings, white.

No. 2
BLACK FURNACE POPPER
Body: Cork, painted black, eyes, white, black centre.
Tail: Four furnace neck hackles.
Hackle: Furnace.
Tag: Silver tinsel.
Markings, white.

No. 3
BLACK AND YELLOW POPPER
Body: Cork, painted yellow; eyes, red and black, markings, black and white.
Tail: Four black neck hackles.
Hackle: Black.

No. 4   GREEN POPPING BUG
Body: Cork, painted green; yellow and black spots.
Tail: Olive and yellow neck hackles.
Hackles: Olive and yellow.

No. 5   GREEN POPPER
Body: Cork, painted green, eyes, white, black centre.
Tail: Six green neck hackles.
Hackle: Green.

No. 6
BLACK AND ORANGE POPPER
Tag: Gold tinsel.
Body: Cork, painted orange, eyes, white, black centre.
Tail: Six black neck hackles.
Hackle: Black.
Body markings, black.

No. 7   YELLOW POPPER
Body: Cork, painted yellow, eyes; red, black centre.
Tail: Six yellow neck hackles.
Hackle: Yellow.
Markings, red and black.

No. 8   BLADES' MINNOW
Tail: White polar bear.
Body: Cork painted white; cut an open mouth and paint red for popping.
Cement four teal body feathers on cork body to imitate the scale effect.

CORK BODIED BUGS
(See Plate LXXII)

No. 1   GRIZZLY POPPER
Body: Cork, painted black, red front in popping recess; eyes, white, black centre.
Tail: Six grizzly neck hackles.
Hackle: Grizzly.
White body markings.

No. 2   POPPING FROG
Body: Cork, painted green; markings, yellow with black centre.
Legs: Grey squirrel dyed green, and inserted into cork body with cement.

No. 3   RED HEAD POPPER
Body: Cork, painted white, head, red, eyes, yellow, black centre.
Tail: Four white neck hackles, and two red in centre.
Hackle: Red and white.
Markings, black and red, optional.

No. 4
RED AND WHITE POPPER
Body: Cork, painted red, eyes, white, black centre.
Tail: Six white neck hackles.
Hackle: White, tag, silver tinsel.
White markings, optional.

[243]

PLATE LXXII. CORK BODIED BUGS.
(See page 243 for descriptions)

No. 5
RED AND YELLOW POPPER
Body: Cork, painted red, eyes, white, black centre.
Tag: Silver tinsel.
Tail: Two red and two yellow neck hackles.
Hackle: White.
Black and white body markings.

No. 6   MINNOW POPPER
(W. F. Blades)
Tag: Silver tinsel.
Tail: Yellow hackle fibres.
Body: Silver tinsel.
Hackle: Scarlet.
Cork painted red, markings, white.
Eyes: White, black centre.

No. 7   MYSTERY BUG
(John Alden Knight)
Body: Cork painted red, make face convex for easy pick-up, or concave for popping more pronounced.
Wings and tail: White bucktail.

No. 8   FISH SCALE POPPER
(W. F. Blades)
Tail: Four grizzly hackles.
Hackle: Grizzly.
Body: Cork painted white, covered with gold scale finish.
Eyes: Black, white centre.

THESE FLORIDA BASS WERE CAUGHT BY FLY FISHERMAN LYMAN BARR.

Chapter XVII

BASS FLIES AND HAIR
BASS BUGS

FOR MOST game fish all over the country the Mississippi Bass Bug is very well known and undoubtedly a "killer." It can be made with almost any kind of hair, and it is made in almost any size.

The hook used in my finished drawing is a No. 1 3X ringed eyed Model Perfect. There is no set rule as to the length of the hair, but I think you get more action with this bug if you make the hair long. By all means take a small amount of hair in each section when making your first bugs; it is much easier to bend the small bunches back.

Take the time to pull the short hairs out of each bunch, and even up the tips by pulling out a few long hairs and put them back in the bunch; this will make the tips even.

Most tyers use a heavy silk such as size A; I prefer 2-0, and I use 4-0 on small sizes.

Place the hook in the vise and coat it with liquid cement, then wrap it with tying silk all the way to the bend. Now take a small bunch of deer

Drawing No. 1

Drawing No. 2

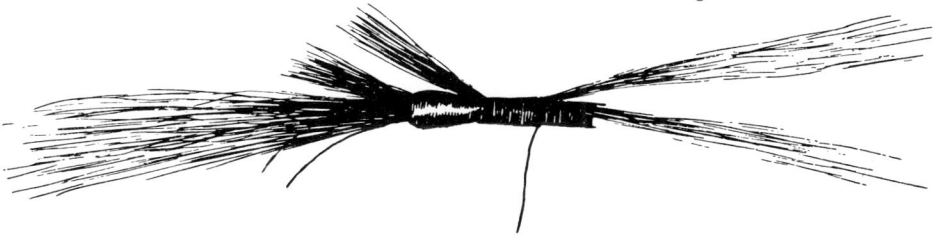

Drawing No. 3

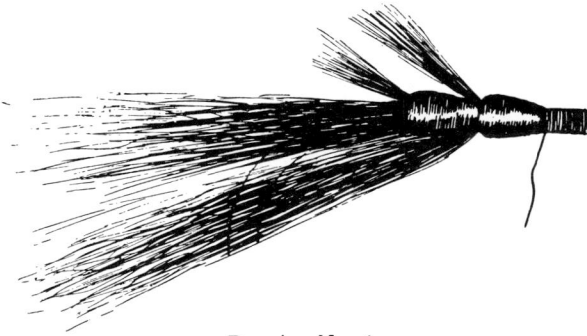

Drawing No. 4

Drawing No. 5

tail hair dyed red, and tie it on, in the position as shown in Drawing No. 1. You will notice that this hair has slipped around the hook, covering the bend of the hook. For a bug tied on a No. 1 3X hook, make the first turn of tying silk over the hair about two and one-quarter inches from the tip, and make fourteen turns to the right and keep the butt ends up; your bug will now be the same as Drawing No. 1.

Take hold of the butt ends and bend them back, pointing to the rear of the hook, winding over them about thirteen times, or to the end of the first winding. Apply a coat of liquid cement over these two windings, then carefully wind the tying silk back to the right, to position shown in Drawing No. 2, completing the first section. Your bug is now the same as Drawing No. 2.

To make the second section, prepare the bunch of hair as previously described and lay it on top of the hook with the tips pointing towards the eye of the hook. Take fourteen turns of tying silk to the right, keeping the hair on top of the hook; this will take a little practice, but will soon become easy. Take the first turn of tying silk approximately two and one-half inches from the tips; your bug will now be the same as Drawing No. 3.

Divide the hair into two equal parts, then pull each part back and down, one on each side of the hook. Hold the hair back with the left hand and carefully wind the tying silk to the end of the windings; apply a little cement, then wind the tying silk to the right to the position shown in Drawing No. 4.

Continue to add the sections of hair until you reach the eye of the hook. I increase the length of the hair about one-eighth of an inch in sections number three and four, then decrease sections five and six about the same amount; this gives the bug a rounded shape.

The amount of hair to use in each section, and the amount of sections, should be established by the tyer, as there is no set rule.

After all the sections are tied in, finish off the head in the usual manner, then cut off any hairs on the sides that may have slipped out of place, and trim the butts as shown in the finished drawing. Take hold of the bend of the hook and cut towards the eye.

Now apply liquid cement on the windings, and the bug will be the same as Drawing No. 5.

When making different sized bugs, be sure to count the first windings you put on each section—whether it be ten or fourteen—this is controlled by the size of the hook you are using and the thickness of the tying silk. If you take too many turns of tying silk in the second windings that are made to the left, you will notice the hair will lay too close to the hook—one turn less than the first windings is generally right.

TYING THE HOLLOW HAIR BODIES

FLIES, MICE, FROGS, MOTHS, GRASSHOPPERS, ETC.

Selecting the proper hair is very essential when making the many different bodies for flies, moths, frogs, etc.

The best way to get this knowledge is to cure a whole deer hide yourself and study the several different kinds of hair. The white hair on the belly is used for the white bodies and is also dyed many other colors. The back hair is long and is used for mice, crawfish, etc.

You can get some very good hair from the face and legs for the fly tails and wings on dry flies. Some deer have a blue dun hair on the body after the brown tips are cut off; that is excellent for small fly bodies such as found on the wet and dry Irresistible.

The caribou and reindeer furnish a very fine hair for this purpose, which is lighter and therefore floats longer than that furnished by the deer.

Drawing No. 1

The big horn mountain sheep furnish us with some very fine hollow hair that is very good for small bodies.

When you are making any of the hair flies or lures, try to obtain a natural and copy it for size and color. I do not mean that you should try to make it exactly the same as the natural, for this we will never do, but try to improve your flies by examining the thing you are trying to imitate.

I will never agree with some of our writers who claim a good imitation of the natural is no better than some of the poor imitations.

I would suggest, for the beginner, to tie a hair bodied moth; it is as easy as any of them, and after tying a few of these you will be able to tackle many different kinds of lures.

Place the hook in the vise, which, in this case, is a No. 6 3X. I used this hook to make the tying easier for the beginner. Put a little liquid cement on the hook, then take two or three light turns of "A" or "C" tying thread, and two whip finish knots. Coat the knot with liquid cement. Cut a small bunch of deer body hair from close to the hide, about one-quarter of an inch through, and cut off the tips; then pull or comb out the fuzz at the roots; place the hair on top of the hook with the centre directly over the tying silk (as shown in Drawing No. 1). Make a turn over the hair and hook, lightly the first time, bringing the hair down on the hook, still holding the hair firmly; open the thumb and first finger tips and make a second turn, and pull the thread down tightly and up towards you; this will make the hair flare up and spin around the hook, making a complete circle. Take the tying silk carefully through the hair; take one turn around the bare hook and make a half hitch; also put on a little cement. Be sure the hair has spun all the way around the hook perfectly, or you will have voids in the body when it is trimmed (See Drawing No. 2).

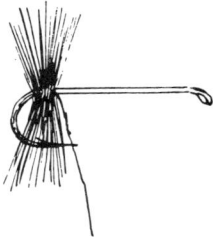

Drawing No. 2

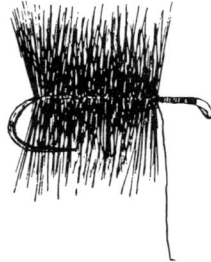

Drawing No. 3

Drawing No. 4

Drawing No. 5

Drawing No. 6

Continue tying on these bunches of hair until the body is the same as Drawing No. 3. Now take a good pair of scissors and trim to shape, same as Drawing No. 4. Notice the slope on the front of the body; this allows the wing to lay down in the proper position.

For the wing, cut a bunch of brown mottled hair from the back of the deer; comb out the fuzz and short hairs. Put a little cement on the part where the wing is to be tied. Now place the wing in position with the curve on the hair, as shown in Drawing No. 5. Now take two or three tight turns of tying silk over the hair, which will make it flare up, as shown in Drawing No. 5; then continue winding the thread through the hair. Now lift up the hair with the left hand fingers and put on several turns of the whip finish and trim the head.

I saturate the head with liquid cement, and when it has taken its initial set, I take my thumb and first finger and press the wing down which will make it fan out.

Give the head another coat of cement. I sometimes make the eyes with yellow and black enamel. Some would rather leave the hair trimmed to the shape of the head, using no cement.

TYING THE HAIR FROG

There are many different ways of tying the deer hair frog and I believe they will all take their share of game fish. The white hair from the deer's stomach, dyed a greenish yellow, is the hair I have used, or dye some the color of the frog you are copying. This hair is hollow and will spin round the hook.

Drawing No. 1

Drawing No. 2

Select a hook suitable for the size frog you wish to tie (size No. 1 hook is suggested) and place it in the vise; put a little cement at the bend and secure size A or C tying silk with a few tight turns and two half hitches. Do not make too much bulk; it is hard to conceal it with the hair body. Cut a portion of deer body hair about ¼ of an inch in diameter; pull out the short hairs and fuzz at the base and cut off the tips; place the hair on top of the hook with the centre over the tying silk, as shown in Drawing No. 1. Make a turn with the tying silk over the hair and hook lightly the first time, bringing the hair down on the hook. Still holding the hair firmly, open the thumb and first finger tips and make a second turn, and pull the thread down tightly and up towards you; this will make the hair flare up and spin round the hook.

Take the tying silk carefully through the hair and put on two half hitches; press them close to the hair; be sure you put your left hand thumb and finger at the back of the hair or you will push it off the hook. Every bunch of hair must spin perfectly around the hook or you will have voids in the body; put a little cement on the half hitches of each bunch. Tie on sufficient hair to make the body to the position of the legs and trim it, as shown in Drawing No. 3.

Put a little cement on the hook and wrap the tying silk round the hook to make a base for the legs; this prevents them from slipping. Select a small amount of pale yellow bucktail; take out the short hairs and tie them in, as shown, splitting the bunch to form the under side of both legs; then tie a piece of strong linen thread on the hook and put each end on the two legs,

Drawing No. 3

Drawing No. 4

now tie in a bunch of brown bucktail dyed green and divide it into two equal parts to form the top of the legs; you will now be in the position as shown in Drawing No. 3.

When tying the first bunch of hair over the base of the legs be sure to press it close to the other body hair; continue tying on each bunch of hair to the eye of the hook, being sure you spin each bunch of hair all around the hook and press each tie close together as in Drawing No. 4. Now trim the body to the desired shape.

The joints in the legs are made by wrapping green silk round the hair. Put cement on the joints, then after it is set you can make the desired kink in the joints. To make the bend in the legs, hold the end of the thread and push the hair up; this will make the bend in the legs. If you desire a decided kink in the joint, put a piece of nylon in before wrapping on the green silk; this will make the kink stay in shape. Before putting on the yellow and black spots (also the eyes) give the hair a coat of clear lacquer where the spots are to be placed; this stops the enamel from running.

Painting the underside with cream enamel makes the frog look more natural and waterproofs the underside. Be sure to trim the underside close to the hook so as not to interfere with the hooking of the fish. If you would like a more natural looking frog, tie in a small pair of front legs in the same manner as you did the rear legs and point them forward.

To make the eyes project, build them up with liquid plastic, then put on the enamel. Plate LXXIII is the finished frog.

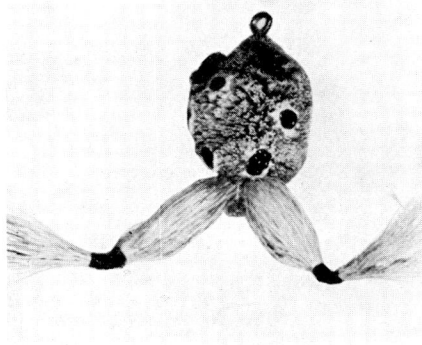

PLATE LXXIII. HAIR FROG.

HAIR BASS BUGS

No. 1 BUCKTAIL BASS BUG
Made of natural brown and white bucktail.

PLATE LXXIV.

No. 2 GREEN HAIR FROG
Legs: Greenish yellow bucktail.
Body: Green deer body hair.
Markings: Yellow and black enamel.
Eyes shaped with plastic, then painted with yellow and black enamel.

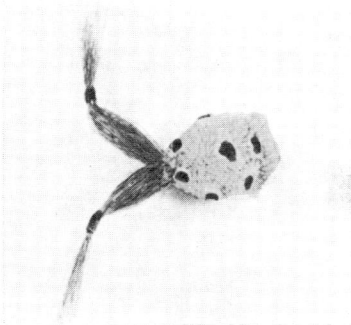

PLATE LXXV.

No. 3 HAIR GRASSHOPPER
(Paul H. Stroud)
Body: Olive yellow deer body hair in rear portion. Front portion, grey hair.
Wings: Small bunch of grey Woodchuck hair overlapped with brown mottled Turkey strands.
Legs: Trimmed scarlet, or fiery brown hackle stems.

PLATE LXXVI.

No. 4 HAIR MOUSE
Tail: Goose wing feather fibres.
Body: Deer body hair.
Whiskers: Porcupine hair.

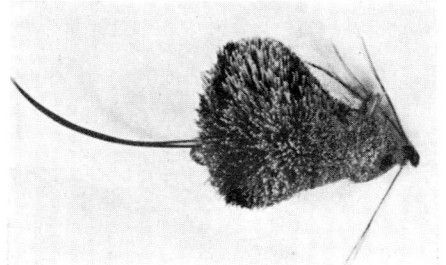

PLATE LXXVII.

No. 5 HAIR MOTH
Body: Yellow kapok for better floating.
Wings: White deer body hair.

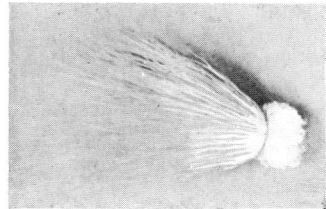

PLATE LXXVIII.

No. 6 **HAIR POPPER**

Tail: Red hackle fibres, or Golden Pheasant breast.
Body: Red chenille, or wool.
Wings and head: Brown Deer body hair.

PLATE LXXIX.

No. 7 **WHITE MOUSE**

Tail: Swan feather fibres.
Body: White Deer body hair.
Whiskers: Moose mane.

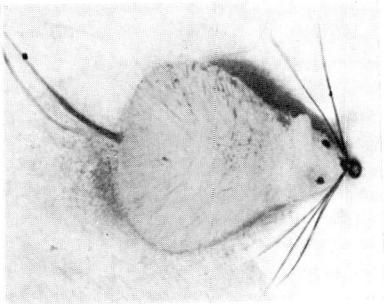

PLATE LXXX.

No. 10 **CRAY FISH**

Tail: Deer body hair.
Body: Deer body hair, tied with long hair so that it will form the legs when the body is trimmed.
Claws: Bucktail.
Antennae: Trimmed brown hackle.

No. 8

WINGED BASS DEVIL BUG
(O. C. Tuttle Devil Bug Co.)

Made of deer body hair in almost any color.

PLATE LXXXI.

No. 9 **WHISKER BUG**
(Weber)

Made of deer body hair.

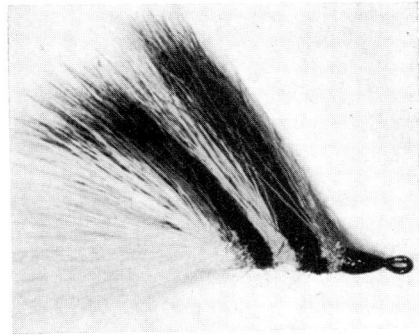

PLATE LXXXII.

PLATE LXXXIII.

[255]

LARGE BASS FLIES

(See Plate LXXXIV. Reading left to right, top to bottom.)

No. 1   BADGER FURNACE
Tail: Red goose.
Body: Trimmed furnace hackle.
Wing: Badger hair.
Hackle: Furnace.

No. 2   COCKATOUCH FLY
Body: Four sections of Peacock herl.
Hackle: Four sections of ginger hackle, the section at the head is a little larger than the first three, commence at the rear with Peacock herl.

No. 3   COWDUNG
Tail: Scarlet hackle fibres.
Body: Orange wool.
Wings: Brown mottled Turkey.
Hackle: Brown.

No. 4   FOX SQUIRREL BUG
Tail and body: Fox squirrel tail.
Hackle: Ginger furnace.

GREY SQUIRREL BUG
(Not Shown)
Tail and body: Grey squirrel tail.
Hackle: Badger.

No. 5   HACKLE BASS FLY
Tail: Brown hackle points.
Body: Brown hackle palmered.

No. 6   JOHNSON'S FANCY
Tail: Two brown hackle tips and red wool "short," also a few fibres of Peacock sword.
Body: Brown hackle palmered, wound closely.
Wing: Brown mottled Turkey tied down wing, over this tie in about twenty-five strands of Peacock herl.
Shoulder: Peacock sword fibres.
Throat: Red hackle fibres.

No. 7   MARCH BROWN
Tail: Scarlet hackle fibres.
Body: Hare's ear, or brown fur dubbing; ribbing, yellow floss.
Wings: Brown mottled Turkey.
Hackle: Grey-brown Partridge back feather.

No. 8   MC GINTY
Tail: Scarlet goose and grey Mallard.
Body: Yellow and black chenille.
Wing: Grey squirrel.
Hackle: Brown.

No. 9   "REDHEADS" SQUIRREL TAIL FLY—YELLOW
Tail: Short yellow floss or wool.
Body: Yellow floss; ribbing, silver tinsel.
Wings: Grey Squirrel.
Hackle: Grizzly.

"REDHEADS" SQUIRREL TAIL FLY—RED
(Not shown)
Tail: Short red floss or wool.
Body: Red floss; ribbing, gold tinsel.
Wings: Red squirrel.
Hackle: Brown.

No. 10   BUCKTAIL BASS FLY
Tail: White bucktail.
Tag: Gold tinsel.
Body: Yellow floss with red floss tip.
Wing: First portion white bucktail, covered with natural black hackle, then add the second wing portion over the hackle.

No. 11   MISSISSIPPI BUG
Color: Red, brown and white.
See page 246 for tying.

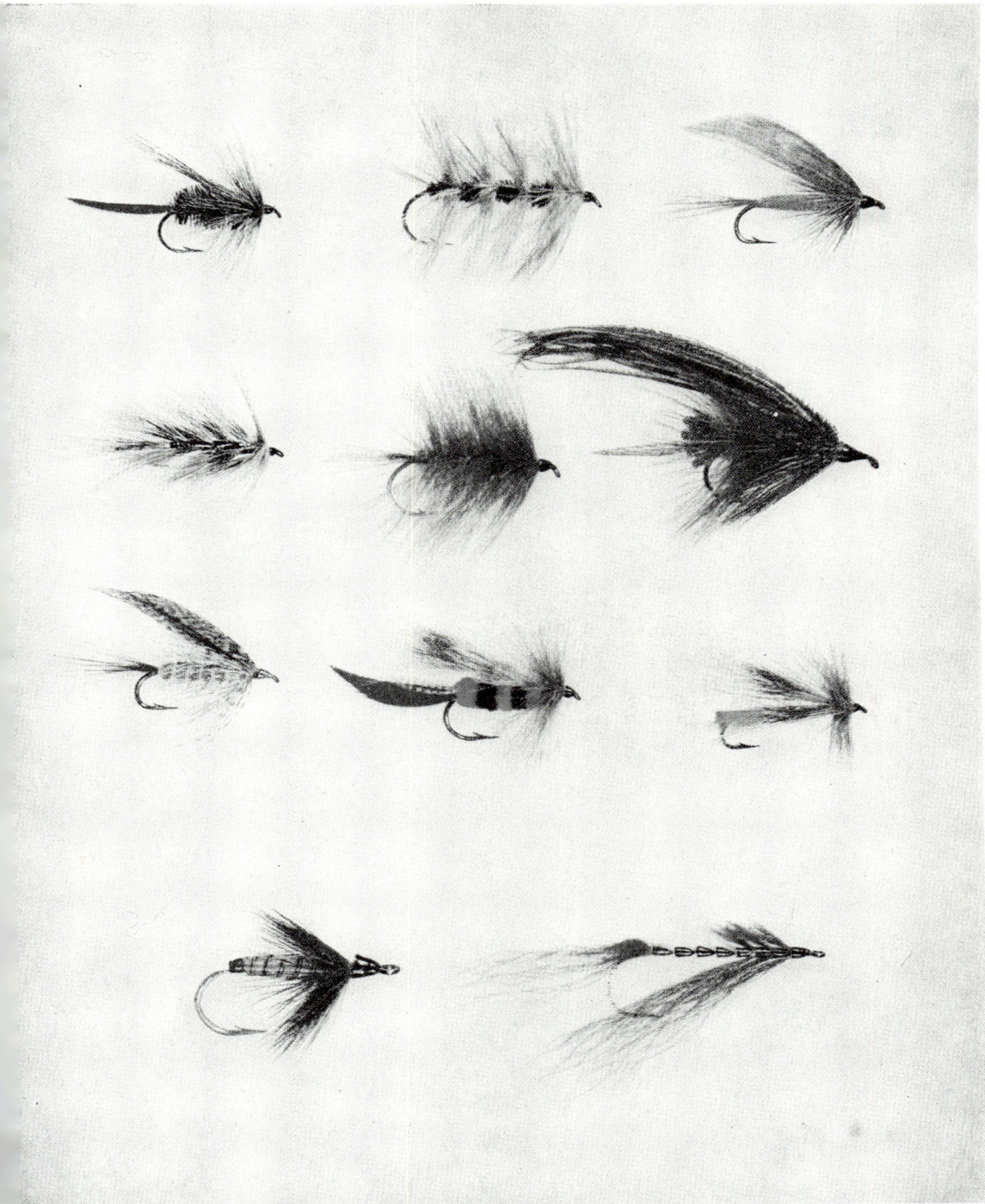

PLATE LXXXIV. LARGE BASS FLIES. (read left to right)
(See opposite page for descriptions)

No. 1 BLADES' MULTI-VARIANT
Tail and Hackle: Multi-variant.
Butts: Peacock herl. Hook, 5/o—6x long.
No. 2 Same as No. 1 except the body is red silk.
Tail: Red deer tail.
This fly can also be tied with red and white hackle tails.
Body: Red and white hackle tied on together. No Peacock herl.
All yellow fly is also very good.
All Cochy-bondhu is also excellent.

PLATE LXXXV. LARGE BASS FLIES.

Chapter *XVIII*

JETS

BASS bugging is steadily gaining in popularity because it is a joy and a thrill to play a husky bass on the fly rod. The floater is spectacular to employ because the angler not only feels the strike, but he sees and hears it as well. The old, time-tested, smooth-bodied feathered lure will always rate high with the man who goes after bass with the fly rod. He can get a high gloss finish on these lures and construct them in such a way that they produce an enticing surface commotion when given rod-tip action, yet they can be picked up cleanly from the water for the next cast.

This is a great lure to fish around fields of pads by daylight and in the shallow shorelines after dark. The now-common farm pond is a great new area for bugging. You trout anglers who love the fly rod but have not applied it to bass waters are missing some fine sport.

In keeping with the times, let's call this wonderful bass popper a "Jet."

BLADES' JETS
(See Plate LXXXVI)

No. 1
Cork: Black.
Wings: White bucktail, two badger hackles on each side.
Hackle: Badger.
Tail: Badger.

No. 2
Cork: White.
Wings: Yellow bucktail, two furnace hackles on each side.
Hackle: Yellow.
Tail: Yellow bucktail.

No. 3
Cork: Yellow.
Wings: Yellow bucktail, two furnace hackles on each side.
Hackle: Olive green.
Tail: Red bucktail.

No. 4
Cork: Yellow.
Wings: Yellow bucktail, two furnace hackles on each side.
Hackle: Multi-variant.
Tail: Red bucktail.

No. 5
Cork: White.
Wings: White bucktail, two grizzly hackles on each side.
Hackle: Badger.
Tail: Red bucktail.

No. 6
Cork: Yellow.
Wings: Yellow bucktail, two black hackles on each side.
Hackle: Yellow.
Tail: Red bucktail.

PLATE LXXXVI. BLADE'S JETS.

PLATE LXXXVII. STREAMER ADDED TO JET'S WINGS.

Chapter XIX

BASS AND BONEFISH FLIES

Many of us take a trip to Florida in the winter and enjoy some fine fishing. It is not a trip for certain species but to enjoy variety to the utmost. Time is divided between fresh and saltwater—bass and bonefish. Either can be taken on the same equipment right on down the line to and including the fly. For the sake of convenience, which turned out to be for the sake of efficiency, too, an assortment of flies was tied for the dual role. One day they would be cast in the bonefish flats, the next day in a bass lake or river.

Included in this group are streamer flies, tube flies, and bugs. The one well-supplied box could be appropriately labeled, For Bass and Bone Fish, and there would be no mixup or disconcerting incident of being at the right place with the wrong ammunition, or vice versa.

BASS AND BONEFISH FLIES
(See Plate LXXXVIII)

No. 1   HACKLE FLY
Tail: Two white hackles, two grizzly, two yellow outside.
Hackle: Cream badger.

No. 2   HACKLE FLY
Tail: Six ginger furnace hackle wisps.
Hackle: Ginger furnace.

No. 3   RED BABOON
Tail: Wood Duck.
Body: Deer or Caribou body hair.
Wing: Red Baboon, Jungle Cock.

No. 4   ORANGE BABOON
Tail: Wood Duck.
Body: Deer or Caribou.
Wing: Orange Baboon.

Nos. 5 and 6   HACKLE FLIES
Make them any size and any attractive color; made the same as No. 1 BLADES' MULTI-VARIANT.

No. 7 MUDDLER MINNOW
BY DON GAPEN
Tail: Speckled brown Turkey wing quill.
Body: Gold tinsel.
Wings: Timber Wolf tail hair and speckled brown Turkey.
Hackle: Deer body hair, which also makes the head.
Excellent for trout and bass.

PLATE LXXXVIII.   BASS FLIES.

PLATE LXXXVIII. BASS FLIES, Continued.

PLATE LXXXIX. GINGER FURNACE AND GRIZZLY BASS WET FLY, YELLOW AND
WHITE POPPER AND GREEN DEER TAIL FROG.

No. 1
Tail: Red deer tail.
Wings: Six variant neck hackles tied to flare out and up.
Hackle: Brown and grey variant.
Head: Red with black and white eyes.

No. 2
Tail: Red deer tail.
Wings: Six yellow neck hackles tied to flare out and up.
Hackle: Four, red, yellow, red, yellow with peacock herl tied in between each one.
Head: Red, with black and white eyes.

No. 3
Tail: Red deer tail.
Wings: Six yellow neck hackles tied to flare out and up.
Hackle: Red and yellow tied on together.
Head: Red, with black and white eyes.

No. 4
Tail: Red deer tail.
Wings: Six red neck hackles.
Hackle: Yellow.
Head: Red, with black and white eyes.

PLATE XC. FLIES FOR BONEFISH AND BASS.

BLADES' EMERITA TALPOIDA (SEA CRAB)

To make the Emerita talpoida (Sea Crab) place a No. 1 or 1/0 3x long hump-shank hook in the vise and wrap it with white nylon thread and copper wire, if you want it weighted. Now tie on the tan deer tail hair for the tail. Pour Duco household cement out of the tube and wrap the thread through it; this speeds up the tying.

I make the body the correct width and about half the thickness. Allow it to set. I then lay the legs, which are natural raffia coated with cement, across the body and pour the cement over them; also put on the antennae which are four light tan hackle stems.

The body is a light tan enamel and Duco household cement. The eyes project at the end of two stems which remind me of periscopes.

This sand bug or mole crab should be excellent for surf fishing for pompano and Florida bass; also bottom fishing. I have on several occasions while surf fishing near Deerfield, Florida seen these sand bugs working near the water's edge for food and immediately bury themselves in the sand with their powerful front legs to hide themselves from the fish and birds that are anxious to devour them.

Make and fish with more of my artificials and conserve the naturals for the fish.

PLATE XCI. SEA CRAB AND THE BLADE'S IMITATION.

Chapter XX

TUBE FLIES

THERE are advantages in using the tube flies. They are lighter than a fly made on a large hook, which means they will not scare the fish as much and will be easier to cast. They are excellent for our floating lines. The hooking qualities are tops. You will observe when you hook a fish the fly slides up the line, which means your fly will last much longer and the fish will not have the leverage to throw the hook; all the fish has in his mouth is the small treble hook. If the hook gets broken you will only have to replace the hook, not discard the fly.

The tube can be made of brass or copper; I have these in sizes from ¼″ to 3/32″. Discarded ball point pens will give several sizes of these tubes. To prevent the metal from cutting your leader, insert a plastic tube in the metal tube; select one that fits tight; also put a little cement on it before inserting it. These plastic tubes can be taken from coated electric wires. Cut this tube off a little longer than the brass or copper tube at each end; this prevents cutting of the leader. Being able to change the size of your hook on your fly is also an advantage with these flies. This method is not new; it has been used on feather jigs for many years. I have read that North American Indians used it with bones.

Possibilities are great. Various nymphs and crustacea can be imitated and flies can be developed for different species of fish. To a degree weight can be controlled, for the tube can be metal, plastic or quill. Those of you who enjoy exercising ingenuity will be fascinated by the possibilities offered. The flies included in this brief chapter are standard with me.

TUBE FLIES
(See Plate XCII)

No. 1. To tie the Spent-Winged May Fly I insert a needle in the plastic tube, leaving it ¼″ longer; this portion is put in the vise and after the fly is made cut it off. This plastic body may not be too durable but it will float well with a small hook.

No. 2. This is my Stone Fly Nymph tied on a piece of Rosin Solder core. I push out the rosin with a needle; insert a needle and tie the nymph on the core. After hooking around twenty rainbow trout I did not damage the lx leader at all. Examine the leader at intervals.

No. 3. This is my small Hellgrammite tied on a small brass tube with plastic inner-tube.

No. 4. Tied and same as No. 3 as to tubes. This Minnow has long fins and two badger hackle stripes, used for action.

No. 5. My Grasshopper with the tubes inserted in the cork body.

No. 6. My Crayfish with tubes covered with plastic.

No. 7. My Stone Fly made on tubes.

No. 8. Same as No. 2 (smaller).

No. 9. *Tail:* Three Moose hairs.
Tube: Brass, plastic lining.
Body: Tan raffia; ribbing, Peacock quill dyed yellow.
Wing: Wood Duck.
Hackle: Brown variant.

PLATE XCII. TUBE FLIES, A REVOLUTIONARY TIE.

PLATE XCIII. THE TUBE FLY STYLE OF TIE APPLIED TO
DIFFERENT TYPES OF FLIES.

TUBE FLIES
(See Plate XCIII)

No. 1

Tail: Yellow and orange hackle fibres.
Body: Red floss, two Peacock herl butts.
Wings: Six fine Peacock herl strands,
Mallard breast dyed orange, topped
with natural Mallard.
Hackle: Dark brown. ⅛″ copper tube
and plastic inner-tube.

No. 2

Ackroyd: See Salmon Fly chapter for
material list. One ⅛″ tube and plastic
inner-tube.

No. 3

Body: Orange floss; ribbing, gold tinsel.
Wings: Tan or Red Squirrel tail. ⅛″
tube and plastic inner-tube.

When using a small propeller or spinner with tube fly or other fly, first thread a
bead on the leader, followed by the blade, then another bead before tying on the fly.

PLATE XCIII, Continued.

No. 4

Body: Cork, painted red. Eyes; white, black centre.

Tail: Six neck hackles, four white, two red.

Hackle: Red and white, tied on together. Tube; 1/8″ brass, plastic inner-tube. In making No. 4 make two cuts in the end of the brass tube about 3/32″ apart and about 1/4″ deep; bend these portions out and file them to a point, file off the other portion of tube. Drill a hole in the cork, insert the tube after setting the two points at a proper angle so that they will pull into the cork and secure it. Insert the plastic tube and make the bug.

No. 5 BLADES' *EMERITA TALPOIDA*
Tie this on a brass tube with a plastic insert and use the instructions given on the *Emerita Talpoida.*

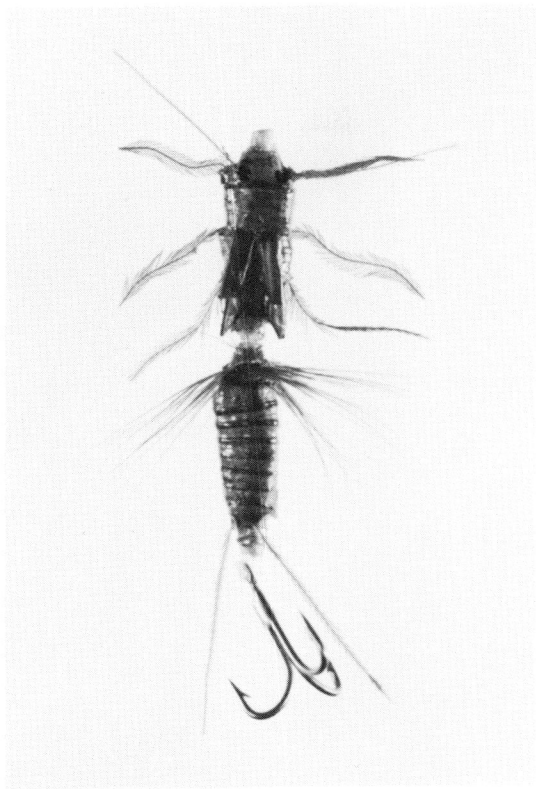

PLATE XCIV. STONE FLY NYMPH, TUBE-STYLE TIE.

BLADES' HEXAGENIA LIMBATA
and
BLADES' STONE FLY NYMPH

I recently had the pleasure of watching about a dozen burrowing type May Fly nymphs that I had placed in a large glass jar filled with water and about one inch of sand at the bottom covered with powdered leaves and small twigs and trash. From this moment on I learned something about action.

These nymphs are very fast and the lower half of the body can swing around in every position so I decided to make the Hexagenia nymph and Stone Fly nymph on two separate tubes for each nymph. This gives the nymphs a very fine action when made by the angler. I also found out I had three nymphs in one; you can use both sections separately; cut the hook off the leader, take off the lower section and put the hook back on the leader again and fish with the top half.

[273]

The only change I made in the Hexagenia nymph was that I put the tail section on a piece of rosin solder core after taking out the rosin. This will give more action.

To tie the jointed nymphs, take a brass tube and pinch the end so that it will go in the vise; see that the tube is long enough to tie the two sections on it. Now tie the Stone Fly and Hexagenia nymphs from my instructions on the tube and cut them apart as shown.

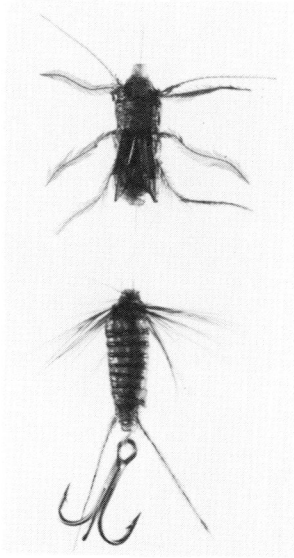

Top two, artificials

Lower two, naturals

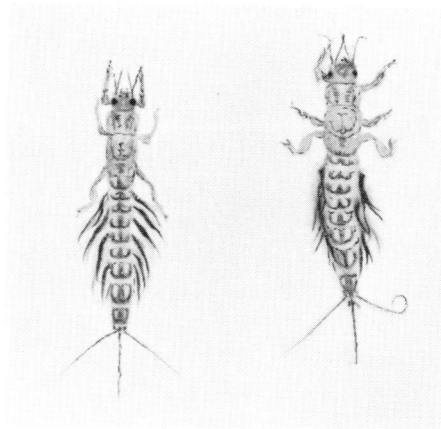

PLATE XCV.   TUBE FLY NYMPHS.

Chapter XXI

SALMON FLIES AND
SALMON DRY FLIES

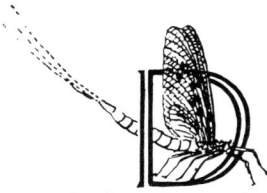

URING WORLD WAR II, I spent two days each week, for about nineteen months, teaching our wounded soldiers how to tie their own flies, and I also taught fly casting and bait casting.

One of the boys told me he had a favorite fly for bass fishing which he thought was called a "Johnson Special," so, as you may know, I asked him to send home for the fly, which he did and I was very much surprised when I saw that it was an old Jock Scott from England or Scotland made on a hook with a gut eye and was a little worn after many years of service.

I offered him several of my flies for his old favorite—in fact, anything in reason including a new Jock Scott, and his answer was, "I think I would like to keep it, Bill."

This proved to me that the Jock Scott is not just a beautiful fly to trim up your hat, but a real fish-getter. The materials used in making salmon flies vary a little by each tyer, but this will not make much difference in respect to taking fish.

Before tying the Jock Scott, lay all of the materials out on a table and when you are laying out the wing material, make two piles, one for the right side and one for the left. This means you must take the strands from a right wing and left wing or they will not marry together. For instance, the red, yellow and blue swan fibres will be taken from six swan feathers.

Now place the desired size salmon fly hook in the vise, coat it with cement, then wind the shank with No. 4-0 tying silk to a point over the point of the barb. Take a piece of fine twist or oval tinsel and carefully pull off about one-eighth of an inch of the silver, then tie it in with the centre core, as shown in enlarged Drawing No. 1.

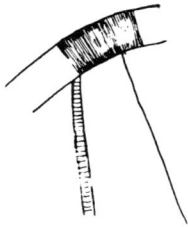

Drawing No. 1

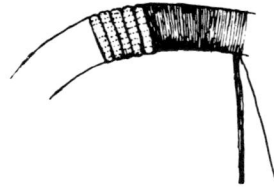

Drawing No. 2

Drawing No. 3

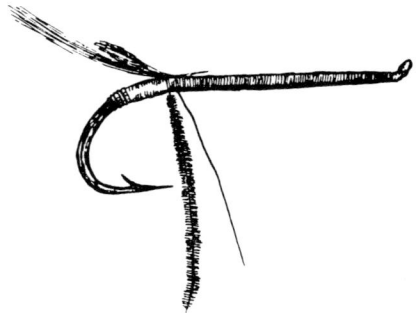

Drawing No. 4

Take hold of the tinsel with the pliers and wind on three to six turns, taking the twist out as you wind and wind it tightly. Make a turn over the tinsel and cut it off a little long, then pull off the silver and cut it off; now wind over the core only and take the tying silk to a point directly over the point of the hook; tie in a single strand of yellow floss, and you will be the same as Drawing No. 2.

Wind the floss to the left, then back to the right, and tie off. Now select a small topping the proper length for the fly you are tying. I advise buying the head of the Golden Pheasant so that the proper size can be selected for the topping and tail topping. This is not easy to tie in as the stem is not flat. I kink this with my thumb nail and first finger tip; in other words, make it more flexible. Cut off the soft fibres at the base and tie it in on top of the hook using a little cement. Cut off the dark soft base of the Indian Crow body feather (see Drawing No. 3) and tie it in. This is laid flat with the best side up. Some persons tie in two on their edge. Tie in a piece of Ostrich herl, and your fly will be the same as Drawing No. 4.

The next step is to wind the herl butt. I continually stroke the fibres back as I make my turns; this prevents winding too many of the fibres under the

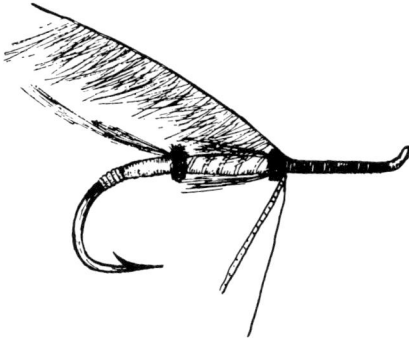

Drawing No. 5

Drawing No. 6

Drawing No. 7

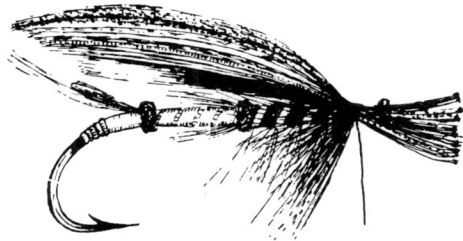

Drawing No. 8

centre quill; tie off the herl and tie in a piece of oval tinsel, about No. 15, which is small, and wind the tying silk to the centre butt. Tie in a narrow strand of yellow floss and wind it to the left and back to the right; tie off and wind the silver oval tinsel and tie this off. The next step is to tie on the Toucan feathers, as shown in Drawing No. 6. This feather is prepared ready for tying in. You can substitute for this feather a hackle tip, or small Golden Pheasant crests, as it is not available at the present time.

Tie three Toucan feathers on the underside and three on the topside, as shown in Drawing No. 5, and prepare a level surface for them or they will stand up too high. Make the natural curve form the appearance, as shown in Drawing No. 5.

Form the second butt the same as the first one; tie in a piece of oval tinsel No. 17 or No. 18, and also a natural black hackle that has been doubled, as shown in Drawing No. 5. To double a hackle, I cut off the soft fibres at the base and stroke the fibres down so that they are at right angles to the stem; now put the thick end of the stem in the vise, hold the hackle vertical, and wet the finger and thumb tips on the left hand; commence to stroke the fibres back so that they are all pointing in the same direction, as shown in Drawing No. 5.

Take the tying silk to the end of the second half of the body and tie in a piece of black floss. Form the floss body and wind the oval tinsel, then tie off.

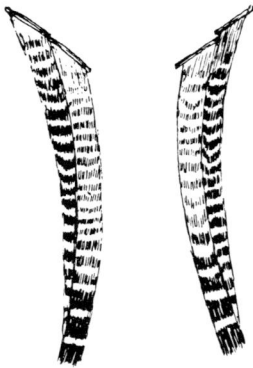

Drawing No. 9

Drawing No. 10

The next step is to wind the hackle tightly following the silver tinsel, and take a few turns at the throat, then cut off the surplus end.

Now tie in a Guinea Fowl body feather of the proper size; stroke the fibres down and tie it in by the tip; stroke the fibres back all the while you are winding. This doubles it the same as the hackle.

Now tie in the two sections of white-tipped Turkey tail feathers, as shown in Drawing No. 7.

You will notice I have left a piece of the quill on these sections. This keeps the fibres together until they are tied in. Your fly will be the same as Drawing No. 7.

The next step is not easy—that is, marrying the fibres together and tying on the wing proper. First of all, do not make the sections large and make as few turns of tying silk as possible. This cuts down the size of the head. Take small sections of yellow, red and blue Swan and marry the three together; then add the sections of Bustard and Florican, then add the sections of cinnamon and grey Turkey.

[278]

To marry these sections together, place them between the thumb and first finger of the left hand, then stroke them together and away from you. Each section should be a little longer than the one next to it.

When you have finished the left side of the wing, make the right side with the other pile of feathers, and *do not mix them at any time*.

I first tie on the far side wing, then tie on the one nearest to me. Some tyers tie them on in three sections on each side—either way can be used.

The next step is to tie on the strands of Peacock sword feathers.

The married sections of Teal and Wood Duck are tied in next, as shown in Drawing No. 9, and No. 11 shows them tied in position.

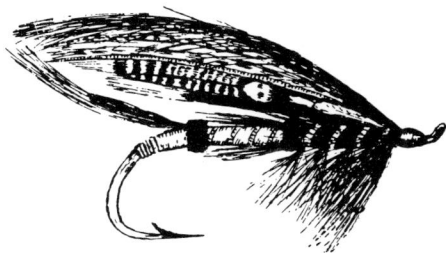

Drawing No. 11

Take a right and left section of brown Mallard with about seven or eight strands in each section, and leave the centre quill on them, as they are not easy to tie on. These form a top for the two wings.

Now tie on the Jungle Cock sides and Blue Chatterer cheeks. I cut the soft base fibres off and put a little cement on the centre quills.

Prepare the topping, as shown in Drawing No. 10, and select the proper size. Tie in the horns with blue and yellow Macaw strands close to the Jungle Cock.

Trim off the surplus ends, tapered as neat and as small as you can get them; then finish off the head in the usual manner, and your fly will be the same as Drawing No. 11.

FISHING WITH SALMON DRY FLIES

Fishing for salmon with the dry fly is a thrilling sport and reminds me of several good spankings I have had with small tarpon on light tackle in Florida.

These flies are not only suitable for salmon; they will take any large trout and most game fish when they are surface feeding. The hackles used in making these flies should be the best obtainable for dry flies; this makes the flies ride high in fast water.

When making these palmered bodies, I double the hackles; this releases all the hackle fibres and for a full body I wind on two hackles at the same time. Some tyers strip off one side of the hackle and wind two hackles together, or one single hackle for a sparsely palmered body.

I then wind a few close turns at the head of the fly and tie off. Take hold of the bend of the hook with the left hand and pull the hackles forward so that they point slightly toward the eye of the hook.

When speaking about the dry fly one cannot forget the name Theodore Gordon, who was born in Pittsburgh, Pennsylvania on September 18, 1854 and who died on May 1, 1915 at Bradley, on the Neversink, Sullivan County, New York. Theodore Gordon was the father of dry fly fishing in America and he spent many hours on the Neversink, casting flies that he had received from Frederic M. Halford, G. E. M. Skues and Mr. Marryat. These English flies will take fish almost anywhere at times, but Gordon got the idea of making a fly to imitate the American insects and he made the "Quill Gordon" which has been a very successful fly for almost any kind of trout. I believe the name of Theodore Gordon will live forever with the "Gordon Fly."

Dry fly fishing for salmon was developed by the late Colonel Ambrose Monell, Mr. George M. LaBranche and Edward R. Hewett, who spent many hours experimenting with many different flies at Colonel Monell's camp on the Upsalquitch River, New Brunswick. The "Colonel Monell," "Pink Lady" and Edward R. Hewett's "Bivisibles," tied on No. 6 and No. 8 hooks have been proved to be excellent killers when salmon are feeding on the surface.

SALMON FLIES

(See Plate XCVI. Read top to bottom, left to right.)

No. 1 KATE

Tag: Silver tinsel, light yellow floss.

Tail: Topping.

Butt: Black herl.

Body: Two turns of crimson floss, remainder, crimson seal fur, palmered with crimson hackle; entire body ribbed with silver oval tinsel.

Throat: Yellow hackle.

Wings: Grey Mallard, tippet strands, Golden Pheasant tail, yellow, crimson and blue swan, brown Mallard; Golden Pheasant topping.

Shoulders: Jungle Cock.

No. 2 JOCK SCOTT

Tag: Silver twist; yellow floss.

Tail: Topping, and Indian Crow.

Butt: Black Ostrich herl.

Body: Two equal parts; No. 1, yellow floss; ribbing, silver twist; veil with Toucan breast feathers. No. 2, Ostrich herl butt black, black floss; ribbing, silver oval (larger than twist) palmered with black hackle.

Hackle: Guinea fowl.

Underwing: Two strips of black Turkey, white tipped, married strands of blue, yellow and red swan, Bustard, Florican and Golden Pheasant tail, two strands of Peacock sword, narrow strips of Teal and Wood Duck.

Wing: Brown Mallard, with Golden Pheasant topping.

Sides: Jungle Cock.

Cheeks: Blue Chatterer.

Horns: Blue and yellow Macaw.

No. 3 THUNDER AND LIGHTNING

Tag: Gold twist yellow floss.

Tail: Topping; Indian Crow.

Butt: Black herl.

Body: Black floss; ribbing, gold oval tinsel, palmered with orange hackle.

Hackle: Blue Jay.

Wings: Brown Mallard with topping.

Shoulders: Jungle Cock.

Horns: Blue and yellow Macaw.

No. 4 BLACK DOSE

Tag: Silver twist orange floss.

Tail: Topping; Teal; Ibis.

Body: Three turns of blue seal fur; remainder, black seal fur palmered with black hackle; ribbing, silver oval tinsel.

Throat: Claret hackle.

Wings: Two tippets veiled with Teal, light mottled Turkey, Golden Pheasant tail, Wood Duck, Peacock sword herl, Ibis, green Parrot, brown Mallard, Golden Pheasant topping.

Cheeks: Blue Chatterer.

Horns: Blue and yellow Macaw.

No. 5 BLACK RANGER

Tag: Silver tinsel yellow floss.

Tail: Topping, Indian Crow.

Butt: Black herl.

Body: Black fur; ribbing, silver tinsel.

Hackle: Black, palmered.

Throat: Light blue.

Wings: Four Golden Pheasant tippets doubled, two projecting Jungle Cock feathers between tippets, topping, Golden Pheasant.

Cheeks: Blue Chatterer.

Horns: Blue and yellow Macaw.

Head: Black.

[281]

PLATE XCVI. SALMON FLIES.
(*See opposite page for descriptions*)

Painting by Wm. F. Blades

No. 6 GREEN HIGHLANDER

Tag: Silver twist canary floss.
Tail: Topping; Teal; Ibis.
Butt: Black herl.
Body: One third yellow floss; remainder green seal fur palmered with green hackle; rib entire body with silver oval tinsel.
Hackle: Yellow.
Wings: Two tippets veiled with Bustard, light and dark, Golden Pheasant tail, dark mottled Turkey, green Swan, brown Mallard; and topping.
Shoulders: Jungle Cock.
Horns: Blue and yellow Macaw.

No. 7 SILVER DOCTOR

Tag: Silver twist and yellow floss.
Tail: Topping, blue Chatterer.
Butt: Scarlet wool.
Body: Flat silver tinsel; ribbing, silver oval.
Hackle: Blue and Guinea fowl.
Underwing: Tippet, Summer Duck, Pintail, Golden Pheasant tail, yellow and blue Swan, Bustard.
Wing: Brown Mallard, and topping.
Horns: Blue and yellow Macaw.
Head: Scarlet and black.

No. 8 BUTCHER

Tag: Silver twist and yellow silk.
Tail: Topping, Teal and blue Macaw, optional.
Butt: Black herl.
Body: In four equal parts, first light red claret seal fur, light blue, dark red claret, and dark blue seal fur.
Ribbing: Silver tinsel.
Hackle: Natural black, palmered from light red claret seal fur.
Throat: Yellow hackle followed by guinea fowl.
Wings: Golden Pheasant red breast feathers and two tippets, sides small strips of Teal, Golden Pheasant tail, guinea fowl, Bustard, Peacock wing, Parrot, and yellow Swan; topped with two strips of brown Mallard.
Horns: Blue Macaw, Cheeks: Chatterer.
Head: Black.

No. 9 DURHAM RANGER
(Silver)

Tag: Silver twist and yellow floss.
Tail: Topping; Indian Crow.
Butt: Scarlet wool or fur.
Body: Silver, ribbed with silver oval tinsel; last two thirds palmered with scarlet hackle.
Hackle: Scarlet.
Wings: Two large Jungle Cock, then two pairs of Golden Pheasant tippets, doubled.
Topping: Golden Pheasant crest.
Shoulders: Jungle Cock (optional).
Cheeks: Blue Chatterer.
Horns: Blue and yellow Macaw.

No. 10 MAR LODGE

Tag: Silver twist.
Tail: Topping and Jungle Cock.
Butt: Black herl.
Body: Three parts; flat silver, black floss, flat silver; ribbing, silver oval entire length.
Hackle: Guinea fowl.
Underwing: Yellow, red and blue Swan, Golden Pheasant tail, Peacock wing strips, Wood Duck, grey Mallard, dark mottled Turkey.
Wing: Brown Mallard and topping.
Shoulders: Jungle Cock.
Horns: Blue and yellow Macaw.

No. 11 RED SANDY

Tag: Silver twist.
Tail: Topping; Indian Crow.
Butt: Scarlet wool.
Body: Two parts; silver oval tinsel; centre butt, Indian Crow and scarlet wool; front half palmered with scarlet hackle.
Wings: Four Indian Crow feathers, doubled, over-lapping each other and enveloping two large Jungle Cock feathers.
Topping: Two Golden Pheasant crests.

No. 12   DUSTY MILLER
Tag: Silver twist and yellow floss.
Tail: Topping, Indian Crow.
Butt: Black herl.
Body: First two thirds; embossed silver tinsel. Balance, orange floss. Ribbing, silver oval tinsel entire length.
Hackle: Guinea fowl.
Wings: Two strips of dark white tipped Turkey; over these place married strands of Golden Pheasant tail, yellow, red and orange Swan, Florican, Bustard, Pintail, Wood Duck, brown Mallard.
Topping: Golden Pheasant.
Cheeks: Blue Chatterer.
Horns: Blue yellow Macaw.

No. 13   LOGIE
Tag and Ribbing: Silver tinsel.
Tail: Golden Pheasant crest.
Body: Claret floss.
Wings: Brown Mallard.
Cheeks: Jungle Cock.
Hackle: Silver doctor blue.

No. 14   SILVER WILKINSON
Tag: Silver twist.
Tail: Topping and tippet fibres.
Butt: Scarlet wool or fur.
Body: Flat silver tinsel; ribbing, silver oval.
Hackle: First, blue, then magenta.
Wings: Two Jungle Cock feathers, veiled with barred Wood Duck and red Swan; topping with a small tippet over it.
Shoulders: Jungle Cock.
Cheeks: Blue Chatterer.
Horns: Blue and yellow Macaw.

No. 15   BLACK FAIRY
Tag: Gold tinsel, yellow floss.
Tail: Topping.
Body: Black seal fur; ribbing, gold tinsel.
Throat: Black hackle.
Wings: Brown Mallard.
Head: Black.

No. 16   DURHAM RANGER
Tag: Silver twist and yellow floss.
Tail: Topping and Indian crow.
Butt: Ostrich herl, black.
Body: Two turns of orange floss, two turns of orange seal fur; the front half black seal fur.
Ribbing: Silver lace and tinsel.
Hackle: From orange fur, palmer with claret hackle.
Throat: Silver doctor blue hackle.
Wings: Two large Jungle Cock, then two pairs of Golden Pheasant tippets, doubled.
Topping: Golden Pheasant crest.
Checks: Blue Chatterer.
Horns: Blue and yellow Macaw.

No. 17   SILVER AND BLUE
Centre fly
(Low Water Salmon Fly)
Tag: Flat silver tinsel.
Tail: Topping.
Body: Flat silver tinsel; ribbing, silver oval.
Hackle: Pale blue.
Wings: Teal.

SALMON FLIES
(See Plate XCVII)

No. 1   AKROYD

Tag: Silver thread.

Tail: Topping and Indian Crow.

Body: Orange mohair; ribbing, broad flat silver tinsel and fine thread tinsel, palmer this first section with lemon colored hackle; front half black floss; ribbing, silver oval tinsel and a blue black heron hackle tied palmer.

Throat: Heron hackle and sometimes Widgeon is added.

Wings: Strips of cinnamon Turkey tail.

Cheeks: Jungle Cock, tied sloping slightly downwards.

No. 2   BEAULY SNOW FLY

Body: Pale blue seal fur dubbing dressed medium thick. Ribbing, broad flat silver tinsel, with gold tinsel over the silver.

Hackle: Black Heron hackle, from back or crest of Heron.

Wings: Peacock herl, or sword fibres.

Head: Bright orange seal fur.

No. 3   BLACK DOCTOR

Tag: Silver tinsel and yellow floss.

Tail: Topping, blue Chatterer.

Butt: Scarlet wool.

Body: Black floss, palmered with black hackle.

Ribbing: Silver oval tinsel.

Throat: Guinea Fowl or English Jay.

Wings: Tippet in strands; yellow, blue and scarlet Swan, dark mottled Turkey, Golden Pheasant tail, Pintail, Guinea fowl, brown Mallard, Golden Pheasant crest topping.

Sides: Jungle Cock.

Horns: Blue and yellow Macaw.

Head: Scarlet wool and black enamel.

No. 4   BLUE BOYNE
(Mr. Kelson)

Tag: Silver twist and claret floss.

Tail: Topping.

Butt: Black herl.

Body: Silver twist in three sections, each butted with black herl. At each joint are Chatterer's feathers sideways, two on each side on top and bottom. The feathers gradually increase in size from the first joint towards the head.

Wings: Five toppings.

Head: Black herl.

No. 5   BLUE CHARM
(Low Water Salmon Fly)

Tag: Narrow silver oval tinsel.

Tail: Topping.

Body: Black floss; ribbing, silver oval.

Hackle: Blue.

Wings: Broad strips of brown Mallard, small band of Teal married to upper edge.

Topping: Golden Pheasant.

No. 6   BLUE DOCTOR

Tag: Silver twist and light orange floss.

Tail: Topping and Chatterer.

Butt: Scarlet wool.

Body: Light blue floss; ribbing, silver oval.

Hackle: Light blue.

Throat: Guinea Fowl.

Wings: Mixed—tippet, Golden Pheasant tail, Bustard, Wood Duck, yellow, red, and blue dyed Swan; two strips of brown Mallard above, topping over.

Horns: Blue Macaw.

Head: Scarlet wool.

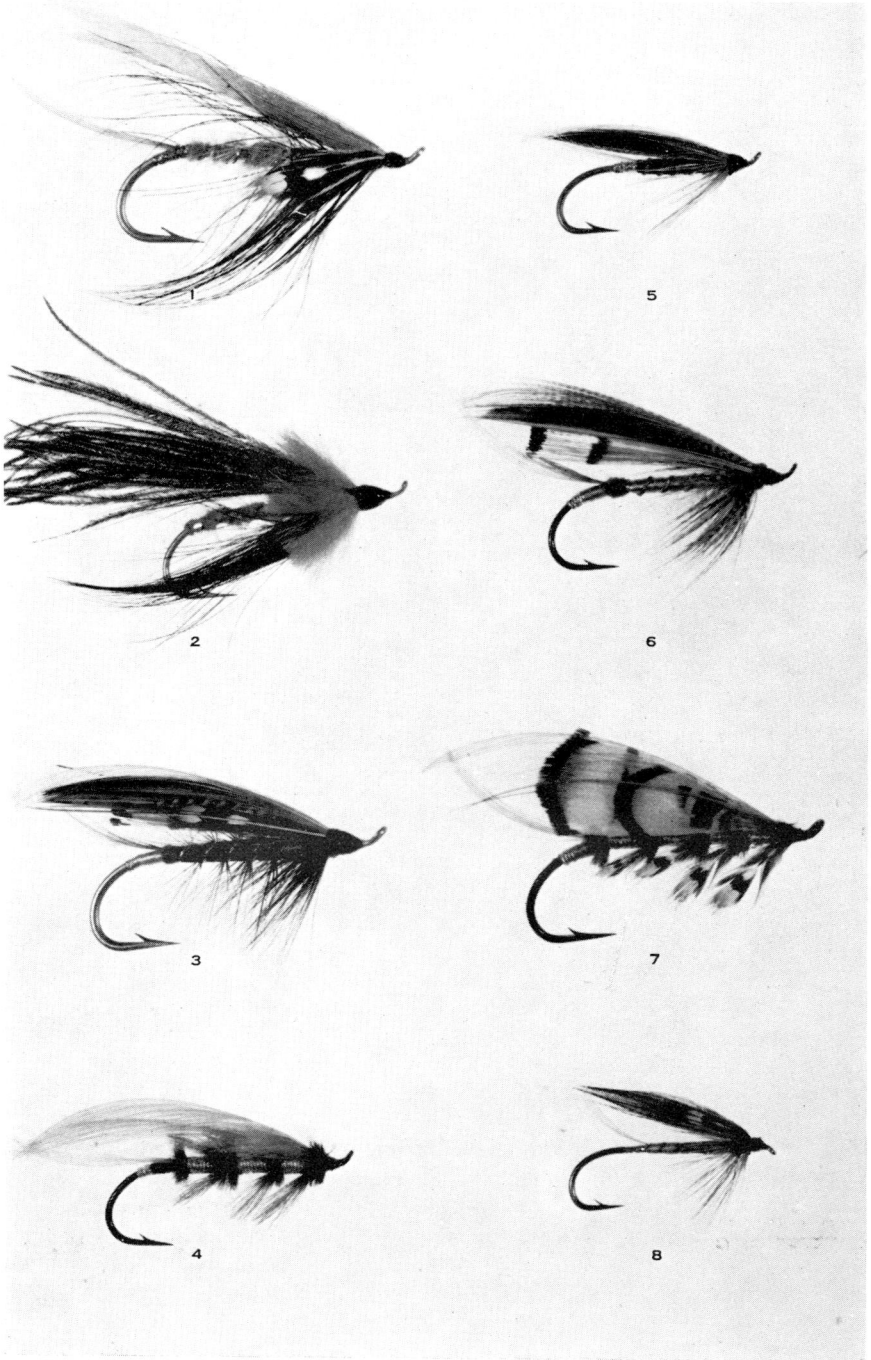

PLATE XCVII. SALMON FLIES.
(*See pages 285 and 287 for descriptions*)

No. 7   EVENING STAR
(Mr. Kelson)

Tag: Silver twist and orange floss.

Tail: Topping.

Butt: Black herl.

Body: In four equal sections: the first three of silver tinsel, each having two Jungle Cock back to back above and below, and butted with black herl; the last section of blue floss, the only one ribbed with silver oval tinsel.

Throat: Jungle as before. These feathers slightly increase in length from the tail to the head.

Wings: Four Amherst Pheasant tippets, back to back; Topping over.

Cheeks: First, Wood Duck tip, then Indian Crow.

Horns: Red Macaw.

No. 8   JOCKIE

Tag and ribbing: Silver tinsel.

Tail: Golden Pheasant crest.

Body: One third at tail, golden yellow floss, red floss in front.

Wing: Brown Mallard.

Cheeks: Jungle Cock.

Hackle: Brown.

SALMON FLIES
(See Plate XCVIII)

No. 1   JUNGLE HORNET

Tag: Gold oval tinsel.

Tail: Red Ibis or breast feather of Golden Pheasant.

Body: Alternate bands of yellow and black chenile tied in two sections.

Hackle: Furnace which is tied in three separate positions, one at the tail, the second occurs in front of first body section, third tie is at the head, increase the size of hackle in ties two and three. One pair of Jungle Cock at each hackle tie which increase in size toward the front.

No. 2   LADY CAROLINE

Tail: Strands of Golden Pheasant breast feather.

Body: Two strands of fine light brown wool and one strand of olive-green twisted together.

Ribbing: Flat silver tinsel, between gold and silver oval twist. The gold oval tinsel is sometimes wound counter-clock-wise.

Hackle: Grey Heron down the body.

Throat: Golden Pheasant breast feather.

Wings: Brown Mallard strips.

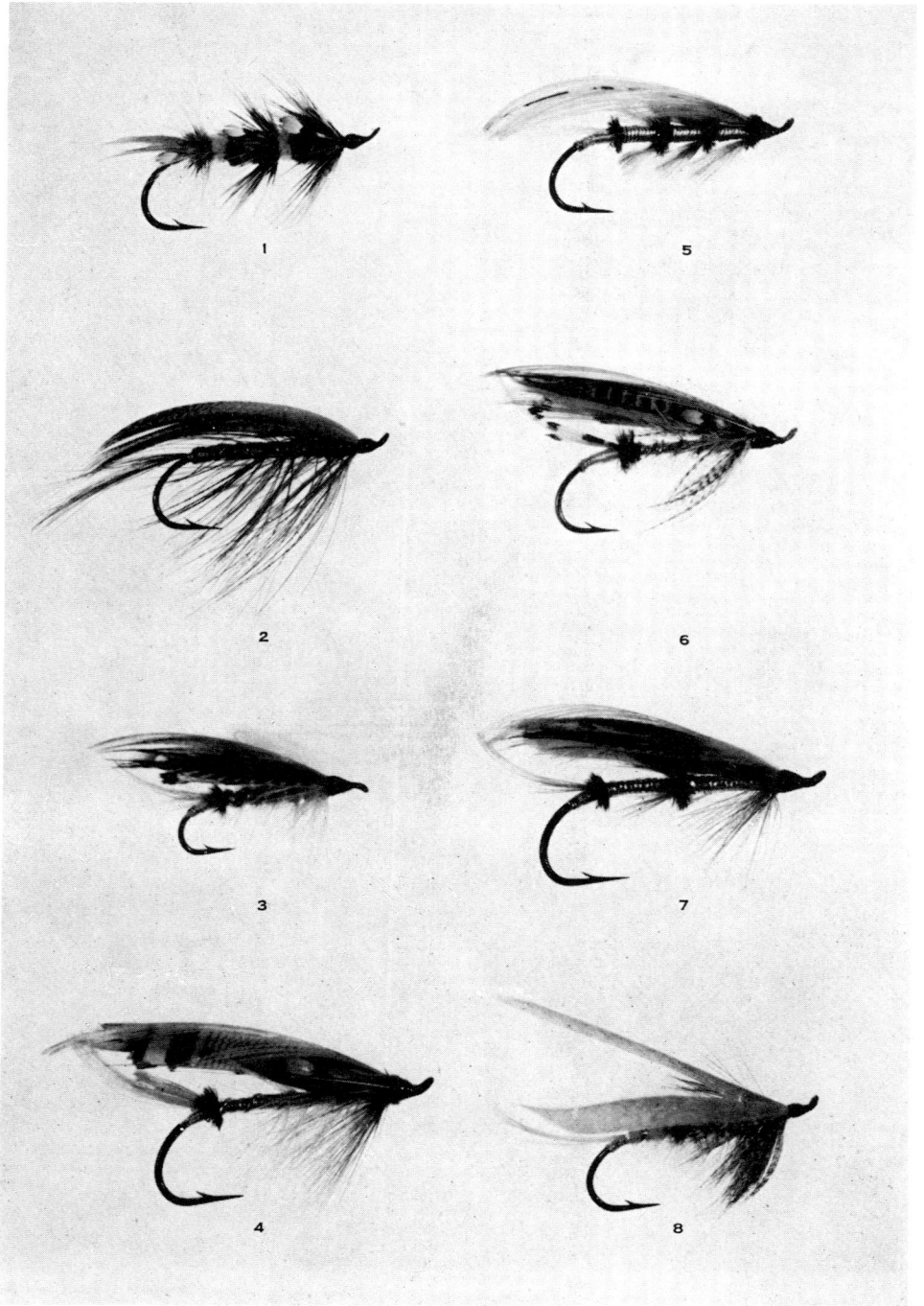

PLATE XCVIII. SALMON FLIES.
(See pages 287 and 289 for descriptions)

No. 3   LEMON GREY

Tag: Silver twist and yellow floss.
Tail: Topping; Indian Crow.
Butt: Black herl.
Body: Silver Monkey fur dubbing; ribbing, silver tinsel.
Hackle: Grey palmered on body.
Throat: Yellow hackle.
Wings: Tippet strands; then strips of Teal, Guinea Fowl, brown Mallard.
Topping: Golden Pheasant.

No. 4   MURDOCH

Tag: Silver tinsel and blue floss.
Tail: Topping, Indian Crow, Blue Chatterer.
Butt: Black herl.
Body: Silver tinsel; ribbing, gold oval tinsel.
Hackle: Yellow palmered.
Throat: Blue and red hackle.
Wings: Tippet strands, Blue Macaw, Turkey, yellow, red, and blue Swan, Peacock, Bustard, Golden Pheasant tail, Wood Duck, Topping over.
Cheeks: Blue Chatterer.
Sides: Jungle Cock.
Horns: Blue Macaw.
Head: Red wool.

No. 5   RED PIRATE
          (Mr. Kelson)

Tag: Silver twist and blue floss.
Tail: Golden Pheasant crest.
Butt: Black herl.
Body: Silver twist, in three sections, each butted with black herl. At each joint are Indian Crow feathers, sideways, two on each side on top and bottom; The feathers gradually increase in size from the first joint toward the head.
Wings: Five Golden Pheasant crests.
Horns: Amherst Pheasant.
Head: Black herl.

No. 6   SILVER GREY
          (Mr. Kelson)

Tag: Silver twist and yellow silk.
Butt: Black herl.
Tail: Golden Pheasant crest and unbarred Wood Duck.
Body: Silver tinsel; ribbing, silver oval tinsel.
Hackle: Badger down the body.
Throat: Widgeon.
Wings: Golden Pheasant tippet and tail, Bustard, Mallard, grey Mallard, yellow and blue Swan; two strips of brown Mallard and a topping over.
Shoulders: Jungle Cock.
Horns: Blue and yellow Macaw.
Head: Black.

No. 7   TORRISH

Tag: Silver tinsel and yellow floss.
Tail: Topping, red Ibis.
Butt: Black herl.
Body: In two parts of silver oval tinsel; first butted with Indian Crow and black herl.
Throat: Red orange hackle.
Wings: Two strips of black Turkey, white tipped. Bustard, Peacock wing, Guinea Fowl, Golden Pheasant tail, red and blue Swan, brown Mallard and topping.
Cheeks: Indian Crow.
Horns: Blue and yellow Macaw.
Head: Black.

No. 8   TURKEY JACKSON

Tag: Silver tinsel.
Tail: Golden Pheasant topping.
Body: Seal fur, lemon, claret, and black in equal sections.
Ribbing: Silver tinsel.
Hackle: Black cock over the black seal fur.
Throat: Speckled Guinea Fowl.
Wings: Two sections of cinnamon or dun Turkey tail feather strips tied on flat.

[289]

SALMON DRY FLIES

No. 1   CAHILL

Tail: Wood Duck fibres.
Body: Grey wool or fur; brown hackle, tied palmer.
Wings: Wood Duck.

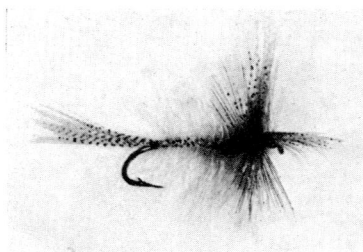

PLATE XCIX.

PLATE C.

No. 2   CINNAMON SEDGE

Tail: Ginger hackle fibres, optional.
Body: Ginger hackle, tied palmer, over yellow-green floss.
Wings: Brown mottled Turkey.
Hackle: Ginger.

No. 3   CLARK SALYER
(Paul Young)

Tail: Grey squirrel dyed pale yellow.
Tag: Silver tinsel.
Butt: Brown grizzly hackle.
Body: Pink wool; ribbing, silver tinsel.
Wings: Grey squirrel dyed pale yellow.
Hackle: Furnace.

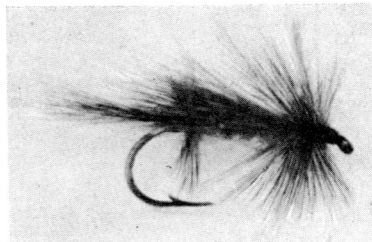

PLATE CI.

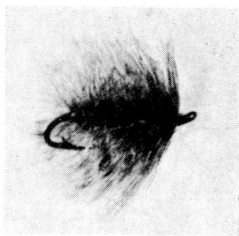

PLATE CII.

No. 4   COLONEL MONELL

Body: Peacock herl; ribbing, scarlet silk floss.
Hackle: Plymouth Rock, tied palmer.

No. 5   GINGER PALMER

Tail: Two ginger hackle tips; optional.
Body: Pale yellow floss; ribbing, silver tinsel.
Hackle: Two ginger hackles tied palmer.

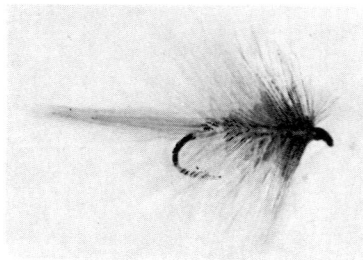

PLATE CIII.

No. 6   GREY WULFF

Tail: Brown bucktail.

Body: Grey Muskrat fur dubbing.

Wings: Brown bucktail tied upright and divided.

Hackle: Blue dun.

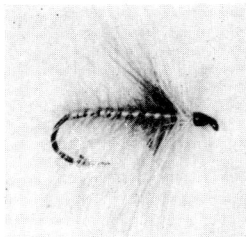

PLATE CIV.

No. 7   PINK LADY
GEORGE M. LA BRANCHE

Body: Pink floss; ribbing, gold tinsel.

Hackle: Ginger, tied palmer; three or four turns of yellow at the head.

PLATE CV.

No. 8   SILVER JUNGLE
(W. F. Blades)

Tag: Silver oval tinsel, and red seal fur.

Tail: Red hackle fibres, and Wood Duck fibres.

Body: Silver tinsel; ribbing, silver oval.

Hackle: Grizzly.

Wing: Grey squirrel.

Shoulders: Jungle Cock.

PLATE CVI.

No. 9   RED JUNGLE
(W. F. Blades)

Tag: Gold oval tinsel, and red seal fur.

Tail: Red hackle fibres, and Wood Duck fibres.

Body: Gold tinsel; ribbing, gold oval.

Hackle: Brown.

Wing: Red squirrel.

Shoulders: Jungle Cock.

PLATE CVII.

No. 10   SOLDIER PALMER

Body: Scarlet fur dubbing; ribbing, silver tinsel.

Hackle: Two fiery brown hackles, tied palmer.

PLATE CVIII.

Chapter XXII

SMUTTING FLIES

SMUTTING FLIES are so small that the drawings of them have been made in two sizes; the small one is the size the fly should be made, and the large fly enables the tyer to see how the fly is tied.

Tying these small flies is just like playing a good fish on them—you have to learn to relax; in other words, do not use those muscles on the fine thread and fine leaders.

Many anglers just can't believe that a good fish can be landed on these small flies, but I have proved it is very difficult for a fish to throw a small hook when it is embedded in its skin.

Other anglers know the necessity of having a few small flies, nymphs, and larvae tied on No. 18 or No. 20 hooks when fish are tailing, which means that they are digging these small nymphs out of the stream bottom with their noses; sometimes their tails are seen above the water. Bulging trout are seen taking the nymphs at the surface, which often are changing to the winged fly. If the fish are taking the nymphs below the surface, my smutter

No. 1 and No. 2 with the wire body may just do the trick fished at different depths. Small weighted nymphs are very desirable for this kind of fishing.

I strongly advise the angler to open the first fish caught so as to determine what the fish are taking.

Fly No. 1, the Badger Quill, is a good fly to commence with. This fly resembles the midge pupa.

I was fishing a small lake in Ontario, Canada when I noticed a few surface rises. I cast a small dry Royal Coachman and brought in two nice brook trout. After opening their stomachs, I found one to be full of black bodied flies, and the other was full of yellow bodied flies. I think this proves that fish can discern color, and I also think that the size of the Royal Coachman was the reason they took it.

When you see trout feeding on these small flies on or near the surface, try a small smutting fly; it may mean success instead of failure.

The above flies are simple to make, except that they should be on a No. 18 or No. 20 hook. Wings: blue dun hackle tips; hackle: blue dun; bodies: one black floss and the other yellow.

SMUTTING FLIES

No. 1   BADGER QUILL
Body: Peacock quill.
Hackle: Badger.

No. 4   HACKLE CURSE
Tag: Silver tinsel.
Body: Black tying silk.
Hackle: Badger.

No. 5 FISHERMAN'S CURSE
Body: A strand of Golden Pheasant tail or brown Turkey.
Wings: Pale Starling.
Hackle: Two cock Starling hackles.

No. 2   CLARET SMUT
Body: Peacock quill dyed claret, or claret hackle stem.
Wings: Pale Starling.
Hackle: Black.

No. 6 W. F. B. SMUTTER No. 1
Tail: Claret hackle fibres.
Body: Maroon colored soft copper wire size .0112 (enameled wire).
Hackle: Claret.
Wing: Light Starling.

No. 3   EMU QUILL
            (W. F. Blades)
Tail: White hackle fibres.
Body: White Emu quill.
Wings: Pale Starling.
Hackle: White.

No. 7 W. F. B. SMUTTER No. 2
Tag: Claret, gray brown dubbing.
Body: Maroon colored soft copper enameled wire size .0112.
Wing: Light Starling.
Hackle: Brown.

MOTH

LEPIDOPTERA PHALAENIDAE HELIOTHIS ZEA (BODDIE) (DET. E. L. TODD). Plate on Page 297.

Wings: Grey and brown white tipped Deer body hair.
Body: Grey Deer body hair trimmed. Markings on back, orange enamel.

MIDGE PUPA

Body: Place a fine needle in the vise; coat the point with cement and lay a piece of 3x or 4x limp nylon on it; tie on the 6-0 tying thread and wind the needle and nylon the length of the body, 5/16″. Tie on a white stripped Emu quill and coat the body with cement, then wind the quill one turn; put on six brown hackle fibres in two tufts, as shown; wind the body and allow it to take an initial set, then slide it off the needle. Tie the nylon on the hook and tie on six brown hackle fibres for legs; put brown enamel on the head.

SMALL MAY FLY NYMPH

Body: Pale tan raffia; length, 5/16″.
Legs: Wood Duck fibres.

Midge pupa   *Small May Fly Nymph*

Chapter XXIII

LAND INSECTS

MODERN dry fly fishermen are attaching greater significance to and manifesting greater interest in imitations of terrestrial insects. The aquatic hatches have pretty well spent their courses by the time hot weather sets in. On the other hand, the quantity and size of the land-born insects is on the increase during this season. Much of the deliberate surface feeding by game fish seen in flat water is to displaced land insects. Unlike the aquatic hatches, they float flush on the surface and are opaque.

JASSID

Body: Black tying silk palmered with black hackle and cut off on the underside.
Wing: One Jungle Cock eye feather tied flat on the body.

Originated by Vince Marinaro

PLATE CIX. IMITATIONS OF TERRESTRIALS.

JAPANESE BEETLE

Body: Black tying silk palmered with black hackle and cut off on the under-side.

Wing: Blue black feather cut to shape; these can be taken from the Mallard or Wood Duck.

(See Plate CX)

No. 1 LEAF HOPPER OR JASSID

Body: Yellow tying thread covered with yellow raffia.

Wings: Pale green Parrot feather.

Legs: Trimmed yellow hackle stems.

Head: Yellow enamel; hook, No. 20; length of insect ⅜″.

No. 2 LEAF HOPPER OR JASSID

Body: Yellow tying thread covered with yellow raffia.

Wings: Green Parrot and two strands of red McCaw body feather on each side.

Legs: Trimmed yellow hackle stems.

Head: Yellow enamel; hook, No. 20; length of insect ⅜″.

[297]

No. 3 LEAF HOPPER OR JASSID

Body: Yellow tying thread covered with yellow raffia.
Wings: English Woodcock.
Legs: Trimmed yellow hackle stems.
Head: Yellow; brown enamel markings.

No. 4   HONEY BEE

Body: Yellow and black chenille.
Wings: Honey dun hackle tips.
Legs: Trimmed greyish-brown hackle stems.

No. 5   HAMMAR FLY

Body: Black raffia and black tying silk; elongated.
Wings: Blue dun hackle tips.
Legs: Trimmed black hackle stems.
Head: Black tying thread and enamel; hook No. 10; length of fly, ⅝″.

No. 6   GREEN BOTTLE FLY

Body: Greenish Peacock herl.
Wings: Light blue dun hackle tips.
Legs: Dark grey trimmed hackle stems.
Head: Green enamel.

No. 7   JAPANESE BEETLE

Body: Wrap the hook with white nylon tying thread and liquid cement. Tie in a flexible trimmed hackle stem; wrap over it on the off-side of the hook, then pull it under the hook and wrap over it on the near side of the hook; continue this a few times using the cement as you wind and flatten the body with pliers; this will make a flat oval body. When the body is to the desired shape tie on a dark Peacock quill, and to get the hairy body, cover it with a white Emu quill and wrap it with the Peacock quill to the first pair of legs which are Peacock sword trimmed a little; tie on the six legs, and a rich-brown feather for the wings. The markings and head are a greenish-black enamel. Hook, No. 12, length of Beetle, ⅜″.

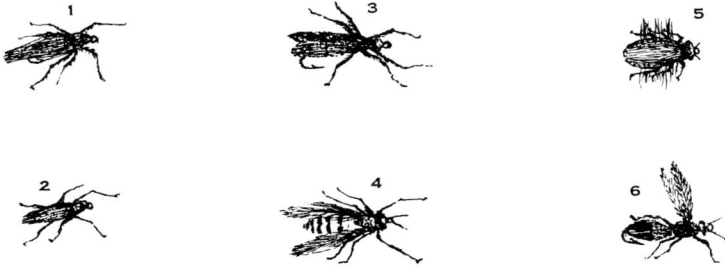

PLATE CXI. MORE LAND-BORN INSECTS.

LEAF HOPPERS OR JASSIDS
(See Plate CXI)

No. 1 POTATO LEAF HOPPER

Body: Green Kapok or Seal dubbing.

Wings: Green Parrot wing quill, one piece of quill saturated with liquid cement.

Legs: Trimmed olive green hackle stems. Green hackle can be added for better floating.

No. 2 ROSE LEAF HOPPER

Body: Yellow and green Kapok or Seal dubbing.

Wings: Yellow Swan or Duck wing quill, one piece of quill saturated with liquid cement.

Legs: Trimmed golden olive hackle stems. Yellow hackle can be added for better floating.

No. 3. LATERAL LEAF HOPPER

Body: Green or brown Kapok or Seal fur dubbing.

Wings: English Woodcock wing quill, one piece of quill saturated with liquid cement.

Legs: Trimmed golden olive hackle stems. Brown hackle can be used for better floating.

No. 4 DEER FLY

Body: Yellow Kapok under-body covered with yellow raffia; Ribbing, brown horse hair; markings, brown enamel.

Wings: Pale honey dun hackle tips. Honey dun hackle can be added.

Legs: Trimmed brown hackle stems.

No. 5 SMALL WATER BEETLE

Body: Black tying thread.

Hackle: Natural black.

Legs: Trimmed black hackle stems.

Top of Beetle: Jungle Cock eye covered with black enamel. Mailed to me from Ashland, Wisconsin.

No. 6 VELVET ANT

Body: Black tying thread and cement. Rear body; back half, black and the remainder, orange. Dubbing; front portion, black.

Wings: Hackle tips, brownish cast.

Legs: Trimmed black hackle stems.

[299]

PLATE CXII. IMITATION WINGED ANT AND HORSE FLY.

ANT (FORMICIDAE)

Lasius sp Det. by M. R. Smith

Body: Brown silk; black enamel on back.
Legs: Trimmed dark brown hackle stems.

Wings: Pale blue dun hackle tips.
Hook: No. 22.

HORSE FLY (FAMILY: TABANIDAE)

Body: To make the body oval I lay a trimmed hackle stem on each side of the body; then wrap this with tying thread; cover it with cement and repeat; build the under-body to size required, then cover it with blue-grey raffia; blue-grey dubbing can also be used.

Wings: Variant hackle tips.
Legs: Trimmed hackle stems; dark grey.

PLATE CXIII. HACKLE TREATMENT FOR REVERSE WINGS.

Hackle prepared for making the pulled-in reverse wings and bodies. Technique developed by Golden, a Canadian fly tyer.

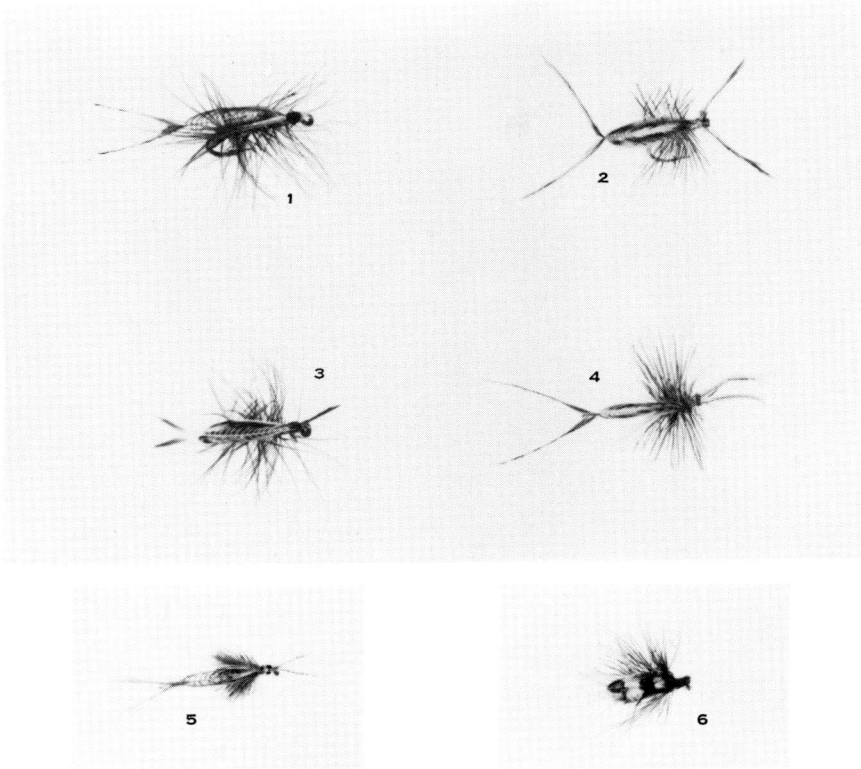

PLATE CXIV. REVERSE HACKLE FLIES.

REVERSE HACKLE FLIES

(See Plate CXIV)

No. 1   DARK BLUE DUN

Body: Black hackle palmered over black silk.

Wing and Tails: Dark blue dun hackle pulled in reverse.

No. 2   PHEASANT SMUTTER

Body: Ginger hackle palmered over black silk. ⅜" long.

Wing, Tail and Feelers: Pheasant body feather fibres pulled in reverse.

No. 3   GINGER BADGER

Body: Black hackle palmered over black silk.

Wings, Tail and Feelers: Ginger Badger hackle pulled in reverse.

No. 4   BADGER SMUTTER

Body and Tail: Badger hackle fibres pulled in reverse.

Hackle and Front Legs: Badger hackle. No body.

No. 5   OSTRICH SMUTTER

Body: Tan or black Ostrich herl palmered the same as a hackle.

Wing, Tail and Feelers: Badger hackle pulled in reverse.

No. 6   JUNGLE SMUTTER

Body: Black hackle palmered over black silk.

Wings: Two Jungle Cock eyes.

[301]

Chapter XXIV

MISCELLANEOUS

BY ALL means try out these small smutting flies if you have not fished with them; the reverse hackle wings improve the floating qualities of these flies and the fine copper wire bodies are excellent for fishing just under the surface; also for taking them down to the bottom in your favorite spring holes.

My good friend Art Besse wrote the following few lines: "Boy, did those tiny weighted smutters of yours finally solve the trout problem in a spring hole that has defied me. That small Grey Shrimp (which was weighted) and the Back Swimmer completed the picture. They are some real armament for problem fishing."

MIDGE PUPA

Tail: Small hackle fibres, brown.
Body: White 6-0 tying silk covered with fine copper wire and white Emu quill.
Legs: Six brown hackle fibres.
Head: Brown enamel. Hook No. 18.

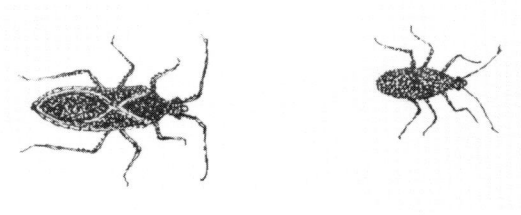

CXVI. COREIDAE, ADULT AND NYMPH.

FAMILY: COREIDAE, ANASA, TRISTIS (ADULT)
(See Plate CXVI)

Body: Cork, cut and filed to size and shape as shown. Coat the body with yellow ochre enamel. The markings are black and dark brown enamel. Tie on the feelers; also the front legs, and form the head with brown tying thread. Length, ¾″.

Legs: Trimmed hackle stems, dark brown, almost black. Lay the middle and rear legs on the underside of the body secured with liquid cement. To get the proper colors get the natural fly and copy it.

FAMILY: COREIDAE, ANASA, TRISTIS (NYMPH)

Body: Pale orange Seal fur dubbing. Dubbing can be mixed with other colors to get the shade you wish. Length, 7/16″. To make the body a flat oval shape read the instructions on the Japanese beetle.

Legs: Trimmed hackle stems, dark brown, almost black.

We have all experienced days in the summer when the trout refuse about everything we cast on the water; when this occurs by all means try small land flies such as Leaf Hoppers, Hammar Head flies, Caterpillars, Grass Hoppers, Moths, Japanese Beetles, Jassids, etc.

The Jassids and Beetles made with the hackle trimmed off on the top and underside, also the single wing laid flat, make excellent floaters.

Bodies made of dubbing and raffia may appear to be a more attractive meal and fished just under the surface will often take the sceptical larger fish.

I prefer dry fly fishing but the fish are not always willing to oblige.

Chapter XXV

FLY FISHING FOR
THE BEGINNER

HAVE been asked by several of my angling friends to include in my book a few pages of advice to the beginner as to what tackle to purchase and how to fish with the artificial fly. My advice is, go to the nearest fishing club that has the facilities for tournament casting and get acquainted with people who have spent many hours perfecting their casting under all conditions.

The action of rods has been very much improved by constant practice. Tapered lines have also been improved by changing the size and length of the different sections, to get greater distance, especially when fishing for large trout in fast water that is too dangerous to wade.

For dry fly fishing I am very well satisfied with the double tapered line that is suitable for the rod I am using. Be sure to have your rod and line checked by an expert for balance, for if it is not balanced you cannot expect to learn how to cast a fly in the proper manner.

I have been asked many times, "Do tournament casters ever go fishing?" The answer is definitely "yes"; many of them are expert fishermen and go fishing as often as they can. But if your ambition is to win the National Tournament prizes, you will have to practice continually. My advice to the beginner is to get as much of this practice and information as you can, for it will be of great help to you when you step in the stream to get your first trout. Many people feel that you have to become a tournament caster when you join a club; this is not the case, for I know many club members who never go in for tournament casting.

If you have taken instructions and practiced fly casting at the club you will be able to place a fly near a rising fish when you go on your first fishing trip; it will also assist you greatly in keeping your fly out of the bushes and trees along the stream; but not entirely; we all do our share of this.

When fishing dry the first time, use a well hackled hairwing fly; this will float easily and also take fish when it is fished just under the surface. A Bivisible tied with a generous amount of hackle is also easy to float. Make your casts short at first, thirty to thirty-five feet is ample, and you will not drown your fly as easily. A very good thing to remember is: do not pick a lot of line off the water; retrieve or float your fly until you can see the leader, then make the pick-up and take a couple of false casts in the air and lay down the fly. This will improve your timing and will save a lot of wear on your rod, as picking long lengths of line off the water just ruins a good rod.

When you are fishing dry you are simply trying to present a winged insect in a most natural way to a feeding fish. I do not wait for trout to rise; I study the stream for deep pools; you will find them at the foot of a small fall, also below and above a beaver dam; a bend in the stream will often bring a deep hole. I also claim you will have a much better opportunity of hooking a fish if you are using a fly that closely resembles the natural fly.

If you are having trouble straightening out the leader when presenting the fly, you will find you are bending your wrist when making the back cast, which means you are taking the rod too far back. Stop the rod at one o'clock and allow the line to straighten out at the back with a high back cast; now make the forward cast and you will notice at once that you are making better casts. If your fly hits you in the back when fishing you are not giving the line time to straighten out in the back cast. When casting a bass bug that has a lot of wind resistance, allow plenty of time for the line to straighten out on the back cast; I believe this will solve most of your troubles.

After you have mastered the overhead cast, get a few lessons from an expert on the following casts. The "roll cast" is used when you have obstructions at your back that will not allow you to make the back cast. In my opinion, this cast disturbs the water which will undoubtedly put down your fish. I only use it when necessary. The "side casts" are very good and should be used often. It is very easy for one to see that if your fly drops lightly a few feet from the line, you will not scare the fish as easily. This cast is used in dry fly fishing to keep the line from dragging your fly under the surface. Many other casts such as the "Steeple cast," the "Spey cast," the "Galway cast," etc., will assist you greatly when fishing almost every trout stream.

A very important thing for the beginner to know is: do not put a rod away that is wet; wipe it dry and leave the cap loose on your rod case. Take your fly lines off the reel to dry every time they are used and never store them on the reel at any time; buy or make a line drier and carrier.

For your first rod buy a 5½ ounce fly rod, with a dry fly action; this will always be a useful rod and is suitable for wet fly fishing, nymph fishing and bass bug fishing. Buy as good a rod as your pocket-book will allow; it will pay off in the long run. If you finally become an ardent fly fisherman you will own several rods of different weights and action to suit your style of fishing. These few lines have been written to start the beginner off on the right foot and not as actual instructions.

MAKING THE OVERHEAD CAST

(See Plate CXVII)

When making your first attempt to cast a fly, assemble your rod and line and tie on a six-foot leader and a fly that has the hook cut off; this is very important. Now lay about twenty to twenty-five feet of your leader and line on the lawn or water. Grip your rod with the thumb on the top and raise your rod to a little above horizontal, as shown in photograph No. 1 and stand with your right foot forward; I put a little more weight on my right foot than my left. I also suggest that you put the line under the fingers of your right hand and grip it so that it is stationary; this will give you less to think about until you have mastered the following instructions.

Now raise the rod up slowly; this takes the slack out of the line; if you pick up a slack line you will not get a good back cast or forward cast. At this point you increase the speed and power and shoot the rod up until your forearm is vertical; stop abruptly at this moment; your rod will be about 22½ degrees past vertical, or one o'clock as you face nine o'clock. This action is up, not back, and keep a stiff wrist at all times. By all means, turn your head to the right and look to see if your rod is at one o'clock; you will be surprised to see that it is, very often, too far back.

PLATE CXVII. MAKING THE OVERHEAD CAST.   Photo by Wilfred Blades

After the abrupt stop, relax and pause until the rod has put your line high and back, and just before the line completely straightens out you start the forward cast. As the line straightens out you will feel a little tug and the rod will drift back a little. You will now be as shown in photograph No. 2.

Start the forward cast slowly with a powerful forward motion, then forward and down; just before you get to the position as shown in photograph No. 3 apply a sharp pressure with your thumb and wrist and stop; this will straighten out your line and leader. At this point release your line slightly and let the fly drop gently on the lawn or water. If you take your aim a little above the water you will notice that your fly will light on the water more naturally.

After you have mastered the preceding instructions try the following cast. When your forward cast is nearly fully extended above the water two or three feet, give the tip of your rod a sharp upward flip; this will put the fly on the water before the line. With a lot of practice this will often take large fish.

FALSE CASTING

When you have practiced the overhead cast and have learned how to deliver your fly on the lawn or water, you want to know how to keep your fly going back and forth in the air; this is called false casting. You use this to dry your line and fly when dry fly fishing, and also to lengthen and shorten your casts.

To false cast use the same method as you learned in the overhead cast except that you stop the forward cast at an angle of 45 degrees above horizontal. Now pause until the line has straightened out in front, then make another back cast; continue this back and forth until your fly is dry, then deliver it on the water.

To extend your line you pull off about three feet of line with your left hand and hold it in your left hand in a loose coil; be sure you are holding your line above this coil. Now make a couple of false casts and at the point where you have applied your thumb and wrist into your forward cast and stopped the rod at 22½ degrees above horizontal, let go of your loose line which will be pulled through the guides by the momentum of your line. Practice this until you get the proper timing and you will have no trouble.

To shorten your line, simply pull the length you desire with your left hand, through the guides. When false casting in the air, shorten it when you start the back cast.

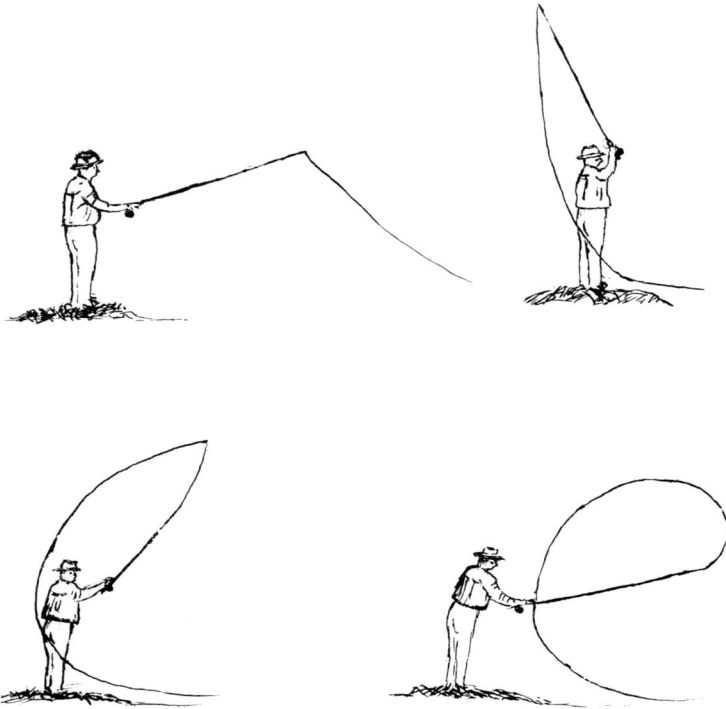

PLATE CXVIII. THE DIFFERENT STAGES OF THE ROLL CAST.

ROLL CAST

The roll cast is used in places where you find that your back cast and side cast are obstructed with trees and bushes.

Start the cast as drawn in figure No. 1 and raise your rod up and back slowly; also tilt the rod to the right so that it is clear of your shoulder and you will be the same as drawing No. 2.

Pause a few seconds until the line has come back to the position shown, then start a decided forward and downward thrust as drawn in figure No. 3, finishing with a stiff wrist and thumb pressure and stop the rod in position as shown in figure No. 4.

If you have followed these instructions perfectly your line will roll out on the water; all you need is a little practice and patience. Use about twenty to twenty-five feet of line and leader on your first casts.

To practice the roll cast stand in the stream and select a calm day.

Chapter XXVI

IN RETROSPECT

I HAVE often been asked, "Do you fish with the flies you make?" Well, my first lessons on fishing were given to me by my grandfather on the River Trent in England.

I came to Chicago at the age of twenty-three and seriously attended to my business on the buildings and became a contractor at the age of thirty-three. Not until I passed forty did I have the time to fish. At this time I met a real pal in Earl Steinmetz; he persuaded me to buy some fishing tackle and spend a couple of weeks at Rooney Lake near Spooner, Wisconsin. This was Paradise; the lake teemed with bass up to 6½ pounds, northern pike around 14 pounds and blue gills. I have never fished a lake that I liked better.

My first bait was minnows and frogs but I soon used spoons and plugs, and entirely forgot live bait. I took a third prize in the State of Illinois in the ⅝ bait casting event. I received my first fly casting lessons at a couple of fishing clubs before I entered the streams and rivers; my first experience was a creek in Spooner, then a river in Superior, Wisconsin; next, the Brule where I nearly got a ducking; this is a tough river for a beginner.

I spent a whole season on the Indian Reservation at Flambeau in the depression; this gave me a lot of experience in operating a boat and outboard motor in these good-sized lakes. I also caught my first muskellunge on Clear Lake. I traveled 2,700 miles on one of these trips fishing out of Knife River for brook trout and trolling Lake Superior for lake trout. I fished the Gun Flint Trail for trout and landlocked salmon, and finally landed in Port Arthur, Ontario, Canada.

My next step was fishing in Ontario, Canada, out of Basswood Lake, twelve miles out of Thessalon at Bill Phillips' Camp. Here we fished the Rapid, Gravel, Snowshoe and Little Thessalon Rivers, and many lakes. I caught and released one hundred and two smallmouth bass in 5½ hours in one of the above mentioned beautiful lakes.

During the winter months I fished in Florida for twenty-five weeks, fishing all the coastline from Clearwater to Cape Sable and over the Keys to Key West where we stayed for a couple of weeks each trip. I landed my first shark on No-Name Key; it was eight feet long. I coaxed it into shallow water and it had at least thirty coils of my line around its body before being gaffed.

The next stop was Miami and Fort Lauderdale. I have caught three sail fish here. Catching a good-sized sail fish is a thrill; I will always remember my first.

A day my wife and I will always remember was when I hired a couple of guides with a good-sized cruiser and rowboat to catch tarpon on bass tackle, about twenty miles south of Everglades City. We had to lie down in the boat to get to this little piece of open water in the mangrove swamp. This is a thrill; try it sometime and take a couple of extra lines; you may need them.

*   *   *   *   *

I sincerely hope the contents of my book will bring help and happiness to many fishermen all over the world; if this is accomplished I feel that my labor in writing and illustrating this book will not have been spent in vain.

INDEX TO FLIES
AND MATERIALS USED IN
THEIR PRODUCTION

Errata

The caption for the first color plate should read:

STREAMER AND STEELHEAD FLIES
(Read left to right)
Blades' Weighted Bucktail Streamer No. 3, Ginger Furnace Frey, Thor, Red Optic Fly, Dot, Paint Brush Two Wing, Cains River Silver Grey, New Trier, Roaring Rapids, Supervisor, Furnace Grey, Blades' Weighted Bucktail Streamer No. 2

The second color plate is inverted. The caption should read:

REALISTIC DRY FLIES AND NYMPHS
(Read clockwise from top)
Blades' Crane Fly Parachute, Damsel Fly Nymph, Dragon Fly Nymph, Blades' Ephemera Simulans, Blades' Stone Fly Nymph, Blades' Stenonema Vicarium

The caption for the third color plate should read:

WET FLIES
(Read top to bottom, left to right)
Clare Flatt, Jungle Cock, Nations Shiner Tip, Squash Bug, Golden Olive, Wood Duck and Black, Royal Coachman, Watson's Fancy